BEYOND MARKET LIBERALIZATION

Beyond Market Liberalization

Welfare, income generation and environmental
sustainability in rural Madagascar

Edited by
BART MINTEN
MANFRED ZELLER

Ashgate

Aldershot • Burlington USA • Singapore • Sydney

Published by
Ashgate Publishing Ltd
Gower House
Croft Road
Aldershot
Hants GU11 3HR
England

Ashgate Publishing Company
131 Main Street
Burlington
Vermont 05401
USA

Ashgate website: http://www.ashgate.com

British Library Cataloguing in Publication Data
Beyond market liberalization : welfare, income generation
  and environmental sustainability in rural Madagascar
  1.Agriculture - Economic aspects - Madagascar 2.Agriculture
  - Environmental aspects - Madagascar 3.Agriculture and
  state - Madagascar 4.Madagascar - Economic policy
  I.Minten, Bart II.Zeller, Manfred
  338.1'09691

Library of Congress Catalog Card Number: 00-132598

ISBN 0 7546 1237 6

Printed in Great Britain by Antony Rowe Ltd.

Contents

List of Tables

ix

List of Figures

Contributors

Dr Francesco Goletti is a research fellow in the Markets and Structural Studies Division of the International Food Policy Research Institute, Washington DC, USA. He currently leads the IFPRI multicountry research program on Postharvest Activities and Agrofood Based Rural Industrialization. He was trained in mathematics at Rome University and obtained his doctorate in economics from New York University, USA.

Dr Cécile Lapenu is a post-doctoral fellow in the Food Consumption and Nutrition Division at the International Food Policy Research Institute, Washington DC, USA. She received a doctorate in agricultural economics from the Ecole Nationale Superieure Agronomique de Montpellier, France.

Dr Bart Minten is assistant professor in agricultural and environmental economics at the Department of Agricultural and Environmental Economics, Katholieke Universiteit Leuven, Belgium. He has a doctorate in agricultural and environmental economics from Cornell University, USA. Prior to this position he was with the World Bank and the International Food Policy Research Institute, Washington DC, USA.

Eliane Ralison is a researcher at the National Center of Applied Research for Rural Development (FOFIFA) within the Ministry of Scientific Research in Antananarivo, Madagascar. She holds a Masters in Economics from the University of Antananarivo and is currently involved in research on the cost of credit to rural farmers.

Désiré Randrianaivo is division chief of the Socio-economic Unit at National Center of Applied Research for Rural Development (FOFIFA) within the Ministry of Scientific Research in Antananarivo, Madagascar. He holds a Masters in Geography and Philosophy from the University of Antananarivo and has advised international organizations and the Malagasy government on agricultural problems in Madagascar.

Claude Randrianarisoa is a researcher at the National Center of Applied Research for Rural Development (FOFIFA) within the Ministry of Scientific Research in Antananarivo, Madagascar. He holds an agricultural engineering degree from the University of Antananarivo and is currently pursuing advanced studies in agricultural economics at Michigan State University, USA.

Dr Manfred Zeller is professor in agricultural economics at the Institute for Rural Development, University of Goetingen, Germany. He holds a doctorate in agricultural economics from the University of Bonn, Germany. Prior to this position he was a research fellow in the Food Consumption and Nutrition Division at the International Food Policy Research Institute, Washington DC, USA, where he was the leader of the multicountry research program on rural finance and household food security.

Preface

This book brings together the results of a research project on welfare, income generation and environmental sustainability of rural households in Madagascar at the end of the 1990s following the liberalization of agricultural markets. While the empirical analysis focuses on Madagascar, the methodologies used as well as the empirical findings and policy conclusions are expected to be relevant for researchers, national and international development and relief organization staff, and readers generally interested in the problems of agricultural development and food insecurity in rural areas of developing countries. The study was funded by the United States Agency for International Development (USAID) as part of the project 'Structure and conduct of major agricultural input and output markets and response to reforms by rural households in Madagascar'. The research project was carried out by the International Food Policy Research Institute (IFPRI), an international research organization in the Consultative Group on International Agricultural Research (CGIAR), in collaboration with the National Center for Applied Research in Rural Development, Ministry of Scientific Research in Madagascar (FOFIFA).

We would like to thank a multitude of people without whom this exciting project would not have been possible. First, we would like to acknowledge the strong support throughout the study by Mary Norris (USAID), François Rasolo (FOFIFA), and Désiré Randrianaivo (FOFIFA). We would like to thank our IFPRI collaborators in this project, in particular Francesco Goletti and Ousmane Badiane. In Madagascar, we would like to acknowledge the assistance and support by Fidèle Rabemananjara, Jean Razafindravonona, Eugenie Raharisoa, Steve Haggblade, Frank Martin, and Tim Healy. Odette Moria, Josee Verlaenen, and Ria Uyttebroeck carefully put the whole book into its final format while Ann Hartell took care of the final editing. Finally, we thank the participants in the different workshops and seminars in Antananarivo for their suggestions and insights, the enumerators and data operators for the meticulous collection and entry of the data, as well as the hundreds of farmers, private operators, and government officials for their information sharing and participation.

Bart Minten, Leuven, Belgium
Manfred Zeller, Washington, DC, USA
October 1999

List of Abbreviations

2SLS	Two Stages Least Squares
AIDS	Almost Ideal Demand System
BCSR	Bureau de Commercialisation et du Stabilisation du Riz (Office of Rice Marketing and Stabilization)
C/F	Côte/Falaise (Coast/Escarpment)
CMS	Centre de Multiplication des Semences (Seed Multiplication Center)
CPI	Consumer Price Index
EPM	Enquête Permanente auprès des Ménages (Permanent Household Survey)
FAO	Food and Agriculture Organization
FIFABE	Fikambanana Fampandrosoana ny lemak'i Betsiboka (Association for Betsiboka plains development)
FIFAMANOR	Fiompiana Fambolena Malagasy Norveziana (Livestock, Agriculture Malagasy – Norway)
FMG	Franc Malagasy
FOB	Free On Board
FOFIFA	Foibe Fikarohana Ampiharina amin'ny Fampandrosoana ny Ambanivohitra (National Research Center for Rural Development)
GDP	Gross Domestic Product
GPS	Groupement de Paysans Semenciers (Farmer Organization of Seed Multipliers)
HAZ	z-score Height for Age
HT	Hautes Terres (Highlands)
IFPRI	International Food Policy Research Institute
INSTAT	Institut National de la Statistique (National Statistical Institute)
IRRI	International Rice Research Institute
NGO	Nongovernmental Organization
OLS	Ordinary Least Squares
RYMV	Red Yellow Mottle Virus
SECALINE	Sécurité Alimentaire et Nutrition Elargie (Food Security and Better Nutrition)

SINPA	Société d'Interêt National des Produits Agricoles (National Company for Agricultural Products)
SOMACODIS	Société Malgache de Commerce et de Distribution (National Company for Trade and Distribution)
SOMALAC	Société Malgache d'Aménagement du Lac Alaotra (National Company for Lac Alaotra Development)
SURE	Seemingly Unrelated Regression Model
UNDP	United Nations Development Program
US	United States of America
WAZ	z-score Weight for Age
WHZ	z-score Weight for Height

1 Introduction

BART MINTEN and MANFRED ZELLER

Objective of the Study

Most African countries have undergone dramatic agricultural market reforms over the last decades. This has resulted in significant changes in the operation of agricultural markets and consequently in welfare, income generation, and natural resource use of rural households. The challenge facing reform processes in these countries is a need to balance efforts to encourage efficient private participation while facilitating and complementing the role of the public sector. Concerns and suspicions about adverse effects of agricultural liberalization on rural households persist and often leave the policy maker at a loss as to the type of interventions required. Hence, managing the reform processes and assisting policy makers necessitates a good understanding of the operation of agricultural markets and the constraints at the farm household level to the response to market incentives.

In this book we study the case of Madagascar. Madagascar went through significant agricultural market reforms during the 1980s and 1990s. This book aims to explore, through descriptive analysis as well as causal determination, the determinants of welfare, income generation, and environmental sustainabillity in rural Madagascar. Rural income generation activities, household welfare, and natural resource use are determined by a complex network of factors whose relationships need to be understood in order to design optimal policies for rural growth, poverty alleviation, and environmental sustainability. Thus, the purpose of this book is to trace those relationships and add comprehensive factual information thereby assisting policy makers and program analysts in identifying the potentials of different policy interventions based on actual recent field data. While focusing on the case of Madagascar, the methodologies, empirical analysis and findings are also relevant for other Subsaharan African countries that have undergone similar agricultural market liberalization programs without having necessarily led to increasing the income and welfare of poor semisubsistence rural households.

Methodology of the Analysis of Policy Reform

Reforms in agricultural input and output markets result in price changes at the farmgate and consumer level and in changes in transaction costs affecting farm household purchases of inputs, market outputs, and the acquisition of basic food and nonfood items. Other policy reforms which do not directly address the functioning of markets can effect the efficiency of farm and nonfarm rural production and investment or the consumption pattern of rural households. These policies include agricultural research and extension; investments in infrastructure, schooling, and nutrition education; and investments in institutions facilitating the exchange of information and capital. Changes in any of these policies are expected to induce transformations in agricultural and non-agricultural income generation which subsequently result in changes in food and nonfood consumption, nutritional status, and various environmental outcomes such as soil fertility and forest cover.

In order to analyze the direction and magnitude of the effects of policy change, each chapter of the book comprises descriptive and econometric analyses. The descriptive analysis addresses the question 'what', whereas the econometric analysis attempts to address the 'why' question. In the descriptive analysis, we crosstabulate the survey data by region or by socioeconomic group of rural households, and seek to describe the production, consumption, and investment behavior of households and their individual members. Behavior results in outcomes, such as income earned, food eaten, calories and protein consumed, and nutritional status obtained. In this impact analysis of market policy reform, we are primarily interested in investigating the effect of specific policy instruments and related policy variables (such as input and output prices, access to fertilizer and improved seed, access to credit) on household behavior and resulting welfare outcomes.

As a multitude of factors influences the behavior of communities, households and their members, and therefore the resulting welfare status, descriptive analysis can only provide suggestive indications on the causality and effect of policy changes on household welfare. In order to measure the direction and magnitude of the effect of changes in certain policy variables, we therefore employ econometric analysis which seeks to identify the single effect of one policy instrument in conjunction with other policy instruments, and in conjunction with exogenous variables, which are beyond the control of policy. For policy relevance, we focus the interpretation of econometric results mostly on the effect of the policy variables. These variables influence outcomes either directly or, by altering behavior, indirectly.

Structure of the Book

Chapter 2 presents a historical overview of agricultural policies in input and output markets in Madagascar. Madagascar started the gradual liberalization of its agricultural markets in the mid-1980s. We look briefly in this chapter at the impact of the recent liberalization on the functioning of the agricultural trader sector. This is important as since the market liberalization these traders are the providers of inputs to farmers and the buyers of agricultural produce.

In chapter 3 a conceptual framework, which is based on the standard agricultural household model for impact analysis, is presented. Rural households in Madagascar are mostly farm households although in some cases nonfarm income exceeds farm income. The farm enterprises produce crops both for subsistence and for sale so the analysis needs to take into account the interlinkages between production, marketed surplus, and consumption within a household. The conceptual framework allows the analysis to be structured in a sequential way beginning with the production and income generation process of the household, then dealing with the marketing and consumption decisions of the household, and finally evaluating the effects on welfare variables, such as calorie and protein intake, and the nutritional status of individual household members. The book follows this sequential structure of household behavior and outcomes at the household and community levels.

Chapter 4 begins with a description of selected socioeconomic characteristics of the survey households, with a particular emphasis on the possession and utilization of land as the major production asset. We further present data on the change in welfare as perceived by the head of the surveyed household. Moreover, this chapter crosstabulates causes of change in welfare, as perceived by the household head, differentiated by various categories of causal factors, including changes in prices for agricultural inputs and outputs.

Chapter 5 covers farmers' access to and demand for major inputs. We present descriptive and econometric analyses on the utilization of fertilizer, the type of crops it is used on, and the evolution of its use over time. Secondly, improved seed is discussed. We further analyze the effects of modern technology and access to input markets on the yield and production of rice.

Chapter 6 covers the descriptive and econometric analyses of all crop enterprises. We analyze the structure of crop income, its changes over time (by using panel data for two of the survey regions), and identify its critical determinants. As mentioned above, the interpretation of results focuses on the effects of those determinants which can be influenced by policy changes. The descriptive and econometric analyses use plot-level data from all fields cultivated by the survey households. As rice is the major crop in Madagascar, we chose to design detailed survey instruments to address the critical question of productivity of rice production. The results of production and profit function estimations for lowland and upland agricultural production are presented.

Chapter 7 further investigates the marketing decisions of farmers with respect to the timing and volume of major food crop sales and purchases. The characteristics of rice buyers and sellers are looked at as well as the determinants of total commercial surplus.

In chapter 8, we describe the structure and determinants of total household income. Thus, we distinguish between farm and various sources of off-farm income, including income from animal production, wages and salaries, and microenterprises. For all sources of off-farm income, we also conduct analysis at the level of individual adult household members. As in chapter 6, we compare the data of the 1997 household sample with the previous 1992 household sample to obtain a picture of the change over time in the two regions for which panel data are available.

Chapter 9 conducts standard economic consumption expenditure analysis, and presents estimates for income and price elasticities for the major food and nonfood groups consumed. These estimates are made for different income quartiles and they illustrate the differential impacts of price and income changes.

Chapter 10 describes the composition of food consumed and evaluates the consumption of calories and proteins on a per capita and per adult-equivalent basis. In the second part of this chapter, an econometric analysis measures the effects of changes in household income and other variables on caloric consumption. The last part of the chapter presents the survey data on nutritional status of preschool age girls and boys. The results in this chapter are then compared with other recent survey results from Madagascar i.e. Sécurité Alimentaire et Nutrition Elargie (SECALINE) and Enquête Permanente auprès des Ménages (EPM).

Chapter 11 deals with the relationship between poverty alleviation, agricultural growth, and environmental sustainability. The chapter illustrates how these components for sustainable development are intrinsically linked and can not be achieved independently. The chapter also focuses in more depth on questions which relate to the critical issue of environmental sustainability of rural development in Madagascar.

Chapter 12 summarizes the main findings and related policy issues and recommendations. We conclude that market liberalization is necessary, but not a sufficient policy instrument for alleviating rural poverty and food insecurity. Complementary public investments in rural hard and soft infrastructure, education, agricultural research and extension, and social safety nets need to be accelerated so that rural households are better enabled to take advantage of market opportunities created by the liberalization of agricultural input and output markets.

2 Market Liberalization and the Agricultural Marketing System

BART MINTEN and CLAUDE RANDRIANARISOA

Policies in Input and Output Markets

Agricultural market reforms in Madagascar resemble those in many other African countries which have gone through cycles of government interventionism and retreat (see Berg, 1989; Staatz et al., 1989). After Madagascar obtained independence from France, governments initially increased the intervention of the state in agricultural markets (see Dorosh and Bernier, 1994; Shuttleworth, 1989; Berg, 1989; Pryor, 1990; Barrett, 1994; 1995) such that by the end of the 1970s, most trade in agricultural products and inputs was in the hands of the state. A reversal of policy took place in the 1980s with a transition from a state food marketing and distribution system to a liberalized market. This transition, however, was very gradual.

A graph on the evolution of real rice prices in Antananarivo from 1960 until 1996 illustrates the different policy periods (Figure 2.1). Prices are relatively stable during the First Republic (1960-1972). During this period small traders together with the parastatal Bureau de Commercialisation et du Stabilization du Riz (BCSR or Office of Rice Marketing and Stabilization), organized the marketing of rice. The BCSR fixed minimum and maximum prices, provided credit to farmers, and organized rural associations. The nationalization of the rice trade with the creation of the Société d'Interêt National des Produits Agricoles (SINPA or National Company for Agricultural Products) caused a significant price increase in 1974. The rice price decreased to its previous level after the creation of the other parastatal organizations. The price evolution shows how price fixation became unsustainable in the beginning of the eighties when the price of rice reached its lowest level. The gradual liberalization of the rice trade as well as a real exchange rate depreciation resulted in a price increase of more than 100 per cent between 1981 and 1986. Since liberalization, we notice a significant average seasonal movement of 25 per cent in Antananarivo with the highest price in March and the lowest price in June. These seasonal movements were almost nonexistent before price liberalization.

7

Liberalization began in 1983 when the state officially abandoned its monopoly on the commerce of agricultural products. The initial liberalization measures implied that agricultural trading was open to everybody except in the two main production areas (the plains of Marovoay and Lac Aloatra) where two government agencies, FIFABE and SOMALAC, could continue their monopoly. The roles of these two state companies were redesigned only in 1989. At the beginning of the reforms, floor and ceiling prices were maintained. In June 1985 a government decree fixed the floor price of paddy rice, but completely removed the ceiling price. In reality the government still effectively controlled domestic rice trade until 1986. From mid-1983 on, it supplied the large cities with 'riz fokontany', i.e. subsidized rice.[1] In November 1986, the government introduced a buffer stock scheme in response to that year's high seasonal prices and to defend the ceiling price. However, the buffer stock scheme was poorly administered and was ultimately terminated in 1990.

In the 1990s, the government became more concerned with the effect of price policies on producers. For example, in 1991 the government introduced an import tax of 30 per cent on rice to protect local production. This tax was reduced to 10 per cent in 1995. However, the government still occasionally granted tax exoneration for certain companies and shipments to assure a steady food supply. The current situation can be described as one in which private traders have been given free rein to set prices and move agricultural products around the country. The state continues to intervene in agricultural markets through buying and selling operations conducted by agencies such as SOMACODIS, but these agencies now only represent a very small percentage of the total volume of food products transacted domestically.

Input markets reflect the same periodical changes. From 1960 until 1975, state intervention was combined with active participation of the private sector. The state fixed input prices and kept a panterritorial price system supported by subsidies. It also supported the creation of a credit system to facilitate access to equipment, fertilizer, and pesticides. Private operators, however, were in charge of the distribution and marketing of inputs. In 1976, the state took over the distribution of inputs. Within the Agricultural Ministry it created a Direction de l'Approvisionnement Agricole (an office of agricultural supply) with regional branches. This office covered services related to seed production, provision of equipment, and management of agricultural tractors and was in charge of storing and selling agricultural inputs directly to farmers. Market reform in input

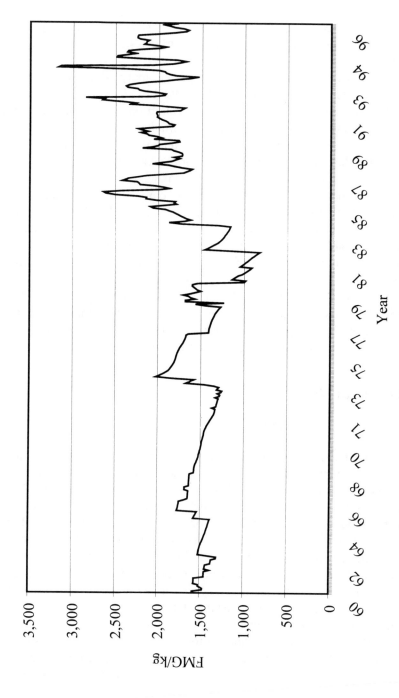

Figure 2.1   Rice prices in Antananarivo, 1960-1996 (deflated prices in 1996 FMG)

distribution started in 1985 and was characterized by a progressive withdrawal of the state from the distribution system, as in the output markets.

Agricultural trade in Madagascar has been analyzed by other authors, most notably Barrett (1994; 1995; 1997a; 1997b; 1997c) and Berg (1989). They illustrate the initial effects of liberalization on prices and marketing. Barrett and Dorosh (1996) show that most Malagasy rural households are deficit producers and must rely on the market for their subsistence. Food markets are thus important not only for urban dwellers but for rural inhabitants as well. Using surveys of Malagasy grain traders, Barrett (1997a) describes agricultural trade in the country as characterized by extreme disparity between large and small traders. He argues that most traders do not have access to the equipment and credit required to penetrate the more profitable segments of the business. As a result, most businesses remain small while a few large traders derive large margins in activities that are secluded from competition. A similar conclusion is reached by Kristjanson and Martin (1991). In the rest of this chapter, the structure, performance, and constraints in the function of agricultural input and output markets are briefly analyzed based on the primary data that were collected at the trader level more than a decade after initial reforms were started.[2]

Beyond Market Liberalization

Structure of the Trader Sector

The liberalized distribution system of agricultural inputs is characterized by a variety of agents including private traders, commercial companies, development organizations, and nongovernmental organizations (NGOs). The barriers to entry seem to be low. Most distribution agents feel optimistic about their sector: they see opportunities for expansion but are constrained by the size of the market. Private distributors are professional, highly specialized in their business, with a level of education at least at the baccalaureat level. About a quarter of the distributors are vertically integrated and have an exclusivity contract with a big local company or the mother company (see Randrianarisoa and Minten, 1997).

The main sources of revenue for input distributors are fertilizers (24 per cent), followed by veterinary products (23 per cent) and pesticides (13 per cent). Most distributors started operations after 1989, long after liberalization policies were put in place, and the number of distributors seems to have peaked in the 1990s. Most retailers and semiwholesalers report a high level of competition while the bigger organizations report competition to be low. This might be due to the fact that bigger organizations usually integrate input distribution with technical and financial support to farmers with purchases of their agricultural products. Only a few organizations combine these activities, thus the level of competition is reported to be low.

The private, output-trading sector has also responded to the liberalization of domestic markets with strong participation (Badiane et al., 1998). An important feature of the postreform output marketing systems is the lack of any significant administrative barriers to market entry. The large majority of traders declare that they face virtually no barriers, either to entry, or to the movement of goods across local markets. They also see competition as fairly high in local markets. The majority of communities report having a choice between traders and communities report more choice compared to five years previously. However, some regions seem to be disavantaged; for example, in the Majunga HT and Fianarantsoa HT less than one-third of the communities report having a choice between traders.

Detailed information at the trader level was available on working capital and equipment, storage capacity and vehicles, telephone usage, labor, management, human capital, and social capital (Mendoza and Randrianarisoa, 1998; Fafchamps and Minten, 1998; 1999b). The data show that the surveyed businesses are fairly unsophisticated by Western standards: average working capital is roughly equivalent to $2,000 US. However, this is still a large figure compared to the annual gross domestic product (GDP) of Madagascar which was $230 US in 1997. The great majority of surveyed traders do not have their own transportation equipment, nor do they often use telephones. Each trading business has an average of four workers, including the owner/manager. Most respondents work full time in trade and remain traders all year round. On average, they are fairly well educated by Madagascar standards.

Malagasy traders in agricultural food products are characterized by their extreme diversity in terms of volume of operation and by their unsophisticated operation (little equipment, few employees).[3] In contrast with the commonly held view that trade in Africa is mostly a secondary activity, most surveyed traders in Madagascar are heavily involved in trade; they have invested a large proportion of their total wealth in it and they derive a significant proportion of their income from it. Given the low level of technical sophistication of the industry as a whole and the relative unimportance of credit, even for large traders, returns to scale are unlikely to be present. As a result, one expects entry to be easy and competition to be fierce. However, constraints to growth and efficiency evidently persist for traders.

Remaining Constraints to Growth and Efficiency in the Trader Sector

Thin input markets The limited demand of most farmers in Madagascar has not allowed the growth of a distribution system needed for intensive agriculture. For example, Madagascar has been importing, on average, around 20,000 tons of mineral fertilizer a year for the last twenty years. Large cotton, sugarcane, and tobacco plantations have used most of those imports (around 50 per cent of total volume). The rest is used by smaller farm holdings. Given that the majority of the population in Madagascar is involved in agricultural activities, this leads to very low levels of fertilizer use per farmer.[4]

High and unstable import prices Farmers' input prices are relatively high in Madagascar. For example, the price of urea is $0.40 US per kg (about 2,000 FMG), 66 per cent higher than the cost of fertilizer in Asia (Goletti et al., 1996). The high cost of agricultural inputs is partly related to high import prices. Import prices of $318 US per ton compare to an FOB price of $205 US per ton out of Western Europe, a reflection of low shipment sizes and high insurance and freight costs. The main concern of traders, however, seems to be related to fluctuations of input prices over the years and they advocate a fertilizer stabilization stock managed by the government (Randrianarisoa and Minten, 1997).

Lack of high yield rice varieties In the case of lowland riceproduction, one of the most limiting factors in input markets is the lack of high yielding rice varieties adapted to the special conditions in Madagascar. The low adoption of available improved varieties by farmers is partly the result of poor yield performance. Even for the most favored farmers, such as the seed multiplication agents, the yield is not much above two tons per hectare (Goletti et al., 1998). This lack of good seed technology is partly the result of insufficient investment in rice research. A significant effort in rice research and the testing of new varieties in different on-farm environments seems to be necessary in Madagascar given the complex agroecological situation. Even though extension could contribute to improving the current situation, the aggregate yield increase with current technology is only on the order of 10 per cent, insufficient to have a strong impact on rural income growth and poverty alleviation (Table 2.1).

Table 2.1   Comparison of irrigated rice yields

	Farmers	Seed farmers (paddy production)	Seed farmers (seed production)
Yield (kg/ha)	1,778	1,864	2,109
Percentage increase	-	4.8	13.1

Source: Data from 1997 IFPRI/FOFIFA survey; after Goletti, Randrianarisoa, and Rich (1998)

High transportation costs   Madagascar shows high transportation costs even when compared to other African countries (Badiane et al., 1997).[5] Prices average $0.20 US per ton per km but could be as high as $1.00 US per ton per km at the time of the survey. It is clear that poor infrastructure contributes to very high transportation costs. Paved roads are available only in 8 per cent of rural communities. Moreover, there are strong seasonal differences in road quality and some regions are completely cut off during the rainy season. Madagascar also lacks market infrastructure. Based on the community survey that was carried out during the study, only 8 per cent of the villages have access to a local market within their community and the average distance and time that it takes to reach a market are, respectively, 10 km or more than 2 hours.

However, even with further infrastructure development, transportation costs might still be high due to lack of economies of scale. A model of transport costs is estimated along the lines of Binkley and Harrer (1981) to test the relative importance of economics of scale. In this model, price per kg is estimated as a function of transport mode, weight, and distance (Table 2.2). Different transport modes show different fixed costs. Motorized vehicles have 110 per cent to 140 per cent higher fixed costs compared to loads carried on the head, while animal-driven vehicles and 'pousse-pousse' (rickshaw) are 100 per cent and 50 per cent more expensive respectively. This implies that more sophisticated means of transport can only be economical if loads are big enough to cover the higher fixed costs.

Given the low commercial surplus, farmers often bring produce to a periodic market, carrying bags on their heads where only bigger traders that buy the produce can achieve economies of scale in transport. Economies of scale in transport are present as the transport price shows an elasticity of 10 per cent with respect to weight. Splitting the regression by paved roads and other roads illustrates that most of the economies of scale are obtained on paved roads (elasticities on paved roads alone amount to 20 per cent) while elasticities are smaller and become insignificant on other types of roads. The elasticity with respect to distance on roads not accessible by vehicles is around 54 per cent compared to 40 per cent on paved roads. Other things equal, an increase in distance does not lead to a proportional change in transport costs. This is further illustrated in the third regression. A doubling of distance reduces hourly per unit transport costs by around 25 per cent. There is no major difference between road types in the decline of the transport cost per kg per hour traveled. This implies equal reduction of the importance of fixed costs for longer distances. In short, high transportation costs in Madagascar, a major cost in marketing and distribution of agricultural products, seem to be caused by two factors: low demand/small commercial surplus of food products as well as bad road quality.

Table 2.2   Determinants of transport prices paid by traders

| | | Log (transport price/kg) | | | | Log (price/kg/hour) | |
| | | All roads | | Paved roads only | | | |
		Coefficient	t-value	Coefficient	t-value	Coefficient	t-value
Intercept		2.100	13.964	2.493	10.333	3.980	21.727
Truck	yes=1	1.200	6.633	1.573	5.878	0.836	3.668
Pickup truck	yes=1	1.101	7.973	1.330	6.111	1.125	6.442
Oxcart	yes=1	0.988	4.907	0.940	2.915	0.208	0.837
Tractor	yes=1	1.473	4.882			1.159	3.120
'Pousse-pousse' (rickshaw)	yes=1	0.532	4.710	0.655	3.409	0.013	0.091
Other mean of transport	yes=1	0.989	7.126	1.229	5.036	0.882	5.070
Weight (kg)	log	-0.097	-3.342	-0.195	-5.399	-0.084	-2.352
Distance on							
all-year dirt road	log	0.478	12.990			-0.224	-4.998
seasonal dirt roads	log	0.385	10.306			-0.250	-5.514
nonvehicle road	log	0.541	7.672			-0.297	-3.461
paved road	log	0.399	13.710	0.399	12.250	-0.267	-7.536
other type of road/river/railway	log	0.412	11.823			-0.370	-8.753

Source: Data from 1997 IFPRI/FOFIFA trader survey

Poor market institutions and high transaction costs Market institutions are poorly developed and not used in Madagascar. The use of trade credit by traders is extremely limited. Most agricultural trade, sales, and purchases, takes place without orders or credit and are cash-and-carry transactions. Invoicing or the use of checks is virtually unheard of. A small proportion of traders nevertheless manage to receive and grant trade credit (15.8 per cent and 13.6 per cent of total grain purchases and sales, respectively) but typically only for one week.

As for credit, the use of formal institutions is also extremely rare for contract enforcement and property rights protection. The direct costs of theft are quite small; on average less than 1 per cent of output traders' annual sales are stolen. On the other hand, 15 per cent of distributors were victims of theft. Some traders occasionally suffer severe losses, especially when goods are stolen at night or during transport. On the basis of these numbers, one may be tempted to conclude that the rule of law prevails in Madagascar and that malfeasance is adequately deterred by existing legal institutions. However, such a conclusion is unwarranted. Fafchamps and Minten (1999a) show that the low incidence of malfeasance owes more to prevention by traders than to legal deterrence.

Traders go to great lengths to minimize the risk of theft and breach of contract. Over one-third of respondents declared they refrained from hiring additional workers for fear of employee theft. The magnitude of this figure and its likely welfare cost in an economy where underemployment is rampant and trade is a major source of employment, perfectly illustrates the idea that the indirect costs of malfeasance are potentially much higher than its direct costs. Among traders who stock agricultural products at night, two-thirds sleep on the premises. Virtually all overnight storage is locked and guarded. Of those traders who transport goods from one town to another, 43 per cent either pay for protection or travel in convoy. In addition, some traders declare that they avoid certain routes for fear of robbery on the road.

Furthermore the trading environment is characterized by high search costs, for both suppliers and for clients. Survey results indicate that finding a supplier or a client is a recurrent problem for traders: between 40 and 50 per cent of them face difficulties, at least occasionally, in identifying potential buyers and sellers. Given that most of the agricultural products are perishable and that storage conditions are often substandard, this could be disastrous for the financial viability of some traders. Fafchamps and Minten (1999b) show that traders who experience many difficulties are those who have the smallest numbers of regular suppliers and clients. In other words, traders with regular sources of supply and a steady clientele are less likely to encounter problems.

Another important transaction cost is imperfect and asymmetric information. Malagasy traders have imperfect access to modern means of communication; the great majority of traders do not have a business phone or fax and there are no public agricultural information services (newspapers, TV, radio). Information is passed mostly by face-to-face communication. Traders also possess imperfect information on product quality, much more so than quantity, as it is more difficult to verify. The evidence indicates that price varies with quality and that quality cannot be perfectly inferred by a product's region of origin. The overwhelming majority of surveyed traders respond to the uncertainty of quality information by inspecting each and every purchase. The importance of quality inspection is further underscored by the fact that the task is virtually never delegated to family helpers, employees, or collection agents.

Low use and high cost of credit   Credit is rarely used in input and output trading. The use of own funds, without outside financing, is the most important way of financing the input distribution for all the actors in input distribution, i.e. retailers, semiwholesalers, and NGOs. The maximum interest rate that distributors are willing to pay is significantly below actual market rates. Hence, most input distributors report not using credit because they consider the interest rate too high (61 per cent of responses) and they report the high cost of credit as one of the major constraints to expansion (Randrianarisoa and Minten, 1997).

The same trends emerge from the output trader survey. Eighty-nine per cent of the traders report that they use only their own funds to support their business operation (Fafchamps and Minten, 1999b). Formal credit as a means to finance trading activities is almost nonexistent; it is mentioned by only 1.5 per cent of the traders representing 6.1 per cent of total sales. The minor importance of formal financial institutions is further illustrated by the fact that only 16 per cent of the surveyed traders have a bank account and one trader out of 100 has a line of credit at a bank. Only 4 per cent of the traders ever asked for credit from a formal institution. When asked why they do not apply for formal credit, half of the traders responded either that they do not know how to apply (28 per cent) or that the application procedure is too complicated (19 per cent). The rest either consider interest rates too high (23 per cent of respondents) or do not possess any collateral (16 per cent). As is often the case in surveys of this type (e.g. Cuevas et al., 1993), a positive relationship between firm size and reliance on formal financial institutions is observed.

Informal credit does not appear to compensate for the limited use of formal credit (Fafchamps and Minten, 1999b). Only one trader out of ten derives part of its working capital from informal credit sources. Less than 2 per cent of the traders are members of savings mutuals and only 1 per cent are members of a 'tontine' (a rotating savings group). The median self-declared opportunity costs of capital reverts to around 20 per cent a year. However, some respondents declare facing a much higher shadow cost of capital. There is no clear relationship between business size and the shadow interest rate perceived by traders.

While there are other constraints to the efficiency of traders, it is clear that those discussed above emerge among the most important. These constraints at the trader level show up in measures of local market performance.

Operation and Performance of Local Markets

High price variability While prices were characterized by relative stability before reform, they are now highly variable (Minten and Mendoza, 1999; Barrett, 1997b; 1997c). High transportation and transaction costs lead to significant spatial price variation for inputs and levels of outputs. Regional prices are 40 per cent higher in the lean period and 27 per cent higher in the harvest period in the higher priced region than in the lower priced region (based on monthly rice prices gathered for the period June 1996-May 1997). These regional differences hide higher differences at the village level as shown by an overall coefficient of variation of 21 per cent during harvest time. Even more unfavorable statistics show up in input prices. For example, the urea price varied from 1,800 FMG per kg in Antananarivo to 3,300 FMG per kg in parts of Fianarantsoa at the time of the survey (Randrianarisoa and Minten, 1997). Hence, a more dynamic input demand by farmers will find bottlenecks in the current high marketing cost and the consequently prohibitive high input prices in certain regions.

Seasonal price variation is also extremely high, especially compared to Asian rice economies. Rural rice prices average 115 per cent higher in the lean period compared to the harvest period. During the survey period, the price was 200 per cent higher in the lean period than in the harvest period in the Majunga Plateaux area while it was smaller in the more accessible Vakinankaratra region (Figure 2.2). As most commercial storage is in towns, a reversal of flows between rural and urban regions is noticed over the year. Hence, seasonal movements are lower in towns than in nearby rural areas and are largest in the most isolated areas (Minten, 1999; Barrett, 1996b). Seasonal variation shows up in other products as well. For instance, before major crop harvests, rural livestock prices are 40 per cent lower than after harvest. This last variation seems almost exclusively linked to demand changes.

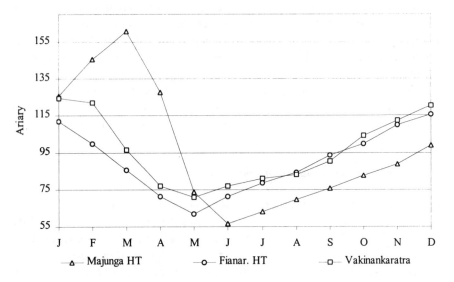

Figure 2.2   Seasonal price of a cup ('kapoaka') of rice, Jun. 1996-May 1997

Low market integration and area coverage   There is little interregional trade and although the capital city Antananarivo occasionally draws food products from outside its own province, most marketed output is consumed within the province where it is produced. Assemblers, defined as traders who gather produce in rural areas and sell it to traders in towns, have an area coverage barely exceeding 100 km. An average wholesaler travels less than 30 km to purchase products (Mendoza and Randrianarisoa, 1998). Results of the market integration analysis confirm that interregional rice trade in Madagascar is still weak, even after reform (Minten and Mendoza, 1999). If liberalization was expected to achieve better integrated markets, the findings suggest that this was not completely achieved.

Traders' response to intermarket shocks remains fragmented and incomplete, as indicated by cross long-run multipliers being less than unitary to greater than one (for methodology, see Minten and Mendoza, 1999). The tests for market integration summarized in Table 2.3 suggest that regional rice markets in Madagascar are linked with each other to some extent. However, the degree of integration is quite limited. Among the ten market pairs estimated for each period, only half yielded significant cross-market multipliers in the prereform and postreform periods suggesting some market linkage between some regional pairs but not others.[6] Reaction time to unanticipated market news is typically sluggish, exceeding one month, although response time is slightly quicker since liberalization suggesting an improvement in the transmission of market news across markets (Minten and Mendoza, 1999).

Table 2.3   Indicators of regional market integration for rice, 1984-1992

Time period	Pairwise market relationship[a]	Cross long-run multiplier[b]	Response time to shocks[c] (months)
Pre-reform (1984-1987)	Antsirabe→Antananarivo	1.24[d]	9
	Majunga→Antananarivo	1.50[d]	1
	Antananarivo→Toamasina	0.68[d]	2
	Antananarivo→Tulear	0.93[d]	2
	Antananarivo→Fianarantsoa	1.12[e]	1
	Fianarantsoa→Antananarivo	0.32[d]	1
Post-reform (1988-1992)	Antsirabe→Antananarivo	0.85[d]	0
	Majunga→Antananarivo	1.82[d]	2
	Antananarivo→Toamasina	0.66[e]	2
	Antananarivo→Tulear	0.93[d]	2
	Antananarivo→Fianarantsoa	1.12[f]	1
	Fianarantsoa→Antananarivo	0.32[e]	1

[a] Indicates the direction of causation such that the market on the left side of the arrow (→) leads the market on the right

[b] Measures the impact of shocks originating from the market on the left side of the arrow on the market on the right

[c] Indicates the time it takes for the market on the left side of the arrow to fully absorb and adjust to shocks coming from the market on the right

[d, e, f] Indicate significance at 1 %, 5 % and 10 % levels respectively

Source: Data from Ministère de l'Agriculture; calculations after Minten and Mendoza, 1999

The reliance on social capital by traders   As indicated before, there is significant variation in size among traders. The fact that small traders are younger and less established but otherwise share a family background similar to that of successful traders, suggests a life cycle explanation for size. However, some of the facts do not fit a simple, free entry, life cycle explanation for the size distribution of trading firms. Fafchamps and Minten (1998) show that traders in the upper tercile of the firm size distribution use fifteen times more working capital and two times more capital, but they get forty-six times more gross margin. Fafchamps and Minten (1998; 1999b) explore in more detail the reasons for these differences.

It seems that one fundamental implication of the institutional and structural deficiencies in the emerging marketing sector is that social capital becomes the key resource used by traders to compensate for these deficiencies.   In other words, the level of familiarity and personal relationship becomes the main determinant of access to critical information related to prices, market conditions and opportunities, access to credit, respect and enforcement of contracts, regularity and reliability of trade flows, and the mitigation of business risk.   In fact, results indicate that traders with better relationships are more prosperous and have much higher profits. Results further indicate that larger traders make more profit than their smaller competitors, not because they abuse their market power, but because their connections make them more efficient in the face of considerable institutional and structural weaknesses in the marketing systems. Social capital allows traders to minimize search costs and enforce contracts, thereby raising their ability to expand exchange beyond cash-and-carry transactions, yielding greater business scale and greater efficiency.

To summarize, input and output markets seem to have responded to the liberalization measures as shown by the increased participation of traders.   However, constraints remain for growth and efficiency of the sector: limited demand for inputs, high and unstable import prices, lack of high yield rice varieties, high transportation costs, high cost or unavailability of credit, as well as poor marketing institutions and high transaction costs. This leads to 'flea market' economies, high reliance on social capital to overcome transaction costs and poor market institutions, high price variability, and low market integration. It is clear that problems in input and output markets affect agricultural producer behavior. In the next chapters, this is studied in more depth.

Notes

1 In Antananarivo, fokontany rice represented more than 60 per cent of household rice consumption until 1986 (e.g. Roubaud, 1997). The subsidy program continued until October 1988 but its importance gradually declined.

2 For a more extensive discussion, see the IFPRI/FOFIFA final report 'Structure and Conduct of Major Agricultural Input and Output Markets and Response to Reforms by Rural Households in Madagascar', October 1998, more specifically Part II, 'Analysis of Input Distribution and Seed Markets', and Part IV, 'Agricultural Output Markets and Price Behavior'. The results in the next section are mainly drawn from these two reports. The sampling frame and survey design for the traders was set up as follows. The input trader survey was organized in January 1997. The sample included 126 input distributors of which 83 per cent were retailers and semiwholesalers and 17 per cent were NGOs and development organizations. Given the small number of input distributors in the survey area, this sample might be considered a census. During February-March 1997, a survey was organized in the seed multiplication subsector. The sample included members of the Groupements de Producteurs de Semences (GPS or group-based seed producers) and individual private seed farmers not part of the GPS. The total sample of 109 farmers includes 61 per cent GPS farmers and 39 per cent individual farmers. The survey at the output trader level consisted of two rounds. The first round was held between May 1997 and August 1997. The questionnaire in the first round survey consisted mainly of questions dealing with the individual characteristics of the traders and with the structure, conduct, and performance of the trading sector. The second round was conducted between September and November 1997. The same traders were visited and they were asked mostly about the nature of their relationships with other traders, clients, and suppliers. A total of 850 traders were surveyed in the first round, 739 of whom were surveyed again in the second round. The sample design was constructed so as to be as representative as possible of all the traders involved in the entire food marketing chain from producer to consumer, wherever located. The survey focused on traders who market locally consumed staples such as rice, cassava, potatoes, beans, and peanuts. Traders involved primarily in export crops, fruits, vegetables, and minor crops were excluded.

3 The coefficients of variation of sales and value added are 2.6 and 3.7, respectively. The corresponding Gini coefficients are 0.761 and 0.702.

4 The Ministry of Agriculture estimated the use of fertilizer on lowland rice at 6 kg per hectare, one of the lowest levels in Africa.

5 Badiane et al. (1997) mention a transport cost per ton per km that is 150 per cent higher than in Benin and 60 per cent higher than in Senegal for similar distances and products.

6 Nonsignificant multipliers are obtained between Antananarivo and Tulear, Antsirabe, and Toamasina, indicating segmentation. Although this can be expected between Antananarivo and Tulear which are naturally separated due to poor roads during that period, the isolation of the nearby regions of Antsirabe and Toamasina from Antananarivo is rather puzzling and difficult to explain.

3 Conceptual Framework, Survey Design, and Sampling Frame for Household and Community Level Analyses

MANFRED ZELLER and BART MINTEN

Conceptual Framework

The performance of local input and output distribution systems and, therefore, their adjustment to changes in the operating environment have strong implications for growth in the agricultural sector and for the welfare of those rural households that directly or indirectly depend on farming for their food security and livelihood. At a given level of technological development, rural households and their members face a set of techniques, of which they choose to apply a subset, depending on the economic, social, cultural, and agroecological environment prevailing in their communities. Of critical importance for the demand for applied techniques is the ability of output marketing systems to absorb marketable quantities and to efficiently transmit price signals across local markets. The extent to which that demand is met, is in turn determined by the supply and availability of the inputs that embody these techniques, that is, by the efficiency (in terms of timeliness and costs) of local input and services delivery systems.

The reforms in agricultural input and output markets result in price changes at the farmgate and household levels and in changes in transaction costs for rural households to acquire inputs and food and to sell farm output or agricultural wage labor. Institutional changes in financial markets, such as changes in the regulatory framework of the financial sector and the recent increase in microfinance projects, influence the household's access to credit and savings options. Furthermore, other complementary services for enhanced supply response and productivity include access to agricultural extension and information. These changes are expected to induce transformations in agricultural and non-agricultural income generation which subsequently result in changes of household farm, nonfarm, and wage income; food and nonfood consumption; nutritional status; and subsequent investment in human and physical capital.

The hypothesized interconnections between changes in farmgate or household gate prices and transaction costs for agricultural inputs and outputs, other goods and services, and household food security (or welfare) are conceptualized in Figure 3.1. The framework of the analysis shows the relationship to factors that are exogenous to the household economy such as macroeconomic and agricultural sector policies which impinge on the structure, conduct, and performance of agricultural input and output markets, on public agricultural extension, and on prices, wages, and interest rates. Other exogenous factors are agroecological and socioeconomic conditions in the community or region in which the household resides which condition the size of the response by farm households to policy changes. Transaction costs in accessing markets and financial and other institutions will be influenced by the overall level of infrastructure, geographic location, characteristics of the rural villages, and the relative abundance of land, water, and other natural resources. In order to control for exogenous effects at the village level in measuring household response to changes in markets, a community level survey which obtains data on these exogenous socioeconomic and agroecological characteristics was designed and implemented.

The household response to changes in input and output prices, wages, and interest rates will be further conditioned by the initial household endowment of physical capital (land, livestock, durables), human capital (labor force, dependency ratio, education), social capital (access to institutions and social networks), and environmental capital (often owned or controlled collectively by the community or certain socioeconomic groups within the community, e.g. access to forests, cultivatable land currently lying fallow, water, grazing land, etc.). Furthermore, the effects of market reforms on household food security are expected to depend on demographic structure of the household (e.g. age, gender, education of household head, dependency ratio, etc.). These factors will impinge on the households' income generation and the mix between agricultural and non-agricultural income sources. Particular emphasis in the research is put on the potentials and constraints of farm households to adopt new agricultural technology (improved seed varieties, fertilizer).

Decisions regarding the marketing and home consumption of agricultural production will be conditioned by household characteristics (wealth, household demography, shocks) and by household level prices and

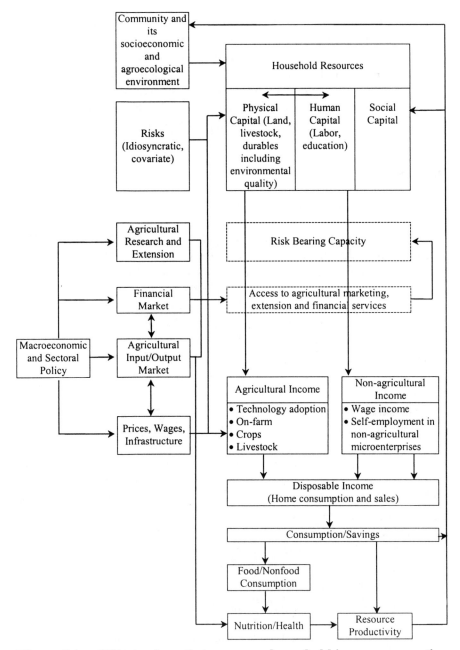

Figure 3.1   Effects of market access on household income generation and food security

transactions costs, particularly in food and financial markets. Disposable income (either generated on- or off-farm) will influence the level and composition of food and nonfood consumption and ultimately, food intake, nutritional status, and residual savings for future investments in physical, human, and social capital. In the long run, these investments will alter the capital base of the household (and of its community through aggregation of other households). This conceptual framework guides our analysis.

Description of Data Sources

Sampling Frame of the 1997 IFPRI/FOFIFA Survey

The survey communities were randomly selected based on a stratified sampling frame that distinguished strata based on agroecological conditions, village size, and the distance from the village to the nearest tarred road. Two types of surveys were organized in the selected villages: a household survey and a community survey. The household survey consisted of two rounds: the first during the period March/April 1997 and the second during the period June/August 1997.   495 households were surveyed in the first round; 30 households were lost in the second round, leaving 465 households in the second round of the survey. During May 1997, 188 communities were surveyed in the community survey.[1]

The surveys were conducted in the faritany of Majunga, Fianarantsoa, and in one subregion of the faritany of Antananarivo (Vakinankaratra)[2]. In the faritany of Majunga, three agroecological strata are differentiated: the Majunga Plains (fivondronana of Maravoay) characterized by the existence of a large irrigation system, the Majunga Plateau (fivondronana of Mampikony), and the Majunga Highlands (fivondronana of Bealalana). In the faritany of Fianarantsoa, three agroecological regions were also differentiated: the highlands region of Fianarantsoa hereafter called Fianarantsoa Hautes Terres (represented by the randomly selected fivondronana of Fianarantsoa II), the Falaise ('escarpement') region (fivondronana of Ikongo), and the Côte ('coastal') region (fivondronana of Manakara). In most tables, we aggregate the latter two regions into a subregion called Fianarantsoa Côte/Falaise. We do the same for the Majunga Hautes Terres region, combining the Majunga Highlands and Plateau. The Vakinankaratra region (fivondronana of Antsirabe and Betafo) has been included in the survey as a major agricultural production region of the country. Moreover, the 1992 IFPRI/CNRE/DSA study 'Credit for the Rural Poor' focused on the Vakinankaratra region (Zeller, 1993) thus, the potential availability of panel data, especially at the household level, called for inclusion of this region in the current study.

Due to the stratified sample set-up, each household and village represents a specific agroecological zone, size of village, and distance to a main road. To ensure that the sample reflects the population as a whole, a weight is assigned to each village and household which reflects the relative importance of each stratum. This weight is used in the calculation of the means, variation, and regression coefficients throughout the study. A demonstration of the sampling and the calculation of the specific weights of each community and household in the respective surveys is given in Tables 3.1. and 3.2. Within a fivondronana, there were six strata in the sample based on the size of the community (3 below and 3 above the median of the particular fivondronana) and on the distance to a paved road (close, medium, far away). The unit of observation for the community survey is the community. Hence, the set-up of the sample implies that each of the strata should represent one-sixth of the total number of communities in the fivondronana. Weights were constructed that reflect this set-up (weighting factor 1)[3]. For the presentation of results, it was decided to merge the Majunga Plateau and Highlands into one stratum and Fianarantsoa Côte and Falaise area into one stratum. To reflect the relative weight of these strata, a second correction was made (weighting factor 2). Then, weights were constructed to reflect the importance of the fivondronana in the fokontany in the whole survey region (weighting factor 3). The final weighting factor for the community survey was obtained through multiplication of these different factors.

The sampling frame for the household survey had to be constructed differently as all the strata within the fivondronana could not be selected because of logistical constraints. The same six strata within the fivondronana were retained as for the community survey based on size of the village and distance to a road. As some fivondronana had to reflect a larger stratum, more households within that fivondronana were sampled. Based on the number of households that were selected in a given fivondronana, the number of villages that could be surveyed was determined taking logistics into account (i.e. at least ten households had to be surveyed in one village). Then, a random selection of the strata in the given fivondronana out of all the strata was made. The unit of observation for the household survey is the household.

Table 3.1   Household sampling and weights in 1997 IFPRI/FOFIFA survey

Stratum Fivondronana	Firaisana	Fokontany	Stratum	Number of households	Population in strata	Weight in the fiv. (WF 1)*	Weight of fiv. in larger strata (WF 2)*	Weight of fiv. in total population (WF 3)*	Total weight
Vakinankaratra									
Antsirabe	Ampatana-Mandriankeni.	Mandriankaniheny	2	23	58,003	0.4255	1	0.7937	0.3377
Betafo	Alarobia Bamaha	Ambohijafy	3	24	58,003	0.6205	1	0.7937	0.4925
Antsirabe	Soanindrariny	Manarintsoa-Sud	6	24	15,587	1.0740	1	0.7937	0.8524
Betafo	Ankazomiriotra	Andratsay Mahamasina	1	13	58,003	1.1455	1	0.7937	0.9092
Betafo	Fidirana	Antampondravola	6	12	150,587	1.0740	1	0.7937	0.8524
Betafo	Betafo	Ambohiambo	4	14	150,587	2.7616	1	0.7937	2.1918
Antsirabe	Ambohidranandriana	Tsaramody	2	12	58,003	0.4255	1	0.7937	0.3377
Total				122					
Majunga – Plaines									
Marovoay	Manaratsandry	Ampijoroa	6	21	61,046	1.0877	1	0.7059	0.7679
Marovoay	Tsararano	Bekalila	3	17	19,551	0.4303	1	0.7059	0.3038
Marovoay	Tsararano	Bepako	4	15	61,046	1.5228	1	0.7059	1.0750
Total				53					
Majunga – Plateau (Majunga HT)									
Mampikony	Bekomatsaka	Bemikondry	4	17	82,641	1.2032	0.9692	0.6964	0.8122
Mampikony	Bekomatsaka	Befotaka	5	19	82,641	1.0766	0.9692	0.6964	0.7267
Mampikony	Ampasimatera	Anovilava	6	19	82,641	1.0766	0.9692	0.6964	0.7267
Mampikony	Ambohitoaka	Sarodrano	1	10	23,506	0.5818	0.9692	0.6964	0.3927
Mampikony	Ampasimatera	Ambodimanga II	3	8	23,506	0.7273	0.9692	0.6964	0.4909
Total				73					
Majunga - Haut Plateaux (Majunga HT)									
Bealanana	Antsamaka	Ambodikakazo	1	15	16,782	0.5743	1.05	0.6964	0.4199
Bealanana	Ambatosia	Ambohimitsinjo	4	15	54,104	1.8514	1.05	0.6964	1.3539
Bealanana	Ambatoriha-Est	Beroitra	2	15	16,782	0.5743	1.05	0.6964	0.4199
Total				45					

Fianarantsoa - Hautes Terres

Fianar. II	Alakamisy Ambohimaha	Ambohimaha	4	17	224,077	1.0644	1	1.9162	2.0396
Fianar. II	Andranovorivato	Sahavanana	5	16	224,077	1.1309	1	1.9162	2.1671
Fianar. II	Alakamisy Itenina	Sangasanga Atsimo	6	17	224,077	1.0644	1	1.9162	2.0396
Fianar. II	Ambalakely	Miandrifekona	1	10	106,151	0.8572	1	1.9162	1.6425
Fianar. II	Andrainjato centre	Ampapana	2	10	106,151	0.8572	1	1.9162	1.6425
Fianar. II	Mahasoabe	Tsararivotra	3	10	106,151	0.8572	1	1.9162	1.6425
Total				80					

Fianarantsoa – Côte (Fianar. C/F)

Manakara	Ambalavero	Ambalavero	5	16	103,552	1.1277	1.2862	1.0357	1.5022
Manakara	Ambahive	Ambandrika	6	16	103,552	1.1277	1.2862	1.0357	1.5022
Manakara	Ambalavero	Tanambao	1	10	39,922	0.6956	1.2862	1.0357	0.9266
Manakara	Ampasimpotsy	Mahatsaratsara	3	8	39,922	0.8695	1.2862	1.0357	1.1583
Total				50					

Fianarantsoa – Falaise (Fianar. C/F)

Ikongo	Ikongo	Ambolomadinika	6	14	43,365	1.2373	0.6593	1.0357	0.8449
Ikongo	Tolongoina	Ambohimahavelona	5	13	43,365	1.3325	0.6593	1.0357	0.9098
	Menatsara								
Ikongo	Ambatofotsy	Ambohitsara	1	15	18,414	0.4904	0.6593	1.0357	0.3348
Total				42					

* Weighting factor

Source: Own calculations based on data from INSTAT (Institut National de la Statistique)

Table 3.2   Community sampling and weights

Stratum	Distance to road	Size of village	Number of fokontany sampled	Weight of fokontany in Fivondronana (WF 1)*	Weight fiv. in larger strata (WF 2)*	Total of fiv. (WF 3)*	Total weight
Vakinankaratra							
	close	small	9	0.926	1.000	0.533	0.494
	medium	small	7	1.190	1.000	0.533	0.635
	far	small	6	1.389	1.000	0.533	0.741
	close	large	11	0.758	1.000	0.533	0.404
	medium	large	7	1.190	1.000	0.533	0.635
	far	large	10	0.833	1.000	0.533	0.444
Total			50				
Majunga - Plaines							
	close	small	3	1.389	1.000	0.363	0.505
	medium	small	3	1.389	1.000	0.363	0.505
	far	small	5	0.833	1.000	0.363	0.303
	close	large	5	0.833	1.000	0.363	0.303
	medium	large	2	2.083	1.000	0.363	0.757
	far	large	7	0.595	1.000	0.363	0.216
Total			25				
Majunga - Plateau (Majunga HT)							
	close	small	5	0.767	1.327	0.926	0.942
	medium	small	2	1.917	1.327	0.926	2.355
	far	small	2	1.917	1.327	0.926	2.355
	close	large	5	0.767	1.327	0.926	0.942
	medium	large	5	0.767	1.327	0.926	0.942
	far	large	4	0.958	1.327	0.926	1.177
Total			23				
Majunga - Haut Plateaux (Majunga HT)							
	close	small	5	0.833	0.699	0.926	0.539
	medium	small	3	1.389	0.699	0.926	0.899
	far	small	6	0.694	0.699	0.926	0.449
	close	large	5	0.833	0.699	0.926	0.539
	medium	large	3	1.389	0.699	0.926	0.899
	far	large	3	1.389	0.699	0.926	0.899
Total			25				
Fianarantsoa - Hautes Terres							
	close	small	4	1.042	1.000	2.364	2.462
	medium	small	3	1.389	1.000	2.364	3.283

far	small	4	1.042	1.000	2.364	2.462
close	large	5	0.833	1.000	2.364	1.970
medium	large	5	0.833	1.000	2.364	1.970
far	large	4	1.042	1.000	2.364	2.462
Total		25				
Fianarantsoa - Côte (Fianar. C/F)						
close	small	4	1.042	1.076	1.218	1.365
medium	small	4	1.042	1.076	1.218	1.365
far	small	2	2.083	1.076	1.218	2.731
close	large	4	1.042	1.076	1.218	1.365
medium	large	5	0.833	1.076	1.218	1.092
far	large	6	0.694	1.076	1.218	0.910
Total		25				
Fianarantsoa - Falaise (Fianar. C/F)						
close	small	4	0.625	0.873	1.218	0.664
medium	small	1	2.500	0.873	1.218	2.658
far	small	4	0.625	0.873	1.218	0.664
close	large	2	1.250	0.873	1.218	1.329
medium	large	3	0.833	0.873	1.218	0.886
far	large	1	2.500	0.873	1.218	2.658
Total		15				
Total number of villages		188				

* Weighting factor

Source: Own calculations based on data from INSTAT (Institut National de la Statistique)

Therefore, more households were surveyed in larger villages. The same weighting procedure as for the village survey was used. Hence, the final weighting factor is obtained through the multiplication of three weighting factors reflecting the importance of the strata within the fivondronana, the correction for the enlarged strata Majunga Hautes Terres and Fianarantsoa Côte/Falaise, and the importance of the fivondronana in the whole survey region.

We point out that while the sample frame allows for reasonable aggregation of the study results for the rural parts of the faritany of Majunga and Fianarantsoa, this is not the case for the faritany of Antananarivo. Finally, the sample includes 12 randomly selected villages for the community survey and 6 randomly selected villages for the household survey (99 households in the first round and 88 households in the second round) in the vicinity of the national park of Ranomafana (in the faritany of Fianarantsoa). However, these villages represent a cluster apart from the overall sampling frame, and are therefore given the weight of zero when tabulating results for the Fianarantsoa region. The villages of Ranomafana were included to allow for some comparative analysis as this area is a major intervention zone of the government of Madagascar for projects aimed at protecting the environment. The selected regions in the survey are shown on Figure 3.2.

Questionnaire Modules of the 1997 IFPRI/FOFIFA Survey

The household survey was a comprehensive survey which obtained data on all the elements described in the conceptual framework. The surveys focused on demography, health, anthropometry, food consumption, income, and wealth (including land possession and tenure, and formal/informal credit and savings transactions). Given the importance of agriculture in rural areas, the survey had a detailed crop-specific enumeration of input and output quantities and prices. To provide insights on the intrahousehold resource allocation and control, the questionnaire for the agricultural production module included questions related to the decision-making process leading to the observed levels of production. For non-agricultural self-employment, such as handicrafts and petty trade, the questionnaire addressed individual household members. This increased not only the accuracy of the results, but allowed also differentiation of these income sources by gender and other individual member characteristics. IFPRI's 1991/1992 survey employed a similar method enabling consistent comparisons.

In order to analyze the effects of changes in income on household food security, the survey enumerated food and nonfood consumption in each of two rounds. For preschoolers, health and anthropometric data were obtained. The structure of consumption and nutrition survey modules were similar to the ones already employed in the previous IFPRI field survey. Apart from consumption, changes in income will affect investment in physical and human capital, such as the buildup of livestock and land assets or the education of children. These effects can only be observed and measured with panel data covering several years. Therefore, households in the previous IFPRI survey were included in our household sample.

The village survey focused on questions related to aggregate and village level variables, such as access to infrastructure and input and output markets, and the evolution of these variables over the last ten years. The questionnaire also included questions on yield levels and their evolution over time, on rural wages and prices, and on environmental issues. The outline of the different modules of the village and household questionnaires are shown in Table 3.3.

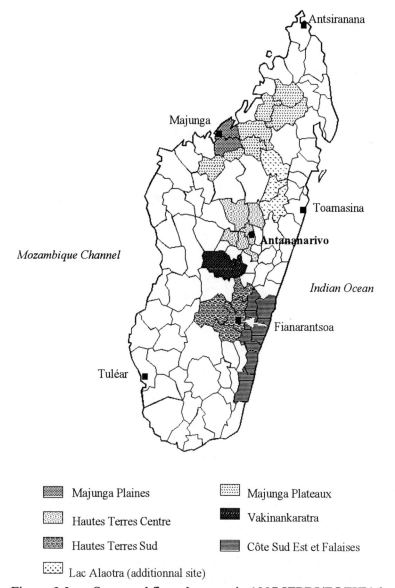

Figure 3.2   Surveyed fivondronana in 1997 IFPRI/FOFIFA household and trader surveys

Table 3.3 Modules of the questionnaires

Community survey	Household survey
Demography of the population	Socioeconomic characteristics of the
Size of the fokontany	households and its members
Ethnic distribution	General information
Access to physical, administrative, and	Characteristics of the different
socioeconomic infrastructure	members, e.g. activities, education,
Access to input markets, agricultural	health
product markets, and consumer	Agricultural possessions and
goods	production
Seasonal price of rice, beef, and daily	Land and forest possession
agricultural salary	Land renting and leasing
Formal credit	Agricultural income of the
Informal credit and organizations	household
Savings group	Agricultural expenditures
Mutual help groups 'Dina'	Livestock income and expenditures
Informal credit	Possession of durable goods (except
Production risk and insecurity	land and livestock)
Cultivated area	Food and nonfood consumption
Use of inputs and agricultural yields	Preparation of food and set-up of
Commercial surplus and own	meal
consumption	Food consumption
Purchasing power	Nonfood expenditures
Access to extension	Access to credit
Feed	Credit obtained
Ecological questions	Credit given
Use of wood and forest products	Gifts received
Land tenure rules	Time allocation of members of
Fires	household
Soil fertility and erosion	Salary and non-agricultural income
Farmers' organizations and	Nutritional status of the children in the
reforestation	household

Source: 1997 IFPRI/FOFIFA household and community survey

1992 IFPRI/CNRE/DSA Sample

The sample of villages in the 1992 survey was drawn using a sample frame that stratified all the villages in the survey regions. Similarly as in 1997, villages were stratified according to two main criteria: population greater or less than the median in region, and region-specific terciles of distance to the nearest main road (Zeller, 1993). In the Vakinankaratra region, altitude was additionally chosen as a stratum to reflect the highly diverse agroecological conditions below and above 1,600 meters. These criteria result in the division of the population into 30 strata: 5 strata covering the different agroecological regions, 2 strata for the size of the village, and 3 strata for the distance to the main road.

The 1992 household survey included three rounds covering seasonal interlinkages between income, consumption and nutrition, savings/ investment, and credit/gift flows. One hundred thirty-five households are located in the Vakinankaratra region and 54 households in three villages in the fivondronana of Marovoay. Household surveys for the first round commenced in mid-January and were completed in Vakinankaratra region by the end of March, and in the Marovoay region by early April. This round covered the peak of the hungry season in the Vakinankaratra region, and the beginning of the hungry season in Marovoay. Household surveys for the second round commenced at the end of April in Vakinankaratra and at the beginning of May in Marovoay and were completed in both regions by the beginning of June. In Vakinankaratra region, it covered the rainy, most productive agricultural season; in the Marovoay region, field preparation and transplanting of rice. As in round 1, income, consumption, credit/gift flows, asset changes (including all categories of assets), and anthropometric and time allocation data were collected. Round 3 was implemented from mid-August until mid-September, and covered most of the dry season income, consumption, and credit/gift flows in Vakinankaratra region. For Marovoay, this survey covered the harvest of early and intermediate rice. The content of the questionnaire was the same as in rounds 1 and 2. In addition, all households members older than 14 years were asked questions on borrowing, differentiated by intended use and source of credit.

Notes

1   Further information on the sampling frame and survey design is contained in the IFPRI/FOFIFA research paper No.1 by Eliane Ralison et al. (1997), titled "Le projet FOFIFA-IFPRI: Présentation - Méthodologie - Echantillon.

2   Madagascar is administratively divided into faritany, fivondronana, firaisana, and fokontany (province, district, subdistrict, and village respectively). We will use the Malagasy names throughout the book.

3   The weighting factors are calculated as follows: $w=(N_i/N)/(n_i/n)$ where N is the total number in the universe, N_i is the total number in the particular strata, n is the total number of units surveyed, and n_i is the number surveyed in that particular strata.

4 Brief Description of Socioeconomic Situation and Changes in Indicators of Welfare

MANFRED ZELLER, BART MINTEN, and CÉCILE LAPENU

In the first part of this chapter we provide a brief description of the socioeconomic characteristics of the survey households. The major focus will be on the possession and utilization of land. We discuss changes in landholding for the panel households during the past five years, and highlight the role of land as a major component of the overall wealth of rural households. In a second section, we present changes in welfare indicators, as reported by the survey households, over the past five years, and report on causes for positive and negative changes as indicated by the household head.

Land Possession, Land Utilization, and Socioeconomic Characteristics of Rural Households

Household Characteristics

Table 4.1 presents data on the average size and dependency ratio of the household, as well as on the age, gender, and education level of the household head.[1] The average household size in all survey regions is 6.16 members, with a dependency ratio of 0.52 dependent children per adult. Larger households with higher dependency ratios are found particularly in the Majunga HT and the Fianarantsoa C/F region. The average age of the head of household varies between 44 and 50 years. About one-eighth of households have women as de facto heads. The average education index is 2.3, implying that the heads obtained six years of primary schooling. However, this average masks the wide variation in this index, as indicated by the standard deviation of 0.96. When comparing education among regions, the Vakinankaratra and the Fianarantsoa HT, as well as the Majunga Plaines

Table 4.1   Means and standard deviations of selected socioeconomic characteristics of survey households, by region

	Majunga Plaines (No.=40)		Majunga HT (No.=87)		Fianar. HT (No.=163)		Fianar. C/F (No.=101)	
	Mean	Standard deviation	Mean	Standard deviation	Mean	Standard deviation	Mean	Standard deviation
Household size	5.84	2.65	6.36	2.66	6.20	2.56	6.30	2.80
Dependency ratio[a]	0.47	0.27	0.56	0.19	0.52	0.18	0.51	0.22
Age of household head	49.93	15.40	45.90	14.83	44.39	11.91	46.73	12.77
% of households with female heads	9.2	-	4.2	-	15.5	-	15.1	-
Education level of household head[b]	2.38	1.35	2.11	1.07	2.41	0.84	2.20	0.94

	Vakinankaratra (No.=103)		Ranomafana (No.=99)		All regions (No.=495)	
	Mean	Standard deviation	Mean	Standard deviation	Mean	Standard deviation
Household size	5.92	2.31	5.97	2.67	6.16	2.58
Dependency ratio[a]	0.52	0.20	0.50	0.19	0.52	0.20
Age of household head	44.30	11.64	44.99	14.90	45.03	14.00
% of households with female heads	14.5	-	12.1	-	12.5	-
Education level of household head[b]	2.36	0.86	2.18	0.75	2.30	0.96

[a] Defined as the number of members below age 14 divided by household size

[b] The average value of a variable defined as follows: 1 = never attended school; 2 = did not obtain a CEPE (a six-year primary school degree); 3 = obtained CEPE; 4 = attended school for nine years; 5 = obtained a baccalaureate (12 years of schooling); 6 = higher education (university, CAP, BTS)

Source: Data from 1997 IFPRI/FOFIFA survey

appear to have higher levels of education than those found in the other regions. The lowest education score is found in the Majunga HT region.

Land Possession

Table 4.2 presents data on the possession of land in 1996. We distinguish three categories of land: (1) irrigable land suitable for rice cultivation (i.e. tanimbary); (2) rainfed, nonirrigable upland cleared for crop cultivation (i.e. tanety); and (3) any other land with forest, bush, or grass cover (i.e. ala-kijana) that has been appropriated by the household. The latter category of land is mostly upland which has been previously cultivated, but at present is idle or reforested. All area measurements are in ares. On average for all regions, households possess 244 ares of land, of which 108 ares are of riceland and upland and the remainder is forest, bush, or grassland. Farm sizes are much larger in the fivondronona of Majunga (an area receiving migrants), ranging from 3.7 hectares to 5.5 hectares, whereas all other regions have average farm sizes of around 1.5 hectares. We note that households living in the Majunga area have at least twice the land than households in the other regions. Moreover, households living in the Majunga Plaines area (i.e. near Maravoay in the Basse Betsiboka) and in the Majunga HT area possess relatively large holdings of riceland of about 2.5 hectares whereas riceland holdings in the other survey areas hover around only 0.5 hectares. The smallest farm sizes and riceland holdings are found in the Fianarantsoa C/F region and in Ranomafana. Chapter 10 will show that these latter regions have also relatively lower food security.

Utilization of Upland and Riceland During the Rainy Season 1995/1996

In order to further appreciate the way rural households utilize their land, Tables 4.3 and 4.4 show data on whether land was cultivated by the owner, rented out, rented in, or left fallow. The last column in Table 4.3 reports the average figure of 108 ares of riceland (tanimbary) owned. Of these 108 ares, 100 ares were cultivated by the owner, 2 ares were rented out, and the remainder was not cultivated, either voluntarily or due to a lack of financial means or labor. On average, the survey households rented in an additional 16 ares so that their cultivated area of riceland is 116; slightly higher than the possessed area of 108. As the survey households are drawn from a random sample, the inequality between land rented out and rented in indicates the existence of absentee landlords who are not part of the sampling frame.

Table 4.3 further shows that the cultivated riceland area is lowest in Ranomafana and Fianarantsoa HT, and highest in Majunga Plaines. The most active rental markets for riceland are found in Majunga Plaines and Vakinankaratra; in the Vakinankaratra, 8 out of 55 ares of cultivated riceland are rented in, whereas this ratio is even higher for the Majunga region (96 out of 332). Our data shows that land prices in these two regions are also the highest.

Table 4.2   Possession of land, by region, 1996, in ares*

	Majunga Plaines (No.=40)	Majunga HT (No.=87)	Fianar. HT (No.=163)	Fianar. C/F (No.=101)
Total area	377	551	150	149
Riceland	246	281	49	58
Upland	102	150	97	88
Forest- or bushland	29	120	5	2

	Vakinankaratra (No.=103)	Ranomafana (No.=99)	All regions (No.=495)
Total area	176	156	244
Riceland	49	46	108
Upland	112	98	108
Forest- or bushland	16	11	29

* 1 hectare = 100 ares

Source: Data from 1997 IFPRI/FOFIFA survey

Table 4.4 shows that the land rental market is less important for upland than for riceland. Of the 102 ares of cultivated upland, only five are rented in. Moreover, we see that the differences in total cultivated land between regions are less for upland than for riceland. Thus, the regional inequality in land cultivation is most pronounced for riceland and less for upland. However, as Table 4.2 shows, households in the Majunga area are able to have longer or more frequent fallow periods on upland as they own more bush and forest land, in particular in the Majunga HT area (see Table 4.4).

Table 4.3   Possession and use of riceland in the rainy season 1995/1996, by region, in ares*

	Majunga Plaines (No.=40)	Majunga HT (No.=87)	Fianar. HT (No.=163)	Fianar. C/F (No.=101)
Owned	246	281	49	58
Owner cultivated	236	244	49	58
Rented out	0	13	0	0
Fallow	10	24	0	0
Rented in	96	20	4	9
Total cultivated area	332	264	53	67

	Vakinankaratra (No.=103)	Ranomafana (No.=99)	All regions (No.=495)
Owned	49	46	108
Owner cultivated	46	45	100
Rented out	1	1	2
Fallow	2	1	5
Rented in	8	1	16
Total cultivated area	55	47	116

*1 hectare=100 ares

Source: Data from 1997 IFPRI/FOFIFA survey

Changes in the Landholding of Panel Households

Of the 182 survey households in the third round of the 1992 IFPRI/CNRE/DSA survey, 150 households could still be surveyed in 1997. None of the former survey households present in 1997 refused to take part in the survey. Rather, the sample attrition of 32 households is entirely due to reasons related to dissolving of households (e.g. death of household head, divorce with the two former partners forming new households); a minor share of households had migrated.   Our analysis of the socioeconomic characteristics of the 32 missing households found no systematic patterns which would indicate that a particular socioeconomic group of households (e.g. the young, the old) was lost in the panel.

Table 4.4   Possession and use of upland in the rainy season 1995/1996, by region, in ares*

	Majunga Plaines (No.=40)	Majunga HT (No.=87)	Fianar. HT (No.=163)	Fianar. C/F (No.=101)
Owned	102	150	97	88
Owner cultivated	95	118	94	87
Rented out	0	2	0	0
Fallow	7	30	3	1
Rented in	6	15	1	0
Total cultivated area	101	133	94	88

	Vakinankaratra (No.=103)	Ranomafana (No.=99)	All regions (No.=495)
Owned	112	98	108
Owner cultivated	95	96	97
Rented out	2	1	1
Fallow	15	1	10
Rented in	10	1	5
Total cultivated area	104	96	102

*1 hectare=100 ares

Source: Data from 1997 IFPRI/FOFIFA survey

Table 4.5 shows data on possession of rice- and upland (including bush and forest) as reported by the household head in 1992 and in 1997. We can see sizable increases in riceland holdings in the Majunga Plaines area. This is possibly explained by the terracing of upland into riceland, but could also be the result of net purchases of riceland and net sales of upland. Overall, one would expect a cohort of representative households to show a relative gain in assets over time through inheritance explaining the increase in landholding for the Majunga area. Moreover, this positive trend of larger farm size is reinforced if uncultivated upland is still available, as is the case in the Majunga Plaines. Grown children leaving the household are less likely to request land from their parents as they can start on their own by taking new land into cultivation.

Table 4.5   Possession of land by panel households in 1996 and 1990, by region, in ares*

	Majunga Plaines		Vakinankaratra	
	1990	1996	1990	1996
	(No.=38)	(No.=38)	(No.=112)	(No.=112)
Riceland	256	317	60	52
Upland (including bush/ forest)	163	120	215	147
Total land	421	437	290	223

* 1 hectare=100 ares

Source: Data from 1997 IFPRI/FOFIFA survey; 1992 IFPRI/CNRED/DSA survey

The situation is completely different in the Vakinankaratra region where both upland and lowland are scarce (except perhaps for upland in West Central villages). For the Vakinankaratra households we see an overall decline in land holdings. Whereas the decline in the riceland area is relatively small and might be caused by simple measurement error, the decline in the upland area is significant (from 215 to 147 ares, about one-third in five years). This large decline could be caused by two factors. First, the error of measurement for self-reported upland is larger than for riceland, which may have caused some of this incidental divergence. However, a good part of the decline must be real. This decline is likely caused by intergenerational transfers of land, i.e. sharing of upland owned by aging parents with younger relatives and grown children leaving the household.[2] Aging parents begin to share some of their land with their adult children who then start up their own households. Table 4.5 suggests that such sharing is more frequently done for upland than for riceland which the parents may prefer to keep as a form of old age security. As land is scarce and expensive in the Vakinankaratra, young families mostly rely on such intergenerational transfers of land.

Balance Sheet of Survey Households

As in 1992, the 1997 IFPRI/FOFIFA survey enumerated all household assets and, through surveys with each adult household member, attempted to obtain a measure of outstanding debt and loan transactions, both informal (i.e. friends, relatives, neighbors, moneylenders) and formal (banks and rural microfinance institutions). Table 4.6 provides a breakdown of assets, and computes the equity position of the household by deducting debt from total assets. All asset values were converted into 1997 values, using various survey methods and assuming linear depreciation and lifetimes for several asset groups. The row 'Total value' reports the value of all assets held by the household. Combined with the data on informal and formal debt, 'Equity' shows the value of assets owned by the household. As indebtedness is very low compared to total assets held, most of the total asset value is funded by equity capital. In terms of equity, it is clear that the households in the Majunga regions and in the Vakinankaratra are much better off than households in the Fianarantsoa regions. The lowest average equity of only 679,000 ariary at 1997 prices is found in Ranomafana (i.e. about $679 US).[3] In all regions, riceland is the most important asset, followed either by cattle, upland, or the house. Little capital is held in the form of monetary savings or food stocks.

It follows from the values of riceland for Majunga Plaines and for the Vakinankaratra (Table 4.6) and from the area of riceland possessed in the two regions (see Table 4.3), that land prices in the Vakinankaratra are roughly double the prices in the Majunga Plaines region. These high land prices are not only explained by the superior fertility of soils, but also by the relatively good infrastructure, better technology, and agro-industrial and market opportunities in the Vakinankaratra which all contribute to higher economic rents for land.

Changes in Landholding and Welfare in Households from 1992 to 1997

In order to obtain a sense of how rural households perceive the recent changes in their livelihood and welfare due to changes in the socioeconomic and agroecological environment, the survey questionnaire comprised a few qualitative questions. Each head of household was asked how, compared to five years ago, his/her welfare had changed.

We used five simple indicators of welfare: (1) quantity of food consumed by the household; (2) quality of food consumed by the household; (3) quality/availability of drinking water; (4) health status of household members; and (5) housing conditions of the family. For each of these indicators, the respondent's answer was recorded either as improving, remaining about the same, or worsening compared to five years ago. In addition, the household head was asked about the change in overall welfare of the household members compared to five years ago.

Table 4.6   Balance sheet of survey households at time of round 1 (April/May 1997), by region*

	Majunga Plaines (No.=40)	Majunga HT (No.=87)	Fianar. HT (No.=163)	Fianar. C/F (No.=101)	Vakinankaratra (No.=103)	Ranomafana (No.=99)	All regions (No.=495)
Riceland	1,741	1,535	416	344	1,189	215	866
Upland	371	491	314	319	496	195	389
Forest/bush	172	112	21	10	27	35	48
Cattle	685	979	222	251	373	97	430
Other	87	47	70	27	51	42	55
House	229	284	470	61	910	61	426
Consumption durables	102	133	33	35	90	19	69
Agricultural production durables	85	111	8	5	59	6	42
Non-agricultural production durables	21	20	3	2	19	3	11
Monetary savings	7	1	1	8	3	5	3
Food stocks	41	14	3	3	0	0	7
Loans lent/receivables	10	6	1	3	3	1	3
Total value	3,628	3,762	1,565	1,093	3,283	683	2,380
Informal debt	39	23	4	26	7	4	15
Formal debt	38	6	0	0	54	0	16
Equity	3,551	3,733	1,561	1,067	3,222	679	2,349

* In 1,000 ariary; 1,000 ariary = 5,000 FMG

Source: Data from 1997 IFPRI/FOFIFA survey

Changes in Welfare as Reported by Households

Table 4.7 reports on the results for each of the five indicators and for the general welfare responses. In the discussion of the results, we first focus on the row on the bottom of the table which represents all regions as a whole. 38 per cent of household heads indicated that overall welfare of the household members had worsened, 30 per cent expressed that it had remained the same, and 31 per cent thought that it had improved compared to five years ago. Thus there were winners and losers over these years, with the aggregate for all regions on average showing a slight, but not overwhelming, worsening of perceived household welfare.

The picture is more diverse when one looks into changes with respect to specific indicators of livelihood. First, it appears that changes in the condition of drinking water were rare. However, improvements outnumber deteriorations by a factor of five (2 per cent worsening and 10 per cent improving). Housing is the only other indicator for which households reported more improvements (17 per cent) than deteriorations (12 per cent). As the improvement of housing conditions is more or less fully under the control of the household itself, this result indicates that households could somewhat improve their home through higher incomes and related repair and construction. On the other hand, for the three indicators regarding food and nutritional security, there were more households who reported a worsening of the situation than those reporting improvement. For the quantity of food consumed, the perceived change is the bleakest: 41 per cent of households report a worsening of the quantity of food they are able to consume, whereas 30 per cent report an improvement. A similarly adverse picture is obtained for the quality of food (as perceived by the household head). For 64 per cent of households, the health status of members remained about the same; 20 per cent reported a worsening; 16 per cent an improvement.

We now turn to the regional differences highlighted in Table 4.7. With respect to drinking water, we note that only the Vakinankaratra reported improvements whereas the situation in the other areas remained the same or worsened. While access to safe drinking water is largely a function of public intervention, the improvement of housing conditions is solely the result of private investment. When poor families build or repair their houses, this indicates an accumulation of household savings. Encouragingly, four of the regions (Majunga Plaines, Majunga HT, Fianarantsoa HT, and Vakinankaratra) have more households which improved their housing

Table 4.7   Changes in household welfare from 1992 to 1997, % of responses

Region	Quantity of food consumed	Quality of food consumed	Drinking water	Health status of household members	Housing conditions	Overall change in welfare
Majunga Plaines (No.=53)						
Worsened	47	45	0	22	13	46
Remained the same	34	39	99	74	72	35
Improved	18	16	1	5	16	19
Majunga HT (No.=118)						
Worsened	45	39	5	22	10	35
Remained the same	32	33	95	65	79	32
Improved	23	28	0	13	11	34
Fianar. HT (No.=80)						
Worsened	45	45	0	16	14	40
Remained the same	31	32	95	70	68	37
Improved	24	23	5	15	17	23
Fianar. C/F (No.=92)						
Worsened	48	40	5	33	18	49
Remained the same	35	49	95	62	77	34
Improved	18	11	0	6	5	16
Vakinankaratra (No.=122)						
Worsened	22	21	0	13	5	26
Remained the same	17	17	57	50	62	11
Improved	62	63	43	37	32	64
Ranomafana (No.=88)						
Worsened	44	26	1	20	9	44
Remained the same	41	59	97	69	86	41
Improved	15	15	2	10	5	15
All regions (except Ranomafana) (No.=465)						
Worsened	41	38	2	20	12	38
Remained the same	29	33	88	64	71	30
Improved	30	29	10	16	17	31

Source: Data from 1997 IFPRI/FOFIFA survey

situation than households with worsening housing conditions. Moreover, the most apparent differences exist with respect to food and nutritional security. Whereas the picture is very positive in the Vakinankaratra, all other regions report clear deteriorations of food security and health status. Particularly disturbing is the reported change in the Fianarantsoa C/F region which reports 48 per cent of households having to eat less compared to five years ago and 33 per cent of households with worsening health status of their members.

We conclude that the households in the Vakinankaratra region report to have improved their living conditions, whereas those in the Majunga HT on average experienced no change, and those in other regions, in particular the Fianarantsoa C/F region, saw their living standards worsening over time.

Perceived Principal Causes of Changes in Welfare

After having enumerated any perceived change in living conditions for each of the five specific indicators, the enumerators further asked what was the probable cause of that change. This question was posed as an open-ended one by the enumerator and he or she was asked to record the two principal causes as given by the respondent. The supervisor and enumerator coded the response after the interview into a list of more than twenty possible causes. For brevity, we focus on the quantity of food consumed which was, according to our regression analysis, the most important determinant for the general well-being of households.

Table 4.8 groups these causes into various subcategories, and reports on the frequency of responses. The data is further differentiated by reported change, positive or negative, in the quantity of food consumed. We note from Table 4.8 that idiosyncratic risk factors (i.e. disease, old age, accident, death) and covariate risks (mainly natural calamities) are the most important self-reported reasons that cause households to slide into greater food poverty. Adverse market changes are important but only explain 30 per cent of the cases (e.g. 59 cases out of 195 households) of increased food insecurity. On the other hand, 51 per cent of improvements in food security (e.g. 72 cases out of 142 households) are caused by improvements in prices or market conditions, and another 3 per cent by direct public interventions and projects. Overall, these results indicate that changes in markets over the five year period have benefited more households than they hurt. At an aggregated level, this indicates that changes in market prices and conditions may have benefited the 'average' rural household in the survey areas.

Table 4.8   Causes of change in quantity of food consumed, % of responses

	Worsened (No.=195)	Improved (No.=142)
Natural catastrophes damaging crops, animals, house, etc.	20	-
Negative idiosyncratic risks (disease, etc.)	33	-
Adverse market/price changes	30	-
Private transfer received (inheritance, gift)	3	-
Public transfer received (social assistance or farm/business extension)	-	2
Favorable market/price changes	-	51
Increase in expenses for social events and schooling	3	-
Positive idiosyncratic events (more household members of working age)	-	31
Other adverse causal factors	14	-
Other positive causal factors	-	13

Source: Data from 1997 IFPRI/OFIFA survey

As Table 4.8 shows, frequent responses were given citing crop failures caused by natural calamities as a reason for decreases in the quantity of food consumed by households. These problems were especially severe in the Majunga HT and in the Fianarantsoa C/F area. As these risks hurt almost everyone in the village at the same time, although not to the same extent, informal social safety nets including informal financial markets, have their clear limits in smoothing consumption (Zeller and Sharma, 1998). The less diversification there is in the rural economy, the more pronounced the limits. Since the formal financial market is quite underdeveloped in rural Madagascar, except in very limited geographic areas of interventions by microfinance NGOs, and since a rural social security system is virtually nonexistent (apart from old-age security for government employees), those regions hit by cyclones, hail, and drought generally must rely on disaster relief or on themselves. However, in many cases, as the data suggest, such disasters can lead to a successive worsening of the food security situation either because natural calamities occur successively or because households are forced to sell productive assets (i.e. land, cattle, equipment) and thus have lower income potential in future years.

A second important cause of a deterioration of the quantity of food consumed was reported by the households as the occurrence of idiosyncratic risk factors which affect individual household members. These factors include illness, old age, accident, or death. All these factors can imply major reductions in the labor force and therefore in the food security of a household or particular members. While informal insurance systems in Madagascar (i.e. community self-help) might mitigate some of the negative effects, in about a third of the cases these risk factors constituted the major cause of a household's slide towards higher food insecurity and greater poverty (Table 4.9). While most of these idiosyncratic risks are insurable, and are in fact insured in developed countries through private insurance or government controlled social security systems, households in rural Madagascar, as in many developing countries, must generally bear such risks on their own. However, while the incidence of the problem is apparent from Tables 4.8 and 4.9, the political response to it is less than obvious. A better understanding of informal networks, i.e. their costs and benefits (in terms of loss in income generation and loss in overall welfare), as well as pilot experiments with member-based financial systems offering services for insurance, precautionary savings, and consumption credit, may offer some directions through which policy might eventually address the problem of missing markets for insurance against idiosyncratic risks. Some of the microfinance organizations in Madagascar already offer services for consumption credit and for precautionary savings (e.g. village banks in Maravoay or credit and savings associations of TSIMOKA/FERT in Vakinankaratra).

In a nutshell it is important to note that the most frequent cause for sliding into food insecurity and poverty appears to be the occurrence of idiosyncratic or covariate risks. In other words, the lack of insurance, credit and savings options, and the shortcomings of the informal and public safety nets mean that much poverty is created simply by bad luck. The third important factor causing a deterioration of food security is adverse changes in input or output prices or in overall market conditions. Thirty-nine per cent of households in the Fianarantsoa HT region report this cause as the major factor in increasing food insecurity. As we later see in chapter 7, many households in this region are net buyers of rice, and market liberalization may have led to reductions of their rice purchasing power.

In Table 4.9, we tabulate the major cause for improvements in household food security. We turn first to positive price and market changes as one of the major reasons given. Most interesting is the fact that price and

Table 4.9   Perceived causes of changes in quantity of food consumed, by region, % of responses

	Majunga Plaines	Majunga HT	Fianar. HT	Fianar. C/F	Vakinankaratra	Ranomafana
Decreases						
Natural catastrophes damaging crops, animals, house etc.	11	42	6	36	6	3
Negative idiosyncratic risks (disease, etc).	27	34	32	32	41	59
Adverse market/price changes	32	19	39	21	32	18
Increase in expenses for social events and schooling	-	-	6	2	-	5
Other adverse causal factors	29	5	17	9	21	15
Increases						
Private transfer received (inheritance, gift)	-	3	-	5	-	-
Public transfer received (social assistance or farm/business extension)	-	-	-	5	-	-
Favorable market/price changes	27	32	50	43	61	46
Increase in expenses for social events and schooling	-	-	6	2	-	-
Positive idiosyncratic events (more household members of working age)	73	65	22	51	19	38
Other positive causal factors	-	-	29	6	10	15

Source: Data from 1997 IFPRI/FOFIFA survey

market changes are a relatively more frequent reasons for improvement than for deterioration of food security, as a simple comparison of results in Table 4.9 reveal. In four out of five regions, a larger share of households perceives price and market changes as a positive rather than a negative cause of changes in food security. Of households in the Fianarantsoa HT region that reported improved food security during the five year period, 50 per cent reported that this change was caused by favorable prices and other market conditions. Even higher is the percentage for the Vakinankaratra, whereas only 27 per cent of 'winners' in the Majunga Plaines area felt that their food security improved because of favorable market conditions.

However, this comparison of relative frequencies is somewhat flawed by the fact that the group of households having to eat less is larger than the group of households eating more compared to five years earlier. On an absolute basis, the ratio of losers to winners due to adverse or favorable market changes is 56 to 73 for all regions as a whole (except Ranomafana). The region-specific ratio of number of losers over winners due to market changes is as follows for the different regions: (1) Majunga Plaines, 8 losers and 4 winners; (2) Majunga HT, 11 losers and 13 winners; (3) Fianarantsoa HT, 14 losers and 11 winners; (4) Fianarantsoa C/F, 8 losers and 9 winners; (5) Vakinankaratra, 15 losers and 36 winners; and (6) Ranomafana, 7 losers and 6 winners. These results suggest that households in the Vakinankaratra gained from recent changes in agricultural input and output markets. The region of Fianarantsoa C/F, Ranomafana, and the Majunga HT have relatively insignificant ratios with almost equal number of losers and winners, whereas households in the Fianarantsoa HT area and in particular in the Majunga Plaines area seem to have been more hurt than helped by recent market changes. Chapters 5 to 10 analyze the price response of producers and consumers of food, and provide a more detailed picture.

Improvements in food security were frequently caused by positive idiosyncratic factors, such as grown children contributing to the enlargement of the family work force or improved health of family members. The role of private transfers, mainly inheritance, and of public transfers or project interventions, was limited in improving the food security of the households. Yet, 5 per cent of households in the Vakinankaratra area, an area with a long-standing project intervention experience, reported that their food security primarily improved because of interventions by government and NGOs (Table 4.9).

Who are the Winners and the Losers: the 'Wealthy' or the 'Poor'?

Table 4.10 addresses this question by disaggregating the responses for the five welfare indicators and the aggregate welfare measure by quartile of household wealth.[4] With respect to quantity of food consumed, 56 per cent of the poorest report to have suffered more food insecurity compared to five years earlier whereas only 17 per cent reported an improvement. Among the highest wealth quartile, the reverse basically holds. The same inequitable pattern persists for quality of food, housing conditions, and, therefore also for the overall welfare measure. The differences between the 'wealthy' and the poorest are quite apparent in Table 4.10. While 56 per cent of the poorest quartile experienced a decline in their living standards (and only 17 per cent an improvement), among the highest wealth quartile the reverse is true. Among the 'wealthy', more than half report to be better off than five years earlier, one-quarter saw no changes, and one-quarter experienced a decline in their living standards.

Are there Systematic Patterns of Causes of Change in Food Poverty with Respect to the Poverty Level?

We previously concluded that for all households as an aggregate, idiosyncratic and covariate risk factors constitute the major cause of sliding into food insecurity and poverty. Does this hold when one disaggregates this information along quartiles of household wealth? In Table 4.11 we first turn to households which experienced a decline in their food security. In roughly one-third of the cases, idiosyncratic risk factors account for the decline, irrespective of the wealth of the household. The incidence of covariate risk factors is higher for the richest households than for the poorest households (26 per cent versus 9 per cent) whereas adverse market price changes or conditions (presumably in food markets for consumers) are relatively more important among the poorer households (33 per cent versus 21 per cent).

When we look at the patterns of causes for households that increased their food consumption, we see that favorable market price changes are the major reason for the positive change in roughly half the cases (Table 4.11). A clear pattern is discernible, indicating that the poorer quartile more frequently had gained from favorable market price changes than the richer quartile (57 per cent versus 49 per cent). Again, the comparison of percentages between winners and losers of market reform is somewhat flawed as the total number of winners and losers is different, implying different bases for the calculation of percentages.

Table 4.10 Welfare changes in quantity of food consumed 1992 to 1997, by quartile of 1992 household wealth, % of responses

| | Quartile of 1992 household wealth | | | |
	Lowest	Low	Upper	Highest
Quantity of food consumed				
Worsened	56	50	32	25
Remained the same	26	33	29	29
Improved	17	17	39	47
Quality of food consumed				
Worsened	51	49	31	21
Remained the same	30	37	32	34
Improved	20	15	37	45
Drinking water consumed				
Worsened	2	1	3	2
Remained the same	90	92	85	84
Improved	8	7	12	14
Health status				
Worsened	29	18	18	14
Remained the same	57	73	63	62
Improved	13	9	19	25
Housing conditions				
Worsened	13	16	11	8
Remained the same	76	74	72	62
Improved	11	10	16	30
Overall welfare				
Got Worsened	56	45	30	23
Remained the same	27	37	30	26
Improved	17	18	40	52

Source: Date from 1997 IFPRI/FOFIFA survey

We have therefore calculated the ratio of winners and losers due to changes in markets in each of the wealth quartiles from the survey data. The ratios for the four wealth quartiles are: (1) for the poorest quartile 16 losers to 20 winners, a ratio of 0.8; (2) for the lower wealth quartile 16 losers to

19 winners, a ratio of 0.74; (3) for the upper wealth quartile 13 losers over 17 winners, a ratio of 0.76; and (4) for the wealthiest quartile of households 10 losers over 18 winners, a ratio of 0.55. These ratios suggest that in all four wealth quartiles those gaining in terms of food security from recent market changes outnumber those losing from the same changes.

Table 4.11 Causes of reduction in quantity of food consumed, as reported by household head, differentiated by quartile of wealth, in %

	Quartile of 1992 household wealth			
	Lowest	**Low**	**Upper**	**Highest**
Reductions (No.=195 out of 465 households)				
Natural catastrophes harming crop, animals, house etc.	9	22	30	26
Negative idiosyncratic risks: disease etc.	36	29	30	38
Adverse market/price changes	33	33	26	21
Increase in expenses for social events and schooling	0	7	2	0
Other adverse causal factors	22	8	12	15
Increases (No.=142 out of 465 households)				
Private transfer received: heritage, gift	5	0	5	1
Public transfer received: (social assistance or farm/business extension)	0	2	0	5
Favorable market/price changes	57	54	48	49
Positive idiosyncratic events: more household members of working age	21	38	27	35
Other positive causal factors	17	5	20	10

Source: Data from 1997 IFPRI/FOFIFA survey

Conclusions

Overall, it appears from these results, that there were more winners than losers for changes in housing conditions and access to drinking water and somewhat negative, but small, changes in health status of household members. However, with respect to the change in the quantity and quality of food, we find a significantly larger number of losers. The negative results for the food situation mainly seem to drive the perceived negative trend in overall welfare. This notion is confirmed by regression analysis. We ran a simple ordinary least squares regression with the overall change in welfare as the dependent variable and the five specific welfare indicators as independent variables. Based on this, we find that the change in quantity of food consumed is by far the most important determinant of welfare, either with respect to the size of the regression coefficient or to its statistical significance. The second most important indicator is the quality of food; the third the health of the household members. The other two determinants are not statistically significant. This confirms that improving food security remains a major concern and policy objective for overall improvement of welfare of rural households in Madagascar.

Qualitative questions that ask about long run changes often run the risk of obtaining opinions rather than facts. While we cannot exclude the possibility that certain answers were given in order to misinform the enumerator in hope for transfers, projects, or the like, we are confident that this constitutes a minor problem mainly for two reasons. First, all the supervisors and enumerators were trained to introduce the survey to the community and the respondents as an undertaking that sought to obtain accurate information for policy formulation and that the sample communities and households were simply chosen to represent all households of a very large region. The survey team was specifically asked to state that the research project would not provide any direct projects or help to the survey villages or to individual households and that the . information would be treated confidentially. Second, when comparing the regional differences discussed below, we note that the self-reported gains in the Vakinankaratra are consistent with the detailed panel household data from this region. Moreover, when we tabulate the self-reported gainers and losers by quartile of household wealth (as shown later in this chapter) we see that gainers were overrepresented among the wealthier quartile whereas losers were relatively more frequent among the poorer quartile. All these qualitative results are consistent with the detailed quantitative results presented in the other chapters.

One cannot deduce from the tabulation of these responses that market liberalization and the resulting changes and adjustments in markets during the five year period covered by the survey were the overriding cause of the observed deterioration of living standards and of increased welfare inequality in rural areas in Madagscar. While changes in prices and other market conditions seem to have hurt more poor than 'wealthy' people, changes in markets also frequently provided opportunities for improvements in living standards among many of the poor. At an aggregate level for all households and for each of the wealth quartiles in the sample, including the poorest, the number of households experiencing improving food security due to recent changes in market prices and market conditions was found to always outweigh the number of losers. However, the ratio of winners to losers is more favorable for the wealthier household quartiles than for the poorer quartiles. In other words, wealthier households seem to have benefited more frequently from recent changes in agricultural input and output markets than poorer ones. Moreover, if we assume that the magnitude of a loss is equal to the magnitude of a gain, we could conclude that overall welfare of rural households has improved due to changes in market conditions during the past five years, but that the observed improvement caused by changes in markets was biased towards the wealthier groups. Yet, we note that this assumption is simplistic at best and such a conclusion may not be valid.[5]

Adverse changes in market prices or in other market conditions are important but only explain 30 per cent of cases of greater food insecurity. Quite disturbing is the picture that risks appear to be the major forces pushing people into poverty. We note that idiosyncratic risk factors such as disease, old age, accident, and death, and covariate risks, mainly natural calamities such as drought and cyclone, are the overriding self-reported reasons that households perceive as having caused deterioration in their living standards.

The lack or inadequacy of health and social services, disaster relief, a formal social safety net, and financial markets may all contribute to the particular vulnerability of the poorest households in dealing with these shocks. Future research appears warranted to explore the costs, benefits, and limits of private and informal markets for providing safety net services, and to identify sustainable policy interventions which can efficiently complement existing private safety net mechanisms.

The self-reported results suggest that market reform and resulting adjustments in rural markets from 1992 to 1997 have had a positive effect on food security, but benefited wealthier households more than poorer ones. The data further suggest that major reasons for increased food insecurity and poverty be related to the occurrence of idiosyncratic risks and, for wealthier households, covariate risks as well. In a word, the overall worsening trend in household welfare is caused by the occurrence of such negative events, and the inability to effectively insure against them at the household and community levels.

Notes

1   While the region of Ranomafana is included to show the average of the 99 survey households in this area, the average data contained in the column 'all regions' does not take into account the Ranomafana data.   As mentioned in the previous chapter, Ranomafana is treated as a separate cluster that does not enter into the calculation for representative figures for the universe of households in the survey areas.

2   In Madagascar, parents pass on some of their land to married children before their death. While the parents remain the legal owners of the land, the children obtain the right to cultivate the land and become de facto owners. Such land was recorded in the 1992 and 1997 surveys as land owned by the household cultivating it.

3   Exchange rate at time of survey was around 1,000 ariary per $1 US.

4   Table 4.6 presented the value of assets, as possessed by the survey households in 1997. The survey modules for assets were designed to allow the calculation of wealth levels up to five years back for fixed, major assets such as land, house, and consumption and production durables. This is basically done by subtracting purchases (and inheritance) of assets which occurred during 1993 to time of first survey round and by adding sales during the past five years from the current 1997 asset value of the household. In the comparison of change in welfare over time by wealth quartile, it is preferable to use initial wealth as a basis.

5   For example, the same marginal changes have greater effects on poorer households than on richer households.

5 Modern Input Use in Agriculture

CLAUDE RANDRIANARISOA, BART MINTEN, FRANCESCO GOLETTI,
and MANFRED ZELLER

In this chapter, we study the level as well as the determinants of the use of modern inputs. The modern inputs discussed concern mineral fertilizer and improved rice varieties. In each section a general overview of the specific situation for the modern inputs in Madagascar is given. Then, the results of the household surveys are discussed. The chapter finishes with conclusions.

Mineral Fertilizer

Introduction

The amount of mineral fertilizers imported by Madagascar has averaged around 20,000 tons a year (including gifts) during the last decades. However, there is high year-to-year variability. Three periods of growth in fertilizer consumption during the last five decades can be distinguished. The first was just before independence, i.e. around 1958. The second period was between 1966 and 1970, i.e. the period when the first major irrigation infrastructure works, such as those in the Lac Aloatra region, were terminated, and more importantly, when the extension of intensive agricultural techniques in the Malagasy Highlands began. The third period of growth was during the socialist period between 1973 and 1986, when fertilizer prices were heavily subsidized by the Malagasy government.

The positive trend in growth of consumption of fertilizer was interrupted each time that there was a radical change in economic policy. This situation occurred in 1958 when the big colonial companies, at that time the main users of imported agricultural inputs, realized that Madagascar would become independent and that future investments looked uncertain. We also notice a drop in 1972, after the national strikes and the start of changes in economic policy towards state nationalized agricultural input and output markets. The third downturn was in 1986 when agricultural markets were liberalized. However, while a strong upward trend was previously seen after each decrease, it seems that the actual situation is different as we only notice a stabilization in total quantities imported, and even a decline in the use of mineral fertilizer if we use the ratio between the total imported quantity of fertilizer divided by the cultivated area.

The analysis on fertilizer use shows significant differences by crop. Almost one-quarter of total imported fertilizer in Madagascar is used on industrial crops, such as sugarcane. The quantity used for cotton is similar, 23 per cent. The rest is divided between the traditional staple and cash crops, including rice. As rice is the most important crop area-wise, it is not surprising to note that the quantity of fertilizer used per unit of lowland is very low. In the survey region, only 8.7 per cent of the total lowland area received mineral fertilizer. The level corresponds to around 3.1 kg of fertilizing elements per hectare of lowland, or 6 to 7 kg of commercial fertilizer per hectare. This level of fertilizer use is far below the recommended doses by extension agencies (Table 5.1) and is low even by African standards.

Table 5.1 Recommended doses and average responses to fertilizer

Crop	Yield average kg/ha	NPK kg/ha	Interval for yield increase	Average increase in yield	Increase in production kg/ha
Irrigated rice	2,100	85/60/40	50-130	90 %	1,900
Upland rice	850	30/30/30	40-100	70 %	600
Maize	800	70/30/25	40-150	95 %	750
Wheat, Barley	700	100/60/45	60-250	15 %	1,050
Peanuts	600	10/50/40	40-80	60 %	360
Potatoes	6,000	80/80/80	60-160	110 %	6,600

Source: Data from FAO (1991)

The Adoption of Mineral Fertilizer

Table 5.2 shows that the number of producers who use mineral fertilizer in the survey region is around 19 per cent representing 8.1 per cent of the total cultivated area. On the one hand, there are small areas such as vegetable gardens or rice nurseries ('pepinières') that are intensive fertilized while some fields or crops receive no chemical fertilizer. Different reasons for this exist and will be discussed in further detail below.

Table 5.2   **Use of fertilizer at the farm level, average of two seasons (1995/1996 and 1996/1997)**

Region	Percentage of farmers using fertilizer[a]	Percentage of area that receives fertilizer	Average dose per hectare[b] (kg per ha)	
			per cultivated ha	per ha receiving fertilizer
Majunga Plaines	2.0	0.9	0.0	2.1
Majunga HT	1.2	0.4	0.3	80.5
Fianar. HT	22.8	13.7	3.9	28.8
Fianar. C/F	0.2	0.0	0.0	40.8
Vakinankaratra	54.1	22.9	17.1	74.6
Total	19.4	8.1	4.5	55.4
Ranomafana	9.8	5.7	1.4	24.2

[a] This is a measure of the adoption rate
[b] The average dose is expressed in kilograms of fertilizing elements ($N+P_2O_5+K_2O$). The total quantity of fertilizing elements divided by total cultivated area gives the average dose per cultivated area. The dose per fertilized hectare is obtained through the division of the total quantity of used fertilizer divided by the total area that received fertilizer

Source: Data from 1997 IFPRI/FOFIFA household survey

There is a clear regional distinction, especially between the central/ southern region including the Vakinankaratra, and the rest of the study region. In these regions, there is a relatively high number of fertilizer users. In the Vakinankaratra region, for example, 54.1 per cent of the producers report the use of chemical fertilizer while in the Fianarantsoa HT, 22.8 per cent of the producers use fertilizer on at least one crop. On the other hand, the level of fertilizer users is close to zero in the Majunga HT and the Fianarantsoa C/F. Despite the good irrigation infrastructure for the Majunga Plaines, only 2 per cent of the farmers are fertilizer users (Table 5.2).

Table 5.3 shows that in most regions rice is the most important crop that receives fertilizer, with the exception of the Vakinankaratra and Majunga HT regions. In the survey region as a whole, 43.2 per cent of total fertilizer use is on rice. In the Majunga HT region, the existence of big industrial companies, such as HASYMA and COTONA for cotton and the group BOLLORE for tobacco, facilitate the use of fertilizer on these crops through vertical integration contracts. In the Vakinankaratra region, the diversification of agriculture and the existence of a significant number of agro-industrial companies help to spread the use of fertilizer on crops other than rice. Barley and wheat, sold directly to brewers and millers, are considered major cash crops in this area. More than 50 per cent of the fertilizer used is used on these crops. Rice consumes 26.7 per cent of total fertilizer use in the Vakinankaratra region.

Table 5.3   Crops' share of fertilizer use in each region, in %

	Majunga Plaines	Majunga HT	Fianar. HT	Fianar. C/F
Irrigated rice	100.0	-	97.5	100.0
Rainfed rice	-	-	-	-
Maize	-	-	0.6	-
Potatoes	-	-	1.2	-
Beans	-	-	0.8	-
Wheat/barley	-	-	-	-
Tubers	-	-	-	-
Cotton/tobacco	-	100.0	-	-

	Vakinan.	Total	Ranomafana
Irrigated rice	27.6	43.2	80.5
Rainfed rice	3.0	2.2	-
Maize	2.6	2.1	-
Potatoes	5.2	4.2	19.5
Beans	2.0	1.6	-
Wheat/barley	52.3	39.3	-
Tubers	-	-	-
Cotton/tobacco	7.3	7.4	-

Source: Data from 1997 IFPRI/FOFIFA household survey

In addition to the descriptive analysis on the percentages of farmers, we identify the determinants of the use of fertilizer by means of a probit regression analysis. The model that is used in the empirical estimation has the following form:

Prob (use) = f(Price; Charhh; Charcom; Systprod).

The probability of the adoption of fertilizer by the household is a function of:
* prices (Price): input prices, output prices, land prices, and wage levels in the village;

- characteristics of the household head and the household (Charhh): gender, age, education level, dependency ratio as measured by the number of dependent people (less than 14 years and more than 55 years) over the number of adults in the household;
- characteristics of the community (Charcom): the economic environment and access to infrastructure, climatic and disease risk, access to credit, and access to agricultural extension services;
- production system of household (Systprod): the cultivated area of tanety as well as tanimbary, irrigation infrastructure, the number of years of experience in agriculture or with respect to particular fields, the characteristics of plots, such as the distance from the field to the house, etc.

Table 5.4 shows the results of the analysis of the determinants of fertilizer use on the farm, independent of the type of crop. The dependent variable is the use of fertilizer on the farm. This variable is a dummy that is 1 if the household uses chemical fertilizer and 0 otherwise. A probit analysis is used to estimate the determinants of the probability of fertilizer adoption. Five variables turn out to be highly significant (at the 1 per cent level): the index of climatic risk, the index of disease risk, the price of lowland, the total area on upland, and the education level of the household head. For the two risk variables, the signs are negative. As expected, the higher the risk level, the lower the probability of fertilizer use. Two examples in the survey region can illustrate this. The first is the case of farmers in the coastal region who each year might experience inundation of their lowlands due to the cyclones.[1] The second example is that of rice producers, especially in the northwestern region (faritany of Majunga), who are often faced with rice virose which can and often does destroy the whole harvest.

The other two significant variables, the price of lowland and the upland area, show positive signs. Higher prices of lowland lead to a greater probability of fertilizer use. Higher lowland prices might be an indication of land quality as well as land scarcity. They both might lead to higher incentives to restore land fertility through the input of elements that have been harvested previously and through the adoption of intensification techniques such as the use of mineral fertilizer (see also next chapter). The positive effect of upland area cultivated seems due to the cash crops that are planted in the Highland region (i.e. Fianarantsoa HT and Vakinankaratra) and the industrial crops in Majunga HT such as cotton and tobacco. The total area often also reflects household wealth and hence, potential access to liquidity for acquisition of fertilizer. Chemical fertilizers have a better chance of being adopted if the household heads received at least some education as illustrated by the significant sign on the education dummy.

Table 5.4   Determinants of the adoption of fertilizer for all crops (results of probit model)

Variable	Coefficient	t-value	Mean of X
Price NPK (ariary/kg)	-0.00309	-1.587	399.58
Price rice (ariary/kg)	0.00062	0.319	174.88
Price cassava (ariary/kg)	-0.00635	-1.574	85.42
Village level wage (ariary/day)	-0.00104	-1.765[a]	642.08
Price lowland (ariary/are)	0.00001	3.523[c]	11,323.34
Price upland (ariary/are)	-0.36343E-05	-0.362	5,457.88
Extension agent in village (1=yes)	0.03413	0.171	0.51
Possible lowland extension (1=yes)	-0.20099	-0.908	0.49
Predicted max. amount to borrow (ar.)	0.26781E-06	1.388	447,588.68
Distance house to distributor (min.)	-0.03846	-1.618[a]	11.56
Age of the household head	-0.00712	-0.902	45.09
Gender of household head (1=male)	-0.23687	-1.167	1.11
Index education level household head	0.63885	2.104[b]	1.85
Dependency ratio	-0.60856	-1.643[a]	0.52
Area lowland cultivated	-0.48685E-04	-0.059	102.29
Area upland cultivated	0.14450E-02	1.981[b]	75.00
Time from house to upland plot	-0.57758E-02	-1.338	21.33
Time from house to lowland plot	0.26306E-02	0.929	27.40
Years of experience with upland plot	-0.11101E-01	-1.011	15.36
Years of experience with lowland plot	0.75895E-02	0.659	15.58
% of lowland area with water problems	-0.24977E-02	-1.128	28.97
Index climatic risk	-0.63412E-01	-3.463[c]	5.93
Index disease risk	-0.72234E-01	-4.271[c]	4.15
Time dummy (1=1995/1996)	-0.17914	-1.172	0.51
Regional dummy Vakinankaratra	2.28346	3.477[c]	0.20
Regional dummy Majunga HT	1.31036	1.654[a]	0.17
Regional dummy Majunga Plaines	1.12401	1.460	0.08
Regional dummy Fianar. HT	1.19814	1.733[a]	0.32

[a], [b], [c] Indicate statistical significance at the 10 %, 5 %, and 1 % levels, respectively; the number of observations is 960

Source: Data from 1997 IFPRI/FOFIFA household survey

Other variables show an impact but to a lesser extent, among them the price of inputs, represented in the regression analysis by the price of NPK; the price of agricultural products other than rice, represented by the price of cassava; the distance between the farm and the closest distributor of fertilizer; and the average wage level in the village. The first two variables show negative signs, meaning that the probability of fertilizer adoption is reduced by a high fertilizer prices and/or high prices of other products that can be substitutes for rice such as cassava. The further away the household is from fertilizer distribution, the less likely it is to use fertilizer. The opportunity cost of travel time to acquire fertilizer would have to be added to the fertilizer price, which would clearly reduce the incentive to use fertilizer. The higher the village wages, the less likely households are to use fertilizer since labor might be a complementary factor to increased intensification and fertilizer use.

The results are not significant for the other variables. However, while one has to be very cautious with interpretation, one can see that a higher rice price is related to a higher probability of fertilizer adoption. The same holds for extension services and the possibility of obtaining credit in case of need. On the other hand, the farms that have a high level of water problems in the lowlands are less likely to use fertilizer, a seemingly logical response to the higher risk for the payoff of fertilizer use. This is also the case for the households that have high dependency ratios, i.e. higher numbers of children and elderly persons in the family. The less a household is able or willing to bear risk, the less likely it is to use fertilizer. For the variables that concern the household head, the probability of adoption is higher for males than for females and higher for younger household heads. The regional dummies confirm that households in the Vakinankaratra and Fianarantsoa HT area are the most likely to use chemical fertilizer.

The Use of Mineral Fertilizer by Crop

Table 5.5 shows the percentage of area that received mineral fertilizer by crop. Even if rice consumes 43.2 per cent (Table 5.3) of the total quantity of fertilizer used, the percentage of the rice area that receives fertilizer is only 8.7 per cent in the lowlands and 10.2 per cent in the uplands. These averages vary significantly by region, as shown by a zero per cent adoption rate in the Majunga HT and Fianarantsoa C/F and 1.1 per cent in the Majunga Plaines area. The highest level is reported in the Fianarantsoa HT area where

30.1 per cent of the lowland area receives chemical fertilizer. The only region where chemical ferilizer is used on upland is the Vakinankaratra region (30.1 per cent of the area). The level of fertilizer use is highly dependent on the type of crop. For peanuts and tubers, except for potatoes, the level is almost zero. For potatoes in particular, the percentage of the area that receives chemical fertilizer is 8.7 per cent in the Fianarantsoa HT region and 46.9 per cent in the Vakinankaratra region. The area of industrial crops that receives fertilizer is respectively 98.8 per cent and 30.2 per cent for wheat/barley (only in the Vakinankaratra) and cotton/tobacco (Vakinankaratra and Majunga HT). Maize only sporadically receives fertilizer, illustrated by its 8.1 percentage, mostly due to the influence of the Vakinankaratra region (14.1 per cent).

The applied quantities per unit of land that receive fertilizer vary widely as well (Table 5.6). On one hand, one can find doses close to the recommended quantity such as for wheat and barley (153.5 kg of fertilizer) and tobacco in Vakinankaratra (238.7 kg). On the other hand, one also finds very small quantities per hectare. For rice, the average dose in the survey region is around 35.3 kg of fertilizing elements, equal to around 72 kg of NPK or urea per hectare that received fertilizer. The dose is rather low in the Majunga Plaines, with a quantity of 2.1 kg of fertilizing elements, which corresponds to the use of fertilizer on the area where young plants are grown ('pepinière').[2]

When we perform the same calculations for the doses on area cultivated, the quantities become very small. For irrigated rice, the average in the survey region is around 3.1 kg of fertilizing elements or around 7 kgs of fertilizer per hectare. For upland or tanety rice, the average is around 6.7 kg of fertilizing elements, and for maize the average is just around 1.0 kg per hectare. High doses can only be found for the industrial crops, i.e. 47.6 kg and 151.6 kg of fertilizing elements per hectare respectively for cotton/tobacco and wheat/barley in the Majunga HT and in the Vakinankaratra.

Table 5.7 illustrates the importance of the two types of fertilizer used in Madagascar: urea and NPK. In the Vakinankaratra region, most of producers use urea as well as NPK as their fertilizer of choice. The farmers of the Fianaranatsoa region prefer NPK while those in Majunga use mostly urea.

Table 5.5   Percentage of area receiving mineral fertilizer

Crop	Majunga Plaines	Majunga HT	Fianar. HT	Fianar. C/F
Lowland rice	1.1	0.0	30.1	0.0
Upland rice	0.0[a]	0.0	-	0.0
Maize	0.0	0.0	1.2	0.0
Potatoes	-[b]	0.0	8.7	0.0
Beans	-	0.0	2.4	0.0
Peanuts	0.0	0.0	0.0	0.0
Wheat/barley	-	-	-	-
Tubers[c]	0.0	0.0	0.0	0.0
Cotton/tobacco	-	21.4	-	-

Crop	Vakinan.	Total	Ranomafana
Lowland rice	27.7	8.7	10.9
Upland rice	30.1	10.2	-
Maize	14.1	8.1	-
Potatoes	46.9	30.4	66.4
Beans	5.0	3.3	-
Peanuts	0.0	0.0	-
Wheat/barley	98.8	98.8	-
Tubers	1.1	0.1	-
Cotton/tobacco	81.5	30.2	-

[a] 0.0 = Level below 0.1 %
[b] Not cultivated in the region
[c] Tubers = Cassava and sweet potatoes

Source: Data from 1997 IFPRI/FOFIFA household survey

Improved Lowland Rice Varieties

Introduction

In the early 1980s, a national seed plan (Plan National Semencier) was put in place in Madagascar. The main policy objective was to increase seed production to help to achieve food self-sufficiency in the country. The Service de Production de Semences et du Materiel Vegetal (SMV or Division for Seed Production) within the Ministry of Agriculture was created to this effect along with some local Centers for Seed Multiplication (CMSs). There was also direct support to seed farmers (see Madagascar Schema Directeur Financier, 1990). This plan benefited from the technical and financial support of the United Nations Development Program/Food and Agriculture Organization (UNDP/FAO) from 1986 to 1990. The results of this intervention were, on average, positive for the performance of the sector as the improved seed variety production increased from 70 tons in 1983 to more than 1,000 tons only two years later. However, despite its early success, the produced quantity remained insufficient at the national level.[3]

At the same time, other organizations such as research centers and private entities have been active in seed production for specific crops, such as potatoes for FIFAMANOR, wheat for KOBAMA, cotton for HASYMA, and peanuts for the FAO. These entities worked closely with the Groupement de Paysans Semenciers (GPSs or seed multiplier groups). Some CMSs that did not have access to enough land also worked with these groups. However, the use of this type of collaboration is still limited as there are effectively only about ten seed-producing organizations that work with the CMSs, most of which are situated in the faritany of Antananarivo, more specifically in the fivondronana of Marinarivo, Arivonimamo, Fihaonana, and Ankazobe. Some individual producers also practice seed multiplication. In most cases they are supported by private or state organizations, like the members of GPSs.[4]

Research on new varieties is done by the research centers, particularly by FOFIFA, and to a lesser extent by FIFAMANOR for specific crops (wheat, potatoes). The seed production sector has traditionally been dominated by the CMSs. However, an increase in the importance of the private sector has recently been noticed, especially since the liberalization measures. There has also been an increase in the total seed quantity produced, as shown in Table 5.8.

The seed subsector shows a relatively transparent structure from research and development to farmer. There are clear, formal, functional, and/or commercial links between the different agents. After the decision to liberalize the distribution of agricultural inputs, a law was put into effect in 1993 to ensure that the CMSs, de facto parastatals, did not sell seed directly to farmers. Thus, they were obliged to go through the private distribution network. In practice, however, the law was difficult to implement given that some CMSs, still formally linked with the Ministry of Agriculture, do not receive any external assistance from the Ministry or other donors.

Table 5.6 Dose of fertilizer per hectare receiving fertilizer

Crop	Majunga Plaines	Majunga HT	Fianar. HT	Fianar. C/F
Lowland rice	2.1	-	29.1	40.8
	(0.0)[a]		(8.8)	(0.0)
Upland rice	_[b]	-	-	-
Maize	-	-	29.0	-
			(0.4)	
Potatoes	-	-	31.0	-
			(2.7)	
Beans	-	-	12.3	-
			(0.3)	
Wheat/barley	-	-	-	-
Tubers[c]	-	-	-	-
Cotton/tobacco	-	80.5	-	-
		(17.3)		

Crop	Vakinan.	Total	Ranomafana
Lowland rice	48.5	35.3	22.8
	(13.5)	(3.1)	(2.5)
Upland rice	65.1	65.1	-
	(19.6)	(6.7)	
Maize	12.0	12.4	-
	(1.7)	(1.0)	
Potatoes	53.9	51.4	32.4
	(25.3)	(15.6)	(21.5)
Beans	39.3	31.8	-
	(1.9)	(1.1)	
Wheat/barley	153.5	153.5	-
	(151.6)	(151.6)	
Tubers	8.2	8.2	-
	(0.1)	(0.0)	
Cotton/tobacco	238.7	157.5	-
	(194.5)	(47.6)	

[a] Values in brackets indicate average dose per ha cultivated
[b] Indicates nonuser of fertilizer for a particular crop or region
[c] Tubers = Cassava and sweet potatoes

Source: Data from 1997 IFPRI/FOFIFA household survey

Table 5.7   Percentage of producers using the two types of fertilizer

Crop	Majunga Plaines	Majunga HT	Fianar. HT	Fianar. C/F
Urea only	100.0	100.0	29.3	-
NPK only	-	-	47.9	100.0
Both	-	-	22.8	-
Total	100.0	100.0	100.0	100.0

	Vakinan.	Total	Ranomafana
Urea only	5.3	18.7	-
NPK only	24.1	34.1	100.0
Both	70.6	47.2	-
Total	100.0	100.0	100.0

Source: Data from 1997 IFPRI/FOFIFA household survey

Table 5.8   Evolution of seed production in Madagascar, 1983 to 1994

Year	Total production (in tons)	Production CMS (%)	Production GPS and private farmers (%)
1983	87	-	-
1984	1,022	-	-
1985	927	-	-
1986	1,119	-	-
1987	1,208	-	-
1991	1,130	82	18
1992	1,750	84	16
1993	1,800	83	17
1994	1,480	75	25

Source: Data from Ministry of Agriculture of Madagascar

Now seeds are supplied to producers in two ways: through the modern subsector where improved varieties originate from the CMSs and/or private farmers or through the traditional marketing system in which seeds are sold or used out of own production. The latter is clearly the most important one as shown by the case of rice; less than 10 per cent of total rice seed, can be considered improved varieties.[5]

Irrigated rice seed production is located in all regions, especially in the Majunga and Fianarantsoa regions, where there is a high number of rice producers. In the Lac Alaotra region, the major rice production region in Madagascar, it seems illogical that there is a low number of rice seed producers. However, the existence of the CMS of Anosiboribory, that produces almost 50 per cent of the rice seed in Madagascar, in this area explains this situation. No GPSs are located in this region.

Table 5.9   Principal crops for seed multiplication, in %

	Vakinankaratra	Majunga Plaines	Fianarantsoa
Lowland rice	6.7	70.0	82.8
Upland rice	23.3	30.0	10.3
Maize	-	-	-
Potatoes	30.0	-	-
Beans	-	-	-
Peanuts	-	-	6.9
Wheat	40.0	-	-
Total	100.0	100.0	100.0

	Majunga HT	Lac Alaotra	All regions
Lowland rice	20.0	10.0	45.9
Upland rice	50.0	10.0	22.9
Maize	-	10.0	0.9
Potatoes	-	-	8.3
Beans	10.0	-	0.9
Peanuts	20.0	70.0	10.1
Wheat	-	-	11.0
Total	100.0	100.0	100.0

Source: Data from 1997 IFPRI/FOFIFA household survey

Improved seed is also produced for crops other than rice. Potato and wheat seed production are particularly important in the Vakinankaratra region (Table 5.9). In the case of wheat, there is a steady demand through the existence of KOBAMA, the wheat miller in Antsirabe, that buys up all the wheat in the region. The organization for potato seed multiplication is in the hands of FIFAMANOR, also located in Antsirabe. These two factors and the regional agroecological characteristics result in a preference of the local seed multipliers for these two crops.[6]

The Adoption of Improved Rice Varieties

The highest number of users of improved rice varieties is found in the Majunga Plaines region where 32.4 per cent of the households use improved seed (Table 5.10). It is second highest in the Majunga HT area with 13.6 per cent. Apart from current use, the household was also asked if it had ever used improved seed. For this last question, the same two regions still appear to lead. Hence, it seems that the continuous work by the agricultural extension services in the Majunga Plaines and by the project IRRI/FOFIFA/ USAID have resulted in adoption of new rice varieties in the region, especially varieties resistant to diseases that once were widespread in that region.

In the other regions, producers use improved rice varieties less frequently. The descriptive analysis of the reasons farmers give for not adopting improved rice varieties (Table 5.11) along with the analysis of the determinants of the adoption through regression analysis (Table 5.12) show that availability of seeds at the right moment is an important factor for adoption. The second most important factor is the price of improved varieties. Price was reported as most important in the Fianarantsoa HT region (39.4 per cent of the responses). In general, anecdotal evidence suggests that producers carefully compare the price of their own production with the prices that they have to pay for improved varieties. On average, the ratio between these products varies between 1.5 and 3 depending on the period that the paddy is sold. As the period when rice seeds are available coincides with the lean period, this often creates budgetary problems for the households, especially in the poorer Fianarantsoa HT region. The third factor is the lack of information; 22.7 per cent of the farmers are not aware of the existence of improved seeds. This level is very high in Fianarantsoa C/F (37.4 per cent) which can be explained through the low density of extension agencies, communication, and other infrastructure in the region.

Table 5.10   Use of improved lowland rice seed at the farm level, average of two seasons (1995/1996 and 1996/1997)

Region	Farmers using improved seeds[a]	Area planted with improved seeds	Average seed dose (kg seed per ha)	Average quantity of improved seeds (IS)	
	(in %)			Tanimbary using IS	Total cultivated tanimbary (kg IS per ha)
Majunga Plaines	32.4 (56.5)[b]	13.9	53	70	9.6
Majunga HT	13.6 (27.2)	5.3	113	74	4.2
Fianar. HT	6.7 (19.5)	5.0	83	46	2.3
Fianar. C/F	5.0 (21.2)	3.2	86	48	1.6
Vakinankaratra	6.0 (21.3)	2.7	69	9	0.2
Total	9.5 (24.5)	6.2	85	63	4.0
Ranomafana	16.9 (24.4)	15.3	80	47	7.2

[a] Adoption rate during the last two seasons
[b] The value in brackets indicate the percentage of producers that used improved lowland rice seed at least once

Source: Data from 1997 IFPRI/FOFIFA household survey

Seed quality does not correspond to producers' expectations in the Vakinankaratra region.   However, one has to acknowledge that the expectations of farmers are often agronomically impossible to fulfill. This is the case, for example, for the demand for high yielding varieties that do not require fertilizer use or varieties that resist drought as well as long submersion in water. It should be noted that agricultural research in Madagascar has come up with some reasonably successful solutions.   Two examples can be mentioned: the rice variety X360, resistant to virose (RYMV), which has permitted producers in the Majunga region to again produce on old lowlands that were abandoned because of infection by the RYMV; and the rice varieties adapted to higher altitudes for the Antsirabe region lowlands that are situated at altitudes of more than 1,300 meters.

Table 5.11   Reasons producers do not use improved seeds, in %

	Majunga Plaines	Majunga HT	Fianar. HT
Too expensive	49.5	2.6	39.4
Not available	4.9	79.1	8.4
Unaware of their existence	4.9	6.1	28.7
Poor quality	20.4	1.4	5.9
Others	20.3	10.8	17.6
Total	100.0	100.0	100.0

	Fianar. C/F	Vakinankaratra	Total
Too expensive	10.3	21.9	23.6
Not available	39.6	7.1	26.3
Unaware of their existence	37.4	15.5	22.7
Poor quality	8.0	23.6	10.2
Others	4.7	31.9	16.2
Total	100.0	100.0	100.0

Source: Data from 1997 IFPRI/FOFIFA household survey

The same explicative variables for the adoption of mineral fertilizer are used for the analysis of the determinants of the adoption of irrigated rice seeds. Hence, the estimated equation has the following form:

Prob (use) = f(Price; Charhh; Charcom; Systprod).

Table 5.12 shows the results of the determinants of the adoption of improved lowland rice seed varieties in the survey region using a probit analysis. The price of agricultural inputs, represented by the price of NPK, the price of lowland, the total area cultivated by the household, and the accessibility to seeds influence the use of improved seeds negatively. The first three variables might reflect allocation problems within the households. An increase in the price of fertilizer could lead to the reduction in spending on items in the budget that are considered less necessary, in particular on seeds that can be obtained from own production. Higher land prices lead to lower adoption rates while better access to seed is a major determinant in the decision to adopt improved varieties. The concept of access can be misleading as it is the accessibility at all times that is very important for adoption. It has been observed that improved varieties are often only available just before the planting season, when the producer is often short in cash as he has to pay for various food and agricultural items.

Table 5.12 Determinants of adoption of improved lowland rice seed (results of probit model)

Variable	Coefficient	t-value	Mean of X
Price NPK (ariary/kg)	-0.00811	-3.286[b]	399.80
Price rice (ariary/kg)	0.00518	2.243[a]	174.60
Price cassava (ariary/kg)	-0.00170	-0.506	85.32
Village level wage (ariary/day)	0.00028	0.883	648.09
Price lowland (ariary/are)	-0.00002	-2.150[a]	11,479.79
Price upland (ariary/are)	-0.61489E-5	-0.442	5,481.45
Extension agent in village (1=yes)	-0.39653	-1.395	0.49
Predicted max. amount to borrow (ar.)	0.66795E-6	2.775[b]	458,905.34
Distance house to distributor (min.)	-0.27916	-2.412[a]	2.33
Age of the household head	0.01097	1.518	45.21
Gender of household head (1=male)	0.35464	1.469	1.10
Index education level household head	0.53279	2.257[a]	1.86
Dependency ratio	0.07480	0.189	0.51
Possible lowland extension (1=yes)	0.14519	0.732	0.50
Area lowland cultivated	-0.00210	-2.533[a]	109.86
Area upland cultivated	0.00123	1.523	79.45
Time from house to upland plot	-0.00353	-0.943	21.64
Time from house to lowland plot	0.00004	1.448	27.35
Years of experience with upland plot	0.00071	0.066	15.37
Years of experience with lowland plot	0.00600	0.544	15.61
% of lowland area with water problems	0.00192	0.935	30.59
Index climatic risk	-0.02616	-1.325	6.04
Index disease risk	-0.00891	-0.378	4.02
Time dummy (1=1995/1996)	-0.86522	-4.489[b]	0.52
Regional dummy Vakinankaratra	-0.37264	-0.836	0.21
Regional dummy Majunga HT	0.21508	0.458	0.18
Regional dummy Majunga Plaines	1.40734	3.038[b]	0.07
Regional dummy Fianar. HT	-0.67296	-1.466	0.32

a, b   Indicate statistical significance at the 5 % and 1 % levels, respectively; the number of observations is 898

Source: Data from 1997 IFPRI/FOFIFA household survey

The factors that influence adoption in a positive way are the price of rice, access to credit measured by the amount that the household would be able to borrow, and the characteristics of the head of the household such as age and education level. Other variables also influence adoption of improved varieties, but to a lesser extent. This holds for water management, climatic risks, and disease risks. These three variables increase the risk of bad production at the plot level but on the other hand are also the subject of intense research to obtain more resistant and well-performing varieties and in that way might induce changes in varieties used. For example, after damage from a cyclone or disease, producers might be obliged to find seeds externally, as their own production might not be sufficient, might not exist, or might be impossible to use as seed.

The variable that measures access to agricultural extension services has a nonsignificant impact on the adoption of improved varieties. These results seem caused by the situation in the Vakinankaratra region, where extension has a negative influence (shown when the extension dummy is split up by region). It seems that agricultural extension in this region, during the period of rice development in the 1980s and 1990s, mostly worked toward other goals than the development of improved varieties. Moreover, the level of sophistication of the farmers in this region might suggest that they know how to obtain better seeds from their own harvests.

Conclusions

In this chapter, we examined the determinants of modern input use in the survey region. We document the small numbers of users of mineral fertilizers and improved crop varieties. The different constraints for higher modern input use are the risks due to climate and plant diseases, lack of irrigation infrastructure, physical access to input markets and distance to the plots, and economic access to inputs (price of agricultural inputs). While changes in climatic or agroecological factors are difficult to achieve, other factors can be influenced by development activities and policies. This is the case, for example, for the reduction of the distance between the seed users and the centers of input distributors, which influences the costs of inputs as well as accessibility. These interventions can be done at the market and market agent level, but also through basic infrastructure development such as roads, communication, etc. Finally, actions with respect to the improvement of water management and the extension of appropriate agricultural techniques seem also to be important for increasing the use of modern inputs.

Notes

1   As was the case in parts of Fianarantsoa C/F in 1997.
2   Unfortunately, in the final calculations per unit of fertilized land, the whole rice area of the household is taken into consideration as no distinction between these areas could be made.
3   The quantity produced in some CMSs is higher than the need in some regions. In such cases, the CMS is unable to sell all the seed and is obliged to use the seed for food.
4   For a good recent overview of the seed multiplication sector, see Goletti, Randrianarisoa, and Rich (1998).
5   The total annual seed needed in Madagascar is around 100,000 tons, assuming that 4 per cent of total production is used as seed. If those seeds are renewed every 4 years, Madagascar would need almost 25,000 tons of improved seeds every year. At this stage, improved seed production is only around 2,000 tons, a level less than 10 per cent of the needed amount.
6   The Vakinankaratara region supplies potatoes to most of Madagascar, from Antsiranana, 1,200 km to the north, to Tulear, 1,000 km to the south.

6 Factor Use and Agricultural Productivity

BART MINTEN, MANFRED ZELLER, and CLAUDE RANDRIANARISOA

Introduction and Conceptual Framework

There is broad agreement that agricultural production levels in Madagascar are low and have been on the decline for several years (Ministère de l'Agriculture, 1997; Roubaud, 1997; Minten et al., 1998; Pryor, 1990; Razafimandimby, 1997). The productivity decline is strongly linked to increasing poverty and environmental degradation in rural areas (Zeller et al., 1999). Despite the recognition of poor agricultural performance few systematic analyses have been done to relate specific household production responses to household and village level characteristics and policy variables following market liberalization. The analysis in this chapter shows which factors are important, qualitatively and quantitatively, in agricultural production in Madagascar using data from the extensive recent household and community survey.

The focus of the analysis is on the causal effect of different household, community, and policy variables on agricultural income. This system is modeled as a recursive system so that the explained upstream variables become explanatory downstream variables in the sequence of decisions that begins with land allocation and leads, finally, to explaining household income levels. Here at the outset, a brief sketch of the rationale and the flow of analysis is given. The first decision taken by the household is to allocate land. The household decides to cultivate possessed lowland or to lease land in or out. For upland area, the same decision must be made as well as whether or not to clear more land or to leave land fallow. In a next stage, depending on household and village level constraints, the household acquires and applies inputs for the different fields and crops. Then, the level of input use and expenditures will determine agricultural production and income.

Hence, the recursive modeling occurs in three stages. The model sketches below are simplified and do not provide the details on variable definitions. They show the concepts of exogenous and endogenous relationships in the analysis. X, Y, and Z are considered vectors of exogenous variables while the other variables are endogenous. Given the distinctive characteristics of upland and lowland area and the interest in the trade-offs of investments between them for environmental reasons, all of the analysis is separated between these production types. The complete system is modeled as follows:

Area lowland/upland cultivated (R) = f (access to credit [A], X)   (1)
Input expenditures on lowland/upland (I) = f (R, A, Y)   (2)
Production = f (R, I, Z)   (3)

Similar recursive systems have also been used by von Braun et al. (1989), Kumar (1994), and Zeller et al. (1998a). Alternative specifications are presented throughout the text to test the robustness of the results.

General Description of Agricultural Input Use and Margins

Table 6.1 shows average monthly gross crop income, input costs, and sales (or cash) income per household in the agricultural year 1995/1996. The reported production and income are based on detailed questionnaires concerning agricultural production, agricultural input levels, and sales. The expenditures shown in the table comprise direct costs arising from the acquisition of seed, organic and mineral fertilizer, pesticides, hired labor, transport, and marketing services. Total gross income amounts to almost 50,000 ariary a month per household for the region as a whole (±$50 US). Sixteen per cent of the value of gross total income is spent on the acquisition of inputs. Production per household is highest in the Majunga Plaines area and lowest in the Fianarantsoa area.

Rice is by far the most important crop, making up almost 60 per cent of the value of total income. However, its importance varies from region to region. In response to the relative land scarcity, households in the highland regions in Fianarantsoa and Vakinankaratra employ more labor- and capital-intensive farming systems. First, they cultivate more labor-intensive crops, such as vegetables and fruits. Second, they use more modern inputs, such as improved seed, fertilizer, and pesticides.[1] However, even by switching to more labor- and capital-intensive systems, it seems that households in land scarce regions are only partly able to bridge the agricultural income gap caused by the more limited access to land. This explains often seasonal or even permanent migration patterns from land scarce regions, mainly the highlands, to other parts of the country (as illustrated by INSTAT, 1998).

As seen by its relative importance in gross income and sales, the share of rice and tubers in total sales income is less than in total income, indicating that these crops are relatively more used as subsistence crops than as cash crops. The lesser importance of tubers in total sales income compared to total income is consistent for all regions.[2] Rice, however, still makes up 45 per cent of agricultural sales income and in the Majunga Plaines region is still the most important cash crop. Upland rice makes up only 1.5 per cent of the total rice production. Hence, the increasing extensification on the uplands documented in previous studies (Zeller et al., 1999; Dorosh et al., 1998) seems to come at the expense of the importance of rice.

Relative land scarcity in the highlands leads not only to intensification of cropping systems but also to more diversification of income sources within agriculture. Vakinankaratra is the most diversified region with vegetables an even more important source of cash income (28 per cent) than rice (26 per cent). On the other hand, Majunga Plaines is the least diversified as four-fifths of cash income is derived from rice. In the Fianarantsoa C/F region, coffee makes up almost half of cash income. Apart from the industrial crops, vegetables (97 per cent), fruits (65 per cent), legumes (especially peanuts), and beans (65 per cent) are used more as cash crops than for home consumption as their share in sales income is significantly higher than their share in total income.

Data on the same households were available in the Vakinankaratra region and the Majunga Plaines region in the periods 1990/1991 and 1995/1996. Table 6.2 shows total and sales income for these households in both time periods.[3] The value of net agricultural income over the five year period increased in Majunga Plaines by 14 per cent but declined in the Vakinankaratra by 4 per cent. It is interesting to note how little the importance of rice in the commercial surplus changed in both regions; it stagnated in the Majunga Plaines region (77 per cent) and increased slightly from 25 per cent to 28 per cent in the Vakinankaratra between 1991 and 1996. The most dramatic change in sales income comes from the fruits and vegetables category, growing in its share of total sales income by almost 8 per cent in Majunga Plaines and by 10 per cent in the Vakinankaratra region. Hence, it seems that increased land scarcity, even for the households that did not migrate, induces households to change to crops with higher margins per hectare.

These results seem to partly contradict the results from the community survey where a more dramatic shift to upland crops and away from rice was noticed over the previous ten years (Minten et al., 1998). Different reasons might explain this discrepancy. First, panel data on a five year interval are

Table 6.1   Monthly agricultural income and input expenditures, by crop and region, 1995/1996

Region	Product	Gross agricultural income (ariary)	Input costs (ariary)	Share in total income	Share in cash income
Majunga Plaines	tubers	563	12	1.0	0.7
	legumes, beans	1,338	480	1.6	2.6
	other cereals	7,043	534	11.8	1.1
	coffee/industrial crops	908	18	1.6	2.2
	fruit	1,066	0	1.9	3.2
	vegetables	1,257	3	2.3	2.6
	early lowland rice	7,831	3,205	8.4	6.3
	medium or late lowland rice	56,811	17,572	71.1	81.2
	rainfed hillside rice	253	85	0.3	0.0
	Total	77,070	21,908	100.0	100.0
Majunga HT	tubers	2,361	220	5.5	3.7
	legumes, beans	3,871	322	9.0	11.5
	other cereals	698	31	1.7	0.6
	coffee/industrial crops	3,753	259	8.9	12.3
	fruit	2,071	0	5.3	8.0
	vegetables	2,953	340	6.7	16.6
	early lowland rice	26,681	5,782	53.2	42.0
	medium or late lowland rice	4,090	827	8.3	4.3
	rainfed hillside rice	680	106	1.5	1.0
	Total	47,157	7,887	100.0	100.0
Fianar. HT	tubers	4,613	84	11.8	10.0
	legumes, beans	4,717	778	10.3	15.5

other cereals	1,053	98	2.5	2.4
coffee/industrial crops	670	119	1.4	2.5
collected crops	11	0	0.0	0.0
fruit	697	6	1.8	3.5
vegetables	3,437	15	8.9	19.8
early lowland rice	4,586	1,153	9.0	4.3
medium or late lowland rice	24,041	3,277	54.2	42.1
rainfed hillside rice	0	0	0.0	0.0
Total	43,826	5,531	100.0	100.0
Fianar. C/F				
tubers	6,273	33	16.3	4.9
legumes, beans	377	80	0.8	0.7
other cereals	68	2	0.2	0.0
coffee/industrial crops	11,298	388	28.6	47.0
fruit	1,541	0	4.0	4.3
vegetables	122	1	0.3	0.3
early lowland rice	9,043	1,948	18.6	16.9
medium or late lowland rice	14,041	2,424	30.4	25.9
rainfed hillside rice	413	124	0.8	0.0
Total	43,175	4,999	100.0	100.0
Vakinankaratra				
tubers	2,491	486	4.7	2.0
legume, beans	4,976	986	9.3	13.0
other cereals	9,155	2,667	15.1	21.7
coffee/industrial crops	664	128	1.2	2.3
collected crops	2	0	0.0	0.0
fruit	2,431	53	5.5	5.7
vegetables	7,335	887	15.0	27.9
early lowland rice	927	183	1.7	0.8

	medium or late lowland rice	24,187	4,520	45.7	25.7
	rainfed hillside rice	1,001	241	1.8	1.1
	Total	53,169	10,152	100.0	100.0
Ranomafana	tubers	8,085	160	30.6	19.2
	legumes, beans	1,346	187	4.5	7.6
	other cereals	379	25	1.4	0.3
	sugar cane and industrial crops	3,666	122	13.7	40.4
	collected crops	12	0	0.0	0.1
	fruit	1,512	0	5.8	10.7
	vegetables	337	0	1.3	2.7
	early irrigated rice	1,360	354	3.9	1.8
	medium or late irrigated rice	11,452	2,137	36.0	15.3
	rainfed hillside rice	856	110	2.9	2.0
	Total	29,005	3,095	100.0	100.0
Total	tubers	3,787	176	8.9	4.7
	legume, beans	3,460	574	7.1	9.5
	other cereals	2,958	637	5.7	6.6
	coffee/industrial crops	3,410	192	7.9	13.6
	collected crops	4	0	0.0	0.0
	fruit	1,503	13	3.7	4.9
	vegetables	3,309	250	7.5	15.2
	early lowland rice	8,903	2,097	16.7	15.2
	medium or late lowland rice	21,133	4,078	41.8	33.1
	rainfed hillside rice	434	101	0.8	0.4
	Total	48,902	8,118	100.0	100.0

Source: Data from 1997 IFPRI/FOFIFA survey

available for the household analysis while the community analysis covered a ten year period. Given that most price changes due to liberalization happened in the beginning of this ten year period, most of the changes might have occurred in those first five years. Second, we have data only on the households that stayed and did not migrate from the village over the previous five years. It is assumed that new immigrants or new households, often poorer ones, might have different agricultural practices than well-established ones due to less access to lowland land (see next section). Hence, given the lesser importance of rice as a upland crop, this shift might indeed be real.

Crop production is plagued in all regions by a high number of covariant and idiosyncratic risk factors (see also chapter 4). Almost 80 per cent of the fields in the lowland area are reported to have experienced some kind of production problem over the previous season (Table 6.3). One-third of the lowland field problems were related to water supply problems, indicating the extent of deficiencies in the irrigation infrastructure. The number of upland fields with problems is significantly lower. However, still almost 50 per cent of the upland fields experienced a problem. On upland as well as lowland, 7 per cent of the fields are reported to have had losses due to phytosanitary diseases.

The numbers in this section give a brief overview of the agricultural production environment in Madagascar. In the next sections, factor use (land and other inputs), modern technology adoption, and agricultural productivity are discussed in more detail through descriptive as well as regression analysis. Table 6.4 shows the definitions of the variables used in the analysis, and their respective means and standard deviations. Further analysis is based on 960 observations, combining data from 495 households in the year 1995/1996 and 465 households in the year 1996/1997.[4]

Land Use

The average area of cultivated upland in the survey region is close to the area of cultivated lowland.[5] However, the magnitude and the relative importance of lowland and upland area varies significantly by region and by household. Lowland areas, absolutely and relatively, are significantly higher in Majunga while upland is relatively more important in the other regions. Most households (86 per cent) cultivate both types of fields. Respectively only 7 per cent and 6 per cent of the households cultivate upland and lowland exclusively.

Table 6.2   Agricultural income and expenditures, 1990/1991 and 1995/1996a

Region	Product	Gross agricultural income (1995/1996 ar.)b	Input costs (1995/1996 ar.)b	Share in total income	Share in cash income
Majunga Plaines 1990/1991	tubers	438	168	0.5	0.4
	legumes, beans	3,390	0	6.4	10.3
	other cereals	540	170	0.7	0.0
	sugar cane and industrial crops	2,274	366	3.6	7.1
	collected crops	0	0	0.0	0.0
	fruit	2,825	0	5.3	3.9
	vegetables	448	16	0.8	1.2
	early lowland rice	6,598	1,967	8.7	9.1
	medium or late lowland rice	48,822	9,598	73.8	67.9
	rainfed hillside rice	68	0	0.1	0.0
	Total	65,404	12,285	100.0	100.0
Vakinankaratra 1990/1991	tubers	6,263	676	13.3	7.9
	legumes, beans	7,759	838	16.5	24.8
	other cereals	7,846	1,770	14.4	21.0
	sugar cane and industrial crops	1,071	184	2.1	4.2
	collected crops	10	0	0.0	0.0
	fruit	2,837	0	6.7	5.5
	vegetables	3,252	245	7.1	11.9
	early lowland rice	905	108	1.9	0.7
	medium or late lowland rice	17,737	3,103	34.8	22.4
	rainfed hillside rice	1,803	498	3.1	1.7
	Total	49,481	7,421	100.0	100.0

Majunga Plaines				
1995/1996	tubers	655	2	1.1	1.2
	legumes, beans	2,635	752	3.1	6.2
	other cereals	6,899	522	10.5	1.3
	sugar cane and industrial crops	944	27	1.5	2.0
	collected crops	0	0	0.0	0.0
	fruit	3,104	0	5.1	9.5
	vegetables	1,605	8	2.6	3.2
	early lowland rice	9,952	3,020	11.4	7.8
	medium or late lowland rice	52,214	13,176	64.4	68.8
	rainfed hillside rice	139	38	0.2	0.0
	Total	78,146	17,545	100.0	100.0
Vakinankaratra				
1995/1996	tubers	3,269	551	6.7	3.1
	legumes, beans	6,576	1,228	13.2	21.8
	other cereals	7,562	1,692	14.5	16.2
	sugar cane and industrial crops	849	156	1.7	3.5
	collected crops	1	0	0.0	0.0
	fruit	2,276	30	5.6	5.6
	vegetables	4,919	416	11.1	21.8
	early lowland rice	807	159	1.6	0.9
	medium or late lowland rice	21,036	3,695	42.9	24.7
	rainfed hillside rice	1,460	390	2.6	2.4
	Total	48,755	8,316	100.0	100.0

a 1,000 ariary=5,000 FMG=$1.10 US; calculations are done on 150 households and are simple averages (nonweighted)

b 1990/1991 income data converted to 1995/1996 values using the CPI of Antananarivo

Source: Data from 1997 IFPRI/FOFIFA survey; 1992 IFPRI/CNRE/DSA survey

Table 6.3   Problems for agricultural production as reported by farmers, agricultural years 1995/1996 and 1996/1997

	Lowland		Upland	
	No. of fields	%	No. of fields	%
Not enough rain	249	20.0	132	5.4
Planted too late	9	0.7	10	0.4
Theft	13	1.1	88	3.6
Losses due to phytosanitary diseases	81	6.5	170	7.0
Lack of inputs (fertilizer, etc.)	313	25.1	468	19.1
Inundation	150	12.1	22	0.9
Other natural calamities	45	3.6	56	2.3
Bad seed quality	17	1.3	39	1.6
Losses due to birds/animals/insects	96	7.7	210	8.6
No major problems	273	21.9	1,250	51.1
Total	1,248	100.0	2,446	100.0

Source: Data from 1997 IFPRI/FOFIFA survey

Table 6.4   Variable definitions

Variable	No. of observations	Mean	Std. Dev.
Area cultivated of upland (are)	960	115.6	135.4
Area cultivated of lowland (are)	960	137.1	206.1
Total input expenditures on lowland (ariary)	960	5,926.3	12,362.8
Total input expenditures on upland (ariary)	960	2,149.7	5,438.0
Net agricultural income (ariary)	960	30,373.6	43,057.0
Gross agricultural income lowland	960	22,669.9	41,224.0
Gross agricultural income upland	960	15,779.7	20,305.0
Area possessed of lowland (are)	960	133.7	232.8
Area possessed of upland (are)	960	126.8	178.0
Value of agricultural equipment (ariary)	960	55,363.7	131,200.0
Dummy fertilizer user (1=yes)	960	0.2	0.4
Dummy improved lowland seed user (1=yes)	908	0.1	0.3
Level of education (1=no education; 6=university)	960	2.2	1.0
Gender household head (1=male)	960	0.9	0.3
Number of children in household	960	3.1	1.9
Number of adults in household	960	2.9	1.5
Number of elderly in household	960	0.4	0.6

Dependency ratio	960	0.5	0.2
Visit of extension agent in village	960	0.1	0.2
Dummy if born in the vilage	960	0.8	0.4
Maximum amount that household can borrow (1,000 ariary)	960	161.2	315.7
Climatic risk	960	6.6	6.8
Disease risk	960	5.0	5.5
Extension possibilities in upland (1=yes)	960	0.6	0.5
Land price upland	960	4,549.9	6,780.8
Land price lowland	960	10,089.4	15,713.6
Irrigation infrastructure index (0=none; 2=fully functional)	960	2.2	0.7
Distance from agricultural lowland plot to house (in minutes)	960	29.0	26.8
Years of experience on lowland field	960	16.8	12.0
Distance from agricultural upland plot to house (in minutes)	960	24.7	38.6
Years of experience on upland field	960	15.8	11.5
Time to paved road (hours)	960	4.0	4.1
Average wage in village, man per day (ariary)	960	720.3	530.7
Price of beans (ariary/kg)	960	394.5	196.1
Price of maize (ariary/kg)	960	217.7	162.9
Price of cassava (ariary/kg)	960	83.4	23.8
Price of rice (ariary/kg)	960	173.6	74.6
Price of NPK (ariary/kg)	960	392.9	38.6
Lowland rice yield (kg/ha)	882	1,688.7	1,111.6
% of lowland area with water problems	960	31.8	44.9
Regional dummy Majunga Plaines	960	0.1	0.3
Regional dummy Majunga HT	960	0.3	0.4
Regional dummy Fianarantsoa HT	960	0.2	0.4
Regional dummy Fianarantsoa C/F	960	0.2	0.4
Time dummy agricultural year 1995/1996	960	0.5	0.5
Number of cattle theft in the village in 1997	960	1.3	2.7
Number of family living in the same village	960	3.8	3.6
Number of family living in a nearby village (1-50 kms)	960	4.4	4.4
Number of family living in a village > 50 kms	960	2.6	3.6
Value of nonland assets (ariary)	960	1,134,011.0	1,896,780.0
Years that household head lives in the village	960	6.5	13.1
Years that spouse of household head lives in the village	960	7.3	11.8
Distance of house to lowlands of parents (km)	960	135.6	369.5
Share of own religion in the village	960	0.6	0.2
Share of own ethnic group in the village	960	0.8	0.3

Source: Data from 1997 IFPRI/FOFIFA survey

Two separate regressions were run that explain the area of lowland and upland cultivated (Table 6.5). The results show the distinctly different determinants of upland compared to lowland area allocation. A dummy that measures if the chief of the household was born in the village was included in both regressions. It is assumed that nativity provides time to acquire more land and higher socioeconomic status. It might be land augmenting in the sense that more land can be cleared or taken into cultivation every year and thus land stock can be accumulated. While the coefficient on this variable is positive, large, and significant in the lowland equation, it is not significant in the upland equation. Native households cultivate on average 61 ares more lowland area.

The larger the family, the more land is cultivated as seemingly more labor is available. One extra adult increases the area cultivated on upland by 20 ares while this variable is insignificant for the lowland area. On the other hand, the coefficient is large and significant for elderly people on lowlands. These results seem to be related to inheritance law in Madagascar and the fact that older households or those native to the village possess more higher valued lowland land compared to younger households or households that more recently migrated into the village (which are often younger households).[6] The acquisition of upland however, seems to be more a question of whether a household has enough labor to take more upland into cultivation.

Availability of fertile but uncultivated land is a major driving force for the area cultivated by the household. The possibility of extension on the upland, a variable that was measured at the community level, increases cultivated upland area by 39 ares. Lack of possible extension is reflected more in the area of upland than in lowland cultivated as changes in lowland area are more difficult to achieve.[7] These extension possibilities are also reflected in the effect of land prices at the village level. If we assume that land prices reflect scarcity as well as quality, the area cultivated by the household decreases very significantly as land prices increase.[8] Their respective elasticities are quite similar, i.e. 0.26 and 0.27 for lowland and upland prices respectively.

Access to more credit increases the area of lowland as well as upland cultivated (but significantly only for upland). A correction for endogeneity was done as access to credit is assumed to be a choice variable of the household as richer households, i.e. households with more land, have better access to credit.[9] Rice prices, without correction, showed an unexpected

Table 6.5   Determinants of land use for agricultural years 1995/1996 and 1996/1997, in are[a]

	Lowland area		Upland area	
	Coefficient	t-ratio	Coefficient	t-ratio
Maximum amount that household can borrow (1,000 ariary)	0.1888	1.184	0.1786	2.832
Gender household head (1=male)	1.6386	0.103	17.2868	1.553
Number of children	1.5839	0.673	5.5629	2.494
Number of adults	-0.4330	-0.059	20.0267	3.743
Number of elder	25.7579	1.726	16.2138	2.030
Dummy if born in the village	61.0472	2.401	11.0774	0.913
Index level of education (1=no education; 6=university)	2.3014	0.229	1.3949	0.322
Price of rice - poor[b]	-0.3107	-1.927		
Price of rice - medium[b]	-0.0931	-0.843		
Price of rice - rich[b]	0.3178	1.785		
Index climatic risk	-2.4679	-1.750	0.6062	0.883
Index plant disease risk	-0.3317	-0.239	0.7273	1.180
Number of cattle theft in the village in previous year	3.0643	0.820	-4.1513	-3.003
Possibility of upland extension (1=yes)	10.5394	0.392	39.0312	4.023
Price land	-0.0035	-2.335	-0.0067	-6.579
Time to paved road (hours)	7.6160	1.076	9.4582	3.467
Time to paved road (hours) - squared	-0.5881	-1.974	-0.3094	-2.788
Regional dummy Majunga Plaines	214.1336	6.664	-21.3512	-1.266
Regional dummy Majunga HT	148.7307	3.895	-11.1631	-0.677
Regional dummy Fianar. HT	-28.5756	-1.062	20.1129	1.687
Regional dummy Fianar. C/F	4.7246	0.163	-17.9665	-1.312
Time dummy (1=agr. year 1995/1996)	4.7150	0.569	6.3785	1.598
Intercept	17.0718	0.425	-40.9646	-1.630
R squared	0.16		0.37	
No. of observations	960		960	

a 2SLS, credit endogenous; robust standard errors with household clusters are reported
b Division along asset values

Source: Data from 1997 IFPRI/FOFIFA survey

negative sign on lowland area cultivated. However, given the methodological problems with this variable, a different specification was tried where the price variable was interacted with the asset value of the household.[10] While poorer households react negatively to rice prices as they are often net rice buyers, they become relatively poorer with rice price increases; richer households react significantly and positively to rice prices, with an area price elasticity of around 0.32. Hence, changes in rice prices have differential impacts on different households, depending on their respective assets.[11] With higher rice prices poorer households might find it rational, given their constraints, to sell or rent out their lowland to richer households. In addition, only richer households might be able to provide sufficient resources to invest in the acquisition of new and previously uncultivated lowland.

Risk management is important for smallholders in Madagascar as shown by the high incidence of problems (Table 6.3). To capture some of these aspects, a risk index was constructed that reflects the incidence of climatic calamities and the incidence of plant diseases in the village over the ten years prior to the survey.[12] Climatic risk is an important issue in Madagascar as cyclones, heavy rainfalls, or late or no rainfall can reduce or sometimes even destroy the whole harvest. Moreover, cyclones strike mostly at the end of the rainy season when most of the agricultural production is in full bloom and still in the field (Oldeman, 1990). As there is clearly a regional dimension to these risks (the east is more often hit by cyclones than the west; the south is more susceptible to drought), the different survey villages show great variation in risk exposure. The results indicate the higher the climatic risk, the higher the upland area and the lower the lowland area. As production in the lowlands seems to suffer relatively more from bad or unfavorable weather conditions, risk-averse rural households seem to diversify away from lowland crops to reduce the impact of these risks. The risk of plant diseases seems not to affect the relative upland/lowland land allocation as upland and lowland crops are equally hit by disease (7 per cent of the fields).

Another dimension of risk is rural insecurity. While rural security has clearly improved in recent years, it remains an important problem in rural Madagascar and has implications for household income, agricultural practices, and natural resource management.[13] For example, Bertrand (1994) documents the use of bush fires as means of protection against rural 'dahalos' (bandits or thieves) while Dodwell (1995) illustrates how certain villages oppose new roads for fear of robbery. Another consequence of rural insecurity is that people are obliged to spend valuable time protecting their agricultural production. One strategy is to produce only on fields within eyeshot (Ramiarantsoa, 1995). As households tend to locate themselves closer to the lowlands, these fields are easier to supervise. Hence, rural security might come at the expense of expansion into the uplands. A variable was constructed that reflects the average incident of theft in the village.[14] This variable shows that for every extra incidence of theft, upland area cultivated is reduced by 4 ares. While the contemporaneous incidences of theft might not be the best indicator of exposure to rural insecurity as households might take protective and preventive measures, more so when more exposed (as illustrated in the case of agricultural traders in Madagascar by Fafchamps and Minten, 1999a), we still conclude that higher rural security leads to less field supervision costs and thus to more extensification into the uplands.[15]

The time required to get to a main road is a significant determinant of the area cultivated, ceteris paribus. Households that are located closer to a paved road cultivate less land. An additional hour of travel time from the paved road increases the upland area by 9 ares. Different reasons might cause this effect. First, the presence of road infrastructure influences input, output, and land prices and therefore relative profitability thus leading to a different factor, i.e. land use. There might be a leveling off of the effect of distance to a paved road, shown by the significant quadratic term, since the further households are from a road, the less incentive to cultivate for commercial surplus due to higher transaction and transportation costs. Second, governments tend to invest in infrastructure in regions with significant agroecological potential (see Binswanger et al., 1993). These regions tend also to be more densely populated. Households in these fertile areas are faced with higher land costs, which might further increase if there is access to a road, and therefore might work the land more intensively and use less land per household.

Area Shares of Different Crops

While lowlands are almost exclusively devoted to rice, this is not the case for the upland where diverse crops can be grown. Equations for the shares in total area of upland cultivated in maize, cassava, and beans (the three most important upland crops in the survey region) were run in a Seemingly Unrelated Regression Model (SURE) (Table 6.6). The SURE specification allows for controlling possible correlations of error terms across equations.

Table 6.6   Determinants of crop area shares in upland cultivation (Seemingly Unrelated Regression Model)

	Share maize		Share cassava		Share beans	
	Coefficient	t-ratio	Coefficient	t-ratio	Coefficient	t-ratio
Area cultivated of upland (are)	0.00018	2.878	-0.00015	-2.021	0.00007	1.654
Possessed area of riceland (are)	-0.00003	-0.708	0.00001	0.239	0.00001	0.400
Own product price (ariary/kg)	0.0000011	0.263	0.0000007	0.035	-0.0000004	-0.162
Index level of education	0.00030	0.036	-0.01389	-1.391	0.00488	0.882
Gender of household head (1=male)	-0.05163	-2.065	0.09897	3.269	-0.01100	-0.656
Number of children	0.00386	0.955	0.00158	0.323	0.00345	1.270
Number of adults	-0.01056	-1.982	0.00746	1.157	-0.00741	-2.074
Number of elder	-0.01708	-1.340	0.01133	0.734	-0.00408	-0.476
Village wage (ariary/day)	0.00007	2.167	0.00013	3.506	-0.00012	-5.792
Price upland (ariary/are)	0.0000007	0.598	-0.0000042	-3.055	-0.0000006	-0.842
Time to paved road (hours)	0.01310	2.624	0.01963	3.248	0.00167	0.500
Time to paved road (hours) - squared	-0.00048	-2.092	-0.00074	-2.641	-0.00010	-0.658
Regional dummy Majunga Plaines	-0.00709	-0.214	0.11118	2.776	-0.13775	-6.204
Regional dummy Majunga HT	-0.25603	-7.516	0.03971	0.963	-0.00574	-0.251
Regional dummy Fianar. HT	-0.23761	-10.095	0.21599	7.577	-0.04068	-2.572
Regional dummy Fianar. C/F	-0.37963	-17.001	0.59453	21.985	-0.13193	-8.800
Time dummy (1=agr. year 1995/1996)	0.00584	0.399	-0.00827	-0.466	0.00273	0.278
Intercept	0.35902	8.917	-0.07207	-1.477	0.22814	8.438
R squared	0.34		0.46		0.21	
No. of observations	836		836		836	
Mean dependent variable	0.212		0.291		0.105	

Source: Data from 1997 IFPRI/FOFIFA survey

Table 6.7   Land area cultivated, input expenditures, and modern input use, agricultural years 1995/1996 and 1996/1997

Region	Total area cultivated (ares)		Input expenditures (ariary/are)*		% of households that use	
	Lowland	Upland	Lowland	Upland	Mineral fertilizer	Improved lowland seeds*
Majunga Plaines	306	89	79.41	8.91	3.22	24.00
Majunga HT	274	136	29.18	14.97	1.85	10.89
Fianar. HT	54	98	84.09	16.37	15.00	4.79
Fianar. C/F	66	90	60.15	5.75	0.00	5.15
Vakinankaratra	56	108	89.49	190.88	52.01	3.69
Total	116	104	69.84	53.42	16.36	7.27

* For the households that cultivate this type of land

Source: Data from 1997 IFPRI/FOFIFA survey

The more area of upland cultivated, the less important is cassava and the more important are beans and maize. Given that cassava is relatively more used as a subsistence crop and beans and maize are more often cash crops (see Table 6.1), it seems that households first try to ensure their own requirements by cultivating cassava and then, if extra land is available, cash crops are planted for extra revenue. On the other hand, there is also a change in consumption behavior as cassava is an economically inferior crop (see chapter 8) and hence, richer households, i.e. households with more land, switch to more expensive calories originating, for example, from maize or beans for home consumption.

The share of upland planted with cassava is also related to lower land prices due to more availability of land, lower land quality, or locations far from output markets. If land is more costly and valuable, households plant more capital- and labor-intensive crops and thus grow less cassava. This is additionally reflected in the regression coefficient for the distance to the main road. As households are located further from the main road, the importance of cassava increases. Every hour further from the main road increases the cassava share in upland area by almost 2 per cent, with significant leveling off of this effect the further from the road one goes.

Acreage responses to changes in output prices are not significant but this is not uncommon for semisubsistence cultivation systems. The higher the wages the higher the importance of cassava and the lower that of beans. Cassava is a relatively more labor-extensive crop than beans, inducing households to switch to cassava if wages increase. The regressions in Table 6.5 have shown that the higher the number of adults, the greater the area of upland cultivated. The presented share equations show that an increased number of adults is related to a lower share of maize and beans while it has no significant effect on cassava. In a nonreported regression, adults are strongly positively related to the other upland crops such as wheat, barley, and industrial crops. These crops seem to receive relatively more labor as is also illustrated by their relatively high input expenditures and higher margins per unit land.

Modern and Total Input Use

Table 6.7 shows the input expenditures per unit land disaggregated for the two land types. In general, input expenditures are significantly higher for lowland than for upland, with the exception of the Vakinankaratra region.

The land area per household is significantly related to the input expenditures per hectare at the regional level. As land is relatively abundant in the Majunga HT, inputs make up only one-third of the expenditures of those in the Majunga Plaines or the Fianarantsoa HT region, where land is scarcer. It is interesting to note the differences in input expenditures in upland agriculture for Fianarantsoa HT and the Vakinankaratra. Although they seem to have similar land constraints, one region seems to invest in upland expenditures while the other does not.

Further division of the type of input expenditures (not reported) reveal that while half of the input expenditures on lowland come from expenditures on hired labor inputs, most input expenditures on upland constitute capital inputs (fertilizer, seeds, pesticides, etc.). This is also reflected by the percentage of households that use fertilizer. This level is especially high in the Vakinankaratra region (52 per cent of the households) where input expenditures on upland are also highest. Overall, 16 per cent of the households in the survey area used mineral fertilizer during the agricultural years 1995/1996 and 1996/1997 combined representing 8 per cent of the cultivated area. The use amounts to around 6 to 7 kg of mineral fertilizer per hectare, one of the lowest application levels in Africa. The table further illustrates that improved lowland rice seed is only used by 7 per cent of the rural households (for a more detailed analysis, see chapter 5).

The intensification or extensification decision of the rural household is determined by different constraints. It is expected that households intensify (subject to availability of intensification technology) if their capital/land or labor/land price ratio is relatively small and that they extensify if capital, availability of technology, or labor is a constraint. Regressions are run to explain total input expenditures at the farm level as a measure for intensification. A distinction is made between upland and lowland input expenditures. An Ordinary Least Squares (OLS) and Two Stages Least Squares (2SLS) specification are presented (Table 6.8).[16] While input expenditures as a whole capture different type of inputs (mineral fertilizer as well as organic fertilizer, pesticides, seeds, etc.), we are also more specifically interested in the use of chemical fertilizer and improved rice seeds given their importance as a means to increase productivity in other countries and continents. Hence, separate probit models were run to determine the characteristics of the households that use these modern inputs. They are reported in the previous chapter.

Table 6.8   Determinants of input expenditures during the agricultural years 1995/1996 and 1996/1997, in ariary[a]

| | Input expenditures lowland (log) | | | | Input expenditures upland (log) | | | |
| | OLS | | 2SLS[b] | | OLS | | 2SLS[b] | |
	Coefficient	t-ratio	Coefficient	t-ratio	Coefficient	t-ratio	Coefficient	t-ratio
Land area (log)[c]	0.8098	8.813	1.0584	4.510	0.7469	6.580	0.4710	1.404
Max. amount hh can borrow (1,000 ar. - log)	0.1684	3.792	0.2345	1.722	0.1446	1.865	0.8013	2.578
Index level of education	0.1460	3.607	0.1027	2.222	0.0813	0.743	-0.0318	-0.239
Gender of household head (1=male)	0.2786	1.570	0.2311	1.360	0.1128	0.409	-0.1733	-0.578
Number of children	0.0142	0.552	-0.0024	-0.072	0.0105	0.245	-0.0155	-0.333
Number of adults	0.0146	0.322	-0.0137	-0.300	0.0292	0.376	-0.0174	-0.175
Number of elderly	-0.1141	-1.191	-0.1890	-2.061	-0.0776	-0.360	-0.0481	-0.214
Visit of extension agent in village	-0.4673	-1.677	-0.1980	-0.577	-0.2232	-0.272	-0.3518	-0.368
Index climatic risk	0.0008	0.135	0.0001	0.019	-0.0296	-1.325	-0.0298	-1.494
Index plant disease risk	-0.0050	-1.168	-0.0116	-1.610	-0.0396	-1.880	-0.0411	-2.224
Wage level village (ariary/day)	-0.0002	-1.252	-0.0004	-1.589	-0.0028	-8.101	-0.0028	-8.345
Price land (ariary/are)[d]	0.000008	3.341	0.000007	3.831	0.000032	2.297	0.000006	0.290
Distance from plot to house (in min.)[d]	-0.0028	-1.254	-0.0030	-1.335	0.0003	0.148	0.0004	0.183
Years of experience on field[d]	0.0017	0.344	0.0023	0.388	-0.0223	-2.300	-0.0166	-1.507
Time to paved road (hours)	-0.0930	-4.986	-0.0845	-3.767	-0.0230	-0.311	-0.0176	-0.235
Time to paved road (hours) - squared	0.0032	4.440	0.0033	4.629	0.0014	0.493	0.0008	0.297
Regional dummy Majunga Plaines	0.0597	0.271	-0.3988	-1.259	-2.3968	-4.637	-2.8394	-4.227
Regional dummy Majunga HT	-0.2758	-1.279	-0.4387	-2.300	-0.6479	-1.391	-0.7983	-1.716

Regional dummy Fianar. HT	0.1669	1.410	0.2007	1.607	-3.0638	-7.925	-2.7808	-7.326
Regional dummy Fianar. C/F	0.1456	1.109	0.1948	1.526	-4.5158	-10.578	-4.2714	-10.853
Time dummy (1=agr. year 1995/1996)	0.2542	3.224	0.2548	3.068	0.6721	2.786	0.6878	2.786
Intercept	3.4212	8.366	2.5767	4.655	5.1365	8.170	4.3777	4.382
R squared	0.38		0.36		0.42		0.36	
No. of observations	908		908		866		866	

a Robust standard errors with household clusters are reported
b 2SLS, credit and land area endogenous
c Zero land observations eliminated
d Depending on upland or lowland expenditures respectively

Source: Data from 1997 IFPRI/FOFIFA survey

Total input expenditures are strongly related to the size of the farm as area cultivated is positive and highly significant indicating that, with increasing land area available to the household, households increase input expenditures. The coefficients are not significantly different from one, for both lowland and upland, implying that input expenditures per unit of land are not related to the size of the farm ceteris paribus. However, it might still be that households with more land apply more inputs than households with less land as they might have better access to equity capital and credit to finance those input expenditures since access to credit shows a significant positive sign in all specifications. The land area might also capture another effect. With a larger quantity of land, the average cost per unit of land of applying inputs, which involves fixed costs, will be reduced and the average net benefit per unit of land will be enhanced.

Land prices have a positive effect on input expenditures. As expected, the higher the quality of the land (due to location, soil fertility, soil type conditions, and the irrigation infrastructure) or the less extensification possibilities, the higher the incentive of the use of improved, but more expensive, techniques (seeds, fertilizer) or of higher labor input. A 1 per cent increase in the price of upland increases input expenditures on upland by 0.14 per cent; 0.08 per cent for the effect of lowland prices on lowland input use. This effect at the farm level is net of the effect that increased land prices lead to less area cultivated. Therefore, input expenditures per unit land are even more sensitive to land prices. It seems that upland intensification is relatively more sensitive to land prices than lowland intensification. This bigger effect of land prices on upland might be related to higher home consumption rates of lowland production (63 per cent) than of upland production (34 per cent). Semisubsistence farmers might prioritize the production for own consumption above income from commercial surplus and might therefore be less sensitive to market conditions for lowland than upland.

Higher wages decrease modern input use. The higher the wage rate, the less hired labor is employed. Higher wages also lead to a lower probability of fertilizer use but have no impact on improved rice seed use. This might be due to the need for additional labor required for fertilizer applications. Input expenditures on lowland by female-headed households are slightly lower than by male-headed households. Female-headed households are, on average, poorer (Dorosh et al., 1998; Minten et al., 1998), have less risk-bearing capacity, and therefore might be less willing or able to invest in higher input expenditures. The further away the household's village is from infrastructure, the lower the input expenditures, controlling for other factors (among which the area cultivated and the land price). Hence, a higher distance to roads in this case reflects the higher cost of inputs, and the lower output prices due to transport and transaction costs. There is also a significant leveling off of this effect as transportation costs increase more slowly over longer distances (Minten, 1999). Distance to fields leads to lower input use on lowlands as the distance between a plot and the family compound raises travel time and the cost of carrying inputs from the homestead. However, the effect is not statistically significant.

The effect of agricultural extension on total input expenditures is shown to be insignificant. However, access to agricultural extension services leads to a significantly higher probability of fertilizer use. Most of the mineral fertilizer use in Madagascar is on industrial crops grown on upland such as wheat, barley, cotton, or tobacco and less often on rice. Such crops are often grown in association with industrial groups providing credit for fertilizer use as well as extension.[17] Climatic risk and risk of plant diseases affect input expenditures mostly negatively in lowland and upland.[18] Risk turns out to be highly significant for the use of fertilizer and the adoption of improved varieties. In both cases, the higher the risk, the lower the adoption rate by risk-averse households.

In the probit regression on fertilizer and improved seed use, significant and expected signs for the probability of mineral fertilizer use are noticed while few of the determinants for improved seed use are significant. In the case that the coefficients in the latter regression are significant, they show different signs than expected (compared to e.g. Kumar, 1994; Zeller et al., 1999; Cameron, 1999). Insights for these results come from the stated reasons for the nonuse of fertilizer and use of improved seed. While the majority of farmers report limited profitability as the major constraint for fertilizer use, availability is given as a major reason for improved seed use; in the case of improved seed, 49 per cent of farmers reported that they did not know of the product's existence or that it was unavailable compared to only 23 per cent in the case of mineral fertilizer. Hence, the low adoption of improved seed compared to mineral fertilizer use seems to be caused more by supply constraints.[19]

Agricultural Productivity

Table 6.9 shows yields, income, input expenditures, and gross margins per crop per hectare. The highest gross margins are obtained for industrial crops, i.e. wheat, barley, and tobacco.   They also show the highest input expenditures per hectare. Most of these crops are grown in connection with organizations that provide credit and payment facilities for the acquisition of inputs (especially seed and fertilizer). Gross margins for rice are highest for main season lowland rice. They are clearly lowest for tavy rice, i.e. the type of rice production based on slash and burn agriculture. However, this kind of rice production is characterized by low labor intensity requirements and low input expenditures and is therefore an economic alternative for regions or households constrained by these factors. Peanuts show the highest gross margin per hectare for nonindustrial upland crops while maize shows the lowest margin.

Table 6.9   Yields, gross income, input expenditure, and gross margins per ha by crop, 1995/1996

Culture	Yield (kg/ha)	Gross income per ha (ariary)	Input expenditure per ha (ariary)	Gross margin per ha (ariary)
Maize (grains)	1,201	187,047	21,350	165,697
Potaoes	3,619	348,410	106,106	242,303
Dried beans	699	333,586	53,378	280,209
Peanuts (unshelled)	1,064	389,634	34,046	355,588
Wheat	3,032	600,459	249,343	351,117
Barley	2,629	471,760	217,743	254,018
Tobacco	816	553,092	134,210	418,882
Coffee	333	173,961	-	173,961
Rice type vary aloha/asara	1,381	249,771	55,207	194,564
Rice type vary vakiambiaty/jeby	2,006	414,670	68,724	345,946
Rice type vary atriaty	1,826	277,692	48,545	229,147
Rice type vary tanety	1,428	333,625	55,579	278,046
Rice type vary tavy	1,030	113,995	17,473	96,521

Source: Data from 1997 IFPRI/FOFIFA survey

Upland and lowland production are analyzed separately in an aggregated agricultural production function. Production is valued at the actual household level prices or, if retained for home consumption, at the village market price. Then, given the specific interest in rice productivity, we look at lowland rice yields in particular. Under the neutrality assumption, the production function may be written as follows:

$$Y=A(E)F(X,Z)$$

where Y is the quantity of output, X is a vector of quantities of variable inputs, Z is vector of quantities of fixed inputs, and E is a vector of household characteristics and of location. For the empirical analysis, the production function is further specialized to the Cobb-Douglas form, so that

$$Y = A\prod_{i=1}^{m} X_i^{a_i} \prod_{i=1}^{n} Z_i^{\beta_i} \prod_{i=1}^{p} e^{\gamma_i E_i}.$$

Taking the logarithms of both sides of the equation, this form is used in the production function analysis. Different specifications are presented to test for robustness, i.e. simple OLS, 2SLS to control for potential endogeneity of land and input use, and OLS with village and time-specific effects to additionally control for variation in factors such as location, market access, soil quality, irrigation, and village structure.[20] Only observations with values of land bigger than zero are included. This results in 908 observations in the case of lowland production and 866 observations for upland production.[21]

Total Upland and Lowland Production

The factors of production show mostly expected signs in the different specifications. It should be noted that input and land uses are measured specifically for lowland and upland production while agricultural equipment and labor (the number of adults in the household) are measured at the farm level. All factors are highly significant in the OLS specification with fixed effects.[22] Input use is significant in lowland and upland production in all specifications. A doubling of input expenditures increases agricultural lowland income by 67 per cent and upland by 26 per cent (Tables 6.10 and 6.11). Evaluated at the mean, this implies that a 1 ariary increase in input expenditures leads to an increase of 1.91 ariary in upland production and of 2.56 ariary in lowland production. These numbers illustrate the high profitability of input use on lowland as well as upland. It is interesting to note that input expenditures, which generally must be made in the lean season, show a pay-off similar to storage of rice as rice prices are from two to three

Table 6.10 Lowland crop production function estimation[a]

	OLS		OLS - time/village fixed effects		2SL[b]	
	Coefficient	t-ratio[c]	Coefficient	t-ratio	Coefficient	t-ratio[c]
Factors of production						
Input expenditures lowland - ariary (log)	0.74619	10.985	0.66993	16.741	0.74617	2.348
Area of lowland cultivated - are (log)	0.09887	0.995	0.15664	2.285	0.09125	0.203
Agricultural equipment assets - ariary (log)	0.04319	1.818	0.04794	2.230	0.04360	1.204
Number of adults (log)	0.28911	1.170	0.34083	2.186	0.29090	1.219
Productivity shifters						
Gender of household head (1=male)	0.44121	1.857	0.51720	2.967	0.44123	1.766
Index level of education	-0.12970	-2.036	-0.09447	-1.707	-0.12925	-2.673
Dependency ratio	-0.18654	-0.643	-0.39887	-1.326	-0.18480	-0.692
Visit of extension agent in the village	-0.85558	-0.763	-1.13794	-0.789	-0.86197	-0.701
Price land lowland (ariary)	0.0000018	0.497	0.0000007	0.179	0.0000018	0.381
Time to paved road (hours)	0.13603	1.979			0.13608	2.163
Time to paved road (hours) - squared	-0.00472	-1.829			-0.00473	-1.778
Regional dummy Majunga Plaines	-2.16520	-3.943			-2.15023	-3.078
Regional dummy Majunga HT	-0.93527	-2.690			-0.92452	-1.419
Regional dummy Fianar. HT	-0.23497	-0.783			-0.23440	-0.801
Regional dummy Fianar. C/F	0.23635	1.514			0.23718	1.336
Time dummy (1=agr. year 1995/1996)	0.70813	2.610			0.70851	2.365
Intercept	1.96707	4.610			1.98833	2.312
R squared	0.42		0.57		0.42	
No. of observations	908		908		908	

[a] Dependent variable is the log of the gross value of crop output; zero land observations have been eliminated

[b] Input use and land use endogenous

[c] Robust standard errors with household clusters are reported

Source: Data from 1997 IFPRI/FOFIFA survey

Table 6.11 Upland crop production function estimation[a]

	OLS		OLS - time/village fixed effects		2SLS[b]	
	Coefficient	t-ratio[c]	Coefficient	t-ratio	Coefficient	t-ratio[c]
Factors of production						
Input expenditures upland - ariary (log)	0.29291	5.076	0.25615	11.075	0.56365	7.271
Area of upland cultivated - are (log)	0.38432	4.625	0.37215	5.536	0.64300	4.234
Agricultural equipment assets - ariary (log)	0.01178	0.638	0.03513	1.459	-0.04750	-2.103
Number of adults (log)	0.72568	2.869	0.55027	3.037	0.32453	1.336
Productivity shifters						
Gender of household head (1=male)	0.42677	1.665	0.47541	2.429	0.32932	1.176
Index level of education	-0.11220	-1.408	-0.13130	-2.099	-0.18410	-2.276
Dependency ratio	1.03365	1.671	0.68162	1.927	0.69810	1.262
Visit of extension agent in the village	0.28739	0.613	-1.76217	-1.087	0.82608	2.622
Price land lowland (ariary)	0.000016	1.974	0.000017	1.735	0.000025	2.174
Time to paved road (hours)	-0.04768	-1.220			-0.07109	-1.942
Time to paved road (hours) - squared	0.00251	1.681			0.00324	2.368
Regional dummy Majunga Plaines	-0.72319	-2.781			0.13256	0.429
Regional dummy Majunga HT	-0.66216	-2.271			0.21264	0.915
Regional dummy Fianar. HT	1.17047	3.705			2.61083	6.535
Regional dummy Fianar. C/F	0.43983	2.199			1.22451	5.259
Time dummy (1=agr. year 1995/1996)	0.54396	4.305			0.35804	2.119
Intercept	3.53989	4.413			1.76060	1.839
R squared	0.37		0.43		0.22	
No. of observations	866		866		866	

a Dependent variable is the log of the gross value of crop output; zero land observations have been eliminated

b Input use and land use endogenous

c Robust standard errors with household clusters are reported

Source: Data from 1997 IFPRI/FOFIFA survey

times as high during the lean season than during the harvest season. Both indicators illustrate the high discount rates faced by rural households in Madagascar.

Land area has a higher impact on production on the uplands than on the lowlands.[23] The elasticies are less than half for lowland production. Given that rental prices and sales prices are twice as high for lowland than for upland, the marginal revenue product of land is significantly higher for upland than for lowland. While this is a surprising result, an explanation might be found in the fact that the coefficients on lowland differ significantly by region. The regions with the highest pay-off to lowland area are the Majunga Plaines and the Vakinankaratra. Both regions are characterized by higher quality lowland, e.g. better soils as well as better irrigation infrastructure, as illustrated by the absolutely and relatively higher lowland prices as well as the better road infrastructure. It seems that the marginal revenue product of land is equalized in the better-endowed, more market-oriented regions while this is not the case in the other regions. Second, the lessened lowland land effect might be partly due to the assigned value of agricultural production as households with less lowland area face higher output prices, reducing the effect of land on gross lowland income. An alternative specification was run where physical rice production was used as dependent variable instead of valued production. In this case the coefficients on land are larger and more significant.[24]

The number of adults in the household affects agricultural production significantly, even after controlling for the higher area cultivation, on upland as well as lowland. It seems that labor markets do not lead to a complete adjustment of the effect of household composition. If factor markets were complete, production decisions affecting total labor supply should be separable from household characteristics (e.g. Benjamin, 1992). It might be that larger households have less difficulty mustering the necessary labor to complete critical tasks during periods of peak demand. The same reasoning holds for female-headed households as they show significantly lower agricultural production on uplands as well as lowlands, with coefficients of similar magnitude, even after controlling for other factors.

Access to agricultural extension, measured by the share of farmers in any village that received a visit by an extension agent in the previous year (excluding the producer under concern), shows in most specifications no significant positive impact on total factor productivity.[25] Education of the household head shows an unexpected negative sign. This might be explained through more off-farm activities by more educated households, especially in microenterprises (see chapter 7). Hence, it is likely that our estimates of the productivity of human capital are biased because individual characteristics which are positively correlated with output are negatively correlated with education. If better educated household heads work more off-farm, an omitted variable bias arises that depresses the estimated effect of schooling on crop productivity. As the measurement of the effect of education on productivity was not the main purpose in this analysis, no attempt was made to correct for this.[26]

Lowland Rice Yields

Previous analysis showed how rice yields in Madagascar declined over the ten year period by between 10 and 30 per cent depending on the type of rice (Minten et al., 1998; Zeller et al., 1999). The highest decline was noticed for upland rice.[27] Separate regressions were run on lowland rice yields, evaluated at the household level (Table 6.12). It is widely assumed in the agronomic and economic literature that irrigation has a large effect on rice yields which we will try to quantify here. Given the difficulty of measuring the availability of irrigation infrastructure, three proxy variables are included in the regression: price of lowland land (as the more infrastructure available the higher the value of the land); the share of the area with water problems (as more irrigation infrastructure would imply less water problems); and an irrigation infrastructure variable as reported by the household.[28] While all the coefficients have the expected sign, only two are significant and their elasticities are small: a 10 per cent increase of the area with water problems leads to a yield reduction of 1.4 per cent and the presence of modern irrigation infrastructure results in 4 to 7 per cent higher yields.

Hence, while we admit that our irrigation infrastructure variables are crude and imprecise, our results indicate that rice yields are not strongly related to irrigation infrastructure itself and that, for example, input use has a much higher effect on yields than does irrigation infrastructure.[29] One of the reasons might be that since the start of liberalization, the Malagasy government has dramatically reduced subsidies for the maintenance and expansion of irrigation systems. This deregulation is reported to have caused significant problems in making the transition from state run irrigation systems to systems run by farmers' organizations (Droy, 1997). This issue deserves further research given its policy importance.

Table 6.12 Determinant of lowland rice yields[a]

	OLS		OLS - time/village fixed effects		2SLS[b]	
	Coefficient	t-ratio[c]	Coefficient	t-ratio	Coefficient	t-ratio[c]
Input expenditures lowland - ariary (log)	0.12521	3.876	0.11572	5.163	0.49142	3.386
Agricultural equipment assets - ariary (log)	0.00898	0.898	0.02173	2.512	-0.00640	-0.620
Number of adults (log)	0.09885	1.533	0.07052	1.112	0.06790	0.907
Area of lowland in possession (are)	-0.00042	-3.964	-0.00037	-3.502	-0.00012	-0.815
Gender of household head (1=male)	0.20638	4.099	0.18820	2.568	0.14467	2.434
Index level of education	0.03535	0.975	0.01506	0.666	-0.01681	-0.417
Dependency ratio	0.04861	0.393	0.07929	0.648	-0.06532	-0.427
Visit of extension agent in the village (1=yes)	0.20177	0.735	1.04270	1.781	0.27942	0.989
Price land lowland (ariary)	0.0000018	0.884	-0.0000002	-0.146	0.0000005	0.399
Index irrigation infrastructure	0.06700	1.756	0.03930	1.256	0.07754	1.926
% of lowland area with water problems	-0.00177	-2.157	-0.00142	-2.630	-0.00182	-2.038
Time to paved road (hours)	-0.00171	-0.058			0.03011	0.850
Time to paved road (hours) - squared	0.00035	0.315			-0.00079	-0.616
Regional dummy Majunga Plaines	-0.64941	-4.157			-0.58856	-4.331
Regional dummy Majunga HT	-0.50908	-4.779			-0.24183	-1.946
Regional dummy Fianar. HT	-0.49508	-3.048			-0.46350	-3.024
Regional dummy Fianar. C/F	-0.19907	-1.909			-0.14633	-1.679
Time dummy (1=agr. year 1995/1996)	0.19703	3.376			0.16906	2.554
Intercept	6.38430	24.452			5.21643	8.872
R squared	0.33		0.43		0.13	
No. of observations	882		882		882	

[a] Dependent variable is the log of the average yield at the household level, 1995/1996 agricultural year
[b] Input use endogenous
[c] Robust standard errors with household clusters are reported

Source: Data from 1997 IFPRI/FOFIFA survey

Rice yields show the typical decline with size of the farm. A 1 per cent increase of the lowland area in possession leads to a 0.05 per cent decrease in rice yields. This confirms the results of Barrett (1996a) who showed similar declines in Madagascar.[30] It seems that differences in land endowments across households are not corrected by land and labor transactions. As we control for purchased inputs, it seems that households with less land presumably work harder on each plot and therefore reach higher yields. However, the caveat of this conclusion is that we can not completely control for land quality except by land price stated by the household itself and by regional dummies.

Net Agricultural Income

As it is typically assumed that farmers maximize farm profits, not farm revenues, a second approach is presented where expenditures on variable inputs are subtracted from farm revenues. Solving for input demand functions in terms of prices results in a restricted net income function. The log of this is estimated as

$$\Pi = \Pi(A, Z, p)$$

where A is a vector of semifixed inputs, Z is a vector of characteristics and location of individual farms, and p is a vector of input and output prices. The profit function approach implies a different stochastic specification from the production function approach. Hence, the two approaches are not necessarily equivalent. The results of this regression are presented in Table 6.13.

The main household-specific factors that seem to influence net agricultural household income are access to credit, access to land, and household composition. A marginal increase of 1 are of land increases net agricultural income by around 50 ariary. Access to credit is highly significant in all specifications. Access to 1,000 additional ariary of credit increases net agricultural income by 61 ariary, implying a net rate of return around 6 per cent in the specification where we try to control for the endogenity of credit. One extra adult member in the household increases net agricultural income by 8 per cent while male-headed households earn 28 per cent more ceteris paribus.

The land price does not directly influence net agricultural income. While land prices influence land allocation, intensification, crop choice, as well as migration decisions (as illustrated in previous sections and by Raison,

Table 6.13　Total crop profit function estimation[a]

	OLS		OLS - time/village fixed effects		2SLS[b]	
	Coefficient	t-ratio[c]	Coefficient	t-ratio	Coefficient	t-ratio[c]
Land cultivated (are)[d]	52.774	3.398	50.940	8.598	42.413	3.069
Share of lowland in total land	-3,743.817	-0.707	-3,924.511	-0.678	-5,916.177	-1.159
Agricultural equipment assets (ariary)	0.023	1.262	0.025	2.238	0.006	0.485
Max. amount hh can borrow (1000 ar.)	15.607	2.315	18.006	4.067	61.302	2.642
Gender of household head (1=male)	9,174.554	5.326	8,529.780	1.955	6,658.705	3.559
Index level of education	-262.803	-0.193	-526.114	-0.377	-1,525.783	-0.837
Number of adults	2,381.462	2.490	2,475.843	2.376	1,311.642	0.834
Dependency ratio	8,553.636	1.550	6,285.771	0.840	4,554.079	0.775
Visit of extension agent in the village (1=yes)	-2,520.855	-0.255	1,160.841	0.031	114.673	0.010
Price land upland (ariary)	0.079	0.297	-0.179	-0.772	-0.183	-0.597
Price land lowland (ariary)	0.073	0.522	-0.008	-0.078	0.018	0.208
Price beans (ariary/kg)	2.484	0.437			2.002	0.319
Price maize (ariary/kg)	27.321	2.221			27.235	2.042
Price cassva (ariary/kg)	-80.429	-1.062			-96.481	-1.190
Price rice (ariary/kg)	130.263	8.209			125.621	10.498
Price NPK (ariary/kg)	-36.182	-1.385			-47.483	-1.764
Wage level village (ariary/day)	-10.934	-2.858			-10.164	-2.019
Time to paved road (hours)	339.134	0.462			-98.853	-0.120
Time to paved road (hours) - squared	14.260	0.416			18.821	0.507
Regional dummy Majunga Plaines	-15,439.460	-2.504			-13,607.680	-2.001
Regional dummy Majunga HT	-8,612.338	-1.356			-1,591.793	-0.213
Regional dummy Fianar. HT	1,015.641	0.179			6,234.623	0.951
Regional dummy Fianar. C/F	-5,685.985	-0.956			-1,971.866	-0.267
Time dummy (1=agr. year 1995/1996)	12,854.180	4.290			13,647.240	4.558

Intercept	-8,884.034	-0.625	3,840.829	0.231
R squared	0.25	0.28	0.15	
No. of observations	942	942	942	

a Dependent variable is total agricultural revenue minus expenditures, except family labor
b Credit use endogenous
c Robust standard errors with household clusters are reported
d Zero land observations have been eliminated

Source: Data from 1997 IFPRI/FOFIFA survey

1984; Ramiarantsoa, 1995; Keck et al., 1994; Zeller et al., 1999), it seems that the combination of these effects leads to an equilibrium in which the land price itself does not directly influence net agricultural household income. The same reasoning holds for the distance to road variable.   While road infrastructure, irrigation, or land improvements might clearly have aggregate effects, they do not individually influence the net income of households. As would be expected in a liberalized market environment, access to infrastructure seems to lead to a variation in relative input and output prices and consequently to an adjustment of the household's choice in factor use as well as migration decisions leading to a relative equalization of agricultural income between the two.

Higher village wages significantly decrease net agricultural production. They might affect net agricultural production through different factors. First, wages are one of the costs entering into the inputs for agricultural production. It can be expected that the higher the wage level, the less profitable is an increase of labor use on existing fields and the less labor is used. Secondly, higher village wage levels might attract household members away from own production and induce them to work as salaried labor. In this way, wage levels would decrease own agricultural production, explaining its negative sign.

Conclusions

This chapter discusses factor use and agricultural productivity in Madagascar. Modern input use and yields are shown to be among the lowest in Africa. While input use is shown to be highly profitable on average – a $1 US investment in inputs results in an increase of output by $1.90 US to $2.50 US – it seems that Malagasy households have shown an insignificant supply response after liberalization of input and output prices due to a host of underlying structural factors, such as low risk-bearing capacity of poor households, the existence of severe crop production risks, credit constraints, high transaction costs in accessing input and output markets, an inadequate agricultural extension system, and small and insignificant productivity effects of available seed technology under on-farm conditions.

The main conclusions, with direct policy relevance, that emerge from the analysis in this chapter are:

- Input use, land allocation, and crop choice are shown to be very sensitive to land prices. They turn out to be a major determinant of land intensification. However, land price in itself does not influence net agricultural income suggesting that households are able to adjust their choices in factor use as well as in migration decisions leading to a relative equalization of agricultural income.

- Price policy seems to have a differential effect for different producers, depending on their respective assets. The small number of households that produce for the market, i.e. the bigger producers, respond significantly and positively to price increases through increased area allocation while smaller producers, usually also net rice buyers, respond negatively.

- The area of cultivated lowland land is mostly explained by access to land measured through variables such as nativity in the village and the number of elders in the household. The other household and policy variables seem to be of minor importance. In contrast, upland area allocation is strongly influenced by possibility for extension and family size. While one obtains lowland area mostly through heritage or through purchase, most of the upland area is obtained through cultivation of virgin areas at the expense of forest, bush, and grassland. This is a result of Malagasy law under which all uncultivated land is property of the state but when newly cleared land is successively cultivated by the same family, it can become private property.

- Access to credit increases land area cultivated, input expenditures per hectare, as well as net agricultural income. This result is consistent with our community level analysis where access to credit is shown to be a major determinant of agricultural production (chapter 11). The significant and sizable effects of access to credit are explained by the severe liquidity constraints which force rural households to choose second-best production strategies.

- Agricultural extension in its existing form seems to have little effect on agricultural production. This might be related to the heterogeneity of extension services offered and demanded in each region. Some regions, such as the Vakinankaratra and the Majunga Plaines region, have been exposed to extension services for a long time and the type of extension services demanded in those areas are different than those in areas where extension has only recently begun. Also, extension in certain areas relates almost exclusively to environmental considerations, is provided by private or other organizations, or is related to specific crops.

Unfortunately, we were not able to distinguish between these different types. Further research should explore this in more detail.

- Irrigation is a significant determinant of agricultural rice yields. However, its direct effect is shown to be smaller than expected. Irrigation increases production directly but, more importantly, indirectly through increasing independence of erratic weather patterns or water supply, and through a decrease of the area that shows relatively more production risks. It is shown that 32 per cent of the lowland fields in the survey region experienced water supply problems.
- Specific household level effects are important as male-headed households and households with more adults show more upland cultivation and higher agricultural incomes. It seems that labor markets do not lead to a complete adjustment of the effect of household composition.
- Distance to a main road determines access to input and output markets and to financial, social, and political institutions. All other factors equal, households closer to such critical infrastructure show higher input use, especially on the lowlands; lower areas cultivated; more orientation towards cash crops; and relatively higher lowland and less upland production. However, distance to a main road does not directly influence net agricultural income.
- Risk, climatic and disease, that rural households are exposed to is a highly important variable for the adoption of modern inputs and for the choice between lowland and upland production. The higher the risk, the lower the adoption rate, and the greater the importance of upland agricultural production. Another dimension of risk, rural security, is shown to lead to lower upland cultivation.

Notes

1   The high level of input costs in the Majunga Plaines region is mostly explained by the cost of hired labor and less by the use of modern inputs.

2   This is also an indication that tubers are mostly grown by poorer, nonselling households. Based on expenditure data of the survey households, expenditure elasticities are estimated based on an Almost Ideal Demand System (AIDS) model to be around 0.75 and 0.42 for rice and tubers respectively compared, for example, to 1.25 for legumes and beans and 2.16 for meat and animal products (chapter 8).

3   Agricultural income and input costs were adjusted through the consumer price index in Antananarivo where the average of the index over the agricultural year 1990/1991 and 1995/1996 was taken. Ideally, this should be done through the use of a producer price

index. However, this index does not exist in Madagascar. We are confident, however, that consistent trends are reflected.

4   The design of the stratified sample typically results in the rejection of the assumption of homoskedasticity as observations within a cluster are likely to have characteristics that are more similar than observations from outside the cluster. The difference between intra- and intercluster correlations will most likely result in heteroskedasticity. Correcting for heteroskedasticity between household clusters is straightforward following the Huber/White correction. This is done for all regressions except in the specification for which community fixed effects are controlled. Sampling was based on a stratified sample and population multipliers would be needed to obtain a representative picture from the sample. While these population multipliers are used in the calculation of descriptive statistics, they are not used in the regression analysis where it is not appropriate to weight the data.

5   The estimates here are different from those averages reported in chapter 4 as the average of two agricultural seasons was considered; the numbers reported in Table 6.4 are different from those in Table 6.7 as these are nonweighted averages.

6   In contrast to the land tenure situation in some other African countries, Malagasy do not need to farm the land in order to maintain their land rights. While land tenure regulations differ between different ethnic groups, a Malagasy family can pass the right of usage (guaranteed by the community) down from generation to generation in most groups. Hence, this often leads to appropriation of land early in the formation of a village (Pryor, 1990; Keck et al., 1994).

7   The results of the community surveys indicate that upland expansion has been five times faster than lowland expansion on average over the last ten years (Lapenu et al., 1998). Dorosh et al. (1998) reach similar conclusions.

8   To avoid potential endogeneity of own land prices, an average community land price was calculated, not taking into account the land price of the household itself. Regressions were run of land prices on road and irrigation infrastructure, closeness to urban centers, and extension possibilities. The coefficients all show expected and significant signs. It is worthwhile to note that one hour further distance to a paved road decreases the land price by 15 per cent for lowland and upland alike. Income gains from lower transport costs are capitalized in land values. Jacoby (1998) and Benirschka and Binkley (1994) show quantitatively the impact of distance to markets on land values in the cases of Nepal and the US respectively.

9   Access to credit is measured by the maximum amount that the adult household members estimate to be able to obtain as loans from informal and formal lenders. In this section, we use the combined credit limit from both the informal (e.g. friends and relatives) and formal sectors (banks, microfinance schemes). The concepts and survey method is described in Diagne et al. (1998); Zeller et al. (1997). The identifiers were share of the same ethnic group in the village; share of the same religious group in the village; number of family (brothers, sisters, daughters, sons) living outside the household's house but in the same village, in a village between 1 and 50 km distant, and further than 50 km distant, the value of non-agricultural assets; the number of years the chief of the household and the spouse have lived in the village; and the presence of 'organizations'.

10   It should be noted that different price specifications for the subsequent analysis were tested and that results were not always satisfactory. This seems due to several reasons.

First, there is limited variability in prices as the number of villages in the sample is limited and there is no time component. Second, household-level prices were used and it can be argued that they are to a certain extent endogenous which causes problems for interpretation. Third, there is no information on the level at which products are sold. Smaller producers might engage in selling smaller quantities at the retail level compared to bigger producers who sell at the wholesale level. This might increase the per unit price for smaller producers and bias the results on the impact of prices. This last reason led us to split the rice price along different asset categories.

11 Barrett and Dorosh (1996) came to a similar conclusion. They conclude that in Madagascar gains from rice price increases are highly concentrated among the largest rice farmers and in particular regions.

12 The risk index is constructed as a simple sum of the incidences of, for the climatic index, drought, cyclone, inundation, and frost, and, for the plant disease index, of rice fleas, virose, and coffee rust.

13 President Ratsiraka made rural security one of the main points of his election campaign in 1996. The results of the community survey in 1997 show that cattle rustling, a good indicator of rural insecurity, is on the decline over the last decade as the average number of cattle stolen per village has dropped from 14 to 2. Less dramatic declines were noticed in theft of small animals, crops, and equipment (Minten et al., 1998). In case studies of villages in east and west Madagascar, Ramiarantsoa (1995) and Fauroux (1989) show the importance of theft in rural Madagascar. Fafchamps and Minten (1999a) show that to avoid robbery almost half of the rural traders travel in groups or are accompanied by guards when traveling.

14 Excluding the household itself as households with more land might more often be victims theft.

15 It has also been suggested that another implication of rural insecurity might be the increasing parcelization of agricultural land (Pryor, 1990). We do not research for this here.

16 Identifying variables for land use are extension possibilities, nativity in the village, as well as the village land price. Given the low explanatory power of the upland land regression, coefficients in the 2SLS are unstable and should be interpreted with caution.

17 Examples include the groups KOBAMA for wheat, HASYMA and COTONA for cotton, BOLLERO for tobacco, and breweries for barley.

18 We did not have a priori expectations on the sign of the coefficient as higher risks might lead to lower investment in inputs such as labor as well as higher investment in risk reducing strategies (such as drought resistant varieties).

19 One important success of improved rice seeds needs mentioning. Most of the improved seed use is in the Majunga where lowlands have been abandoned because of infestation by the red yellow mottle virus (RYMV). FOFIFA, in collaboration with IRRI, was successful in the development and diffusion of a virose resistant variety, X360. It has been reported that more than 10,000 ha have since been returned to cultivation (World Bank, 1997).

20 The identifying variables for land use are nativity in village, village land price, expansion possibilities; those for input use are distance to plots, experience with the fields, and climatic and disease risk.

21   One problem of the Cobb-Douglas specification is that it does not allow any of the inputs to take on a value of zero. In order to avoid takings logs of zero in some cases, all log values for inputs are computed as $\log(x+1)$ except in the case of land. Zero land observations have been eliminated.

22   Unless stated otherwise, we will use the coefficient of this regression for the calculation of quantitative effects in the remainder of the chapter.

23   An alternative specification with the total land area possessed instead of area cultivated was used to avoid the endogenity problem. The results reflect the same conclusions presented here.

24   In this case the coefficient on land shows a significant elasticity of 0.24 and 0.29 in the case of OLS and OLS with fixed effects respectively and an insignificant elasticity of 0.30 in the 2SLS specification. In the first two specifications, the distance to road coefficient becomes insignificant suggesting the above-mentioned price effect.

25   As actual demand for extension by the farmer himself is generally associated with individual specific characteristics that are unobservable to us but that might be correlated to higher output, coefficients that measure individual access would be expected to be biased upwards. There might still be problems even with the variable as it is specified here as extension agents may be allocated to areas with higher agricultural potential (Rosenzweig and Wolpin, 1985).

26   Methodologies to potentially correct for this bias are discussed in Fafchamps and Quisumbing (1999) and Pitt et al. (1990).

27   In this analysis, only lowland rice yields were considered. The results in Table 6.1 show that upland rice production makes up less than 1.5 per cent of total rice production although in terms of area it is more important given the lower yields on the uplands.

28   An area-weighted index between zero and two was constructed where a value of two reflects irrigation infrastructure that makes rice production independent of rainfall patterns. This would include irrigation dams, pumps, and well-maintained irrigation canals. A value of zero would mean that rice production would be completely dependent on rainfall and that infrastructure does not exist or, if it exists, is not functional. A value of one was defined as infrastructure, modern or traditional, that exists and is functional but production still depends on rainfall and water evacuation still causes problems. However, it seems likely that some enumerators and/or households misunderstood this question.

29   Not taking into account that better irrigated areas receive slightly more inputs.

30   Similar results have also been shown to exist in other Subsaharan countries (Udry, 1996; Gavian and Fafchamps, 1996; Benjamin, 1994).

7 Marketed Agricultural Surplus

BART MINTEN, CLAUDE RANDRIANARISOA, and MANFRED ZELLER

Introduction

One of the objectives of agricultural policy in Madagascar is to increase income and food security of rural households by increasing agricultural production and marketed surplus (Ministère de l'Agriculture, 1997). However, Malagasy policy makers are often at a loss in determining the means through which this can be achieved, as determinants of marketed surplus are not well understood. A recent study concluded that no obvious determinants exist for the commercial surplus and that farmers with important commercial surpluses were distributed spatially 'at random' (SARSA, 1996). On the other hand, Robilliard (1998) found high price elasticities, deducted as residuals from demand and supply elasticities, while Barrett (1996a) found significant price, income, and risk effects in commercial surplus decisions.

In this chapter, the commercial surplus and its determinants are analyzed based on recently collected household data in the IFPRI/FOFIFA survey. In contrast to the other chapters, the analysis in this chapter is generally concerned with the agricultural year 1995/1996 (agricultural expenditures are for the agricultural year 1996/1997). This is done to ensure that a whole year's cycle of production and marketing is included. The commercial surplus is explicitly linked to relevant policy factors. We will also specifically focus on seasonal issues as this has often been a forgotten component in previous analytical work. The structure of the chapter is as follows. First, we discuss the level of commercial surplus, its variability over the year, main outlet channels, and market conditions in the survey region. Second, given the importance of rice in production, nutrition, and cash income in Madagascar, we focus on the characteristics of net buyers and net sellers of rice. Then, the determinants of the value of total commercial surplus are analyzed. We finish with conclusions and implications.

The Level of Commercial Surplus

Table 7.1 presents the uses of agricultural production by product group. The two main uses for the harvested products are home consumption and sales. In the survey region, 40 per cent of the value of total gross agricultural production is sold. However, some products are relatively more often home-consumed (tubers, rice) while other products are mainly used as a source of cash income (fruits, vegetables, sugar, industrial crops). The quantities that are used as feed, payment for rent, salary, gifts, etc., are small as combined they constitute less than 5 per cent of the total use of agricultural production. Payment of salaries in kind for hired labor make up 2 per cent of the total rice production.[1] The quantities used for seed make up 4 per cent of the total quantity produced. Use of seed is especially important for rice and beans where it totals more than 5 per cent of the total production. In the remainder of the analysis, we will focus on the specifics of the commercial surplus.

Table 7.1   Uses of agricultural production in % of value terms (agr. year 1995/1996)

	Harvest	Home consump.	Sold	Payment leasing land
Tubers	100.0	69.4	24.5	0.0
Legumes, beans	100.0	36.0	53.9	0.3
Other cereals	100.0	49.8	43.5	0.0
Sugar cane and industrial crops	100.0	17.9	77.9	0.0
Fruit	100.0	36.2	63.8	0.0
Vegetables	100.0	9.7	90.1	0.0
Early irrigated rice	100.0	56.3	26.3	1.0
Medium or late irrigated rice	100.0	56.1	30.7	3.0
Rainfed rice	100.0	67.7	20.0	0.9
All crops combined	100.0	49.1	40.1	1.5

	Feed	Repayment credit	Seed reserve	Gift	Payment salary
Tubers	3.8	0.1	0.8	0.3	1.2
Legumes, beans	0.3	0.1	7.6	0.4	0.4
Other cereals	3.4	0.4	1.7	0.3	0.9
Sugar cane and industrial crops	0.0	0.8	2.3	0.2	0.0
Fruit	0.0	0.0	0.0	0.0	0.0
Vegetables	0.1	0.0	0.2	0.0	0.0
Early irrigated rice	0.0	1.9	7.9	3.0	2.5
Medium or late irrigated rice	0.0	0.9	4.3	1.8	3.2
Rainfed rice	0.0	1.7	6.2	1.2	1.3
All crops combined	0.5	0.8	4.5	1.4	2.0

Source: Data from 1997 IFPRI/FOFIFA household survey

Table 7.2   Total agricultural and sales income by households, ariary per month (agr. year 1995/1996)

Region		Net agricultural income			Agricultural sales inome		
		total	lowland	upland	total	lowland	upland
Majunga Plaines	Mean	55,162	43,865	11,297	27,992	24,504	3,489
	Std. Dev.	56,600	52,278	25,025	36,738	36,522	8,361
Majunga HT	Mean	39,270	24,163	15,107	16,416	7,605	8,811
	Std. Dev.	59,862	55,561	20,839	23,436	16,184	15,397
Fianar. HT	Mean	38,295	24,198	14,097	15,100	7,009	8,091
	Std. Dev.	62,270	61,293	12,504	34,322	33,080	9,073
Fianar. C/F	Mean	38,176	18,712	19,464	20,873	8,947	11,926
	Std. Dev.	46,059	33,488	22,174	35,686	28,451	15,003
Vakinankaratra	Mean	43,017	20,410	22,606	24,920	6,591	18,329
	Std. Dev.	53,854	42,179	22,246	32,273	20,046	19,825
Ranomafana	Mean	25,909	10,321	15,588	7,899	1,348	6,551
	Std. Dev.	21,080	13,378	13,357	9,263	3,122	8,231
Total	Mean	40,783	23,861	16,922	19,598	8,832	10,766
	Std. Dev.	56,607	51,230	19,815	32,916	27,925	14,850

Source: Data from 1997 IFPRI/FOFIFA household survey

The commercial surplus makes up almost 50 per cent of total net agricultural income for the survey region (Table 7.2).   The value of commercial surplus amounts to $25 US per household per month compared to a value of total production of $50 US.   There are significant differences by region and among households.   The absolute value of commercial surplus is highest in the Majunga Plaines region ($40 US per month) while the relative value (commercial surplus over harvest ratio) is highest in the Vakinankaratra region (58 per cent).   The lower the value of agricultural production for a region, the higher the home consumption ratio; for example, 60 per cent of total agricultural production is home-consumed in Fianarantsoa HT.   As expected, variations of the commercial surplus among households, as measured by the coefficient of variation, is higher than for net production as a whole.   This is the case for lowland and upland production.   The commercial surplus coming from upland and lowland is of equal size for most regions except for Majunga Plaines where lowlands make up 87 per cent of total commercial surplus and for Vakinakaratra where upland makes up 73 per cent of the value of total commercial surplus.   The relative variation of commercial surplus and lowland production between households is significantly higher than for the upland.   Hence, commercial surplus derived from lowland contributes to increased inequality in cash income between households.

Table 7.3 Quantities of rice and number of households in rice trade

| Region | Quantity of rice (kg) | | | Net quantity |
	harvested	sold	bought	sold (kg)
Majunga Plaines	3,540.6	1,471.0	251.2	1,219.7
Majunga HT	1,384.2	363.2	159.2	204.0
Fianar. HT	614.6	119.1	215.2	-96.2
Fianar. C/F	890.5	359.7	201.7	157.0
Vakinankaratra	1,009.6	262.0	156.3	105.6
Ranomafana	607.7	247.1	76.0	-172.1
Total	1,124.8	350.1	193.2	156.9

| Region | % of households that, during the last year | | | |
	were net buyers	were net sellers	bought rice	sold rice
Majunga Plaines	19.7	70.8	61.6	76.5
Majunga HT	37.4	53.5	49.9	67.7
Fianar. HT	77.8	17.4	87.9	49.4
Fianar. C/F	65.1	32.5	92.5	55.7
Vakinankaratra	56.4	37.9	80.4	59.8
Ranomafana	76.8	17.2	91.9	33.3
Total	59.3	35.7	77.4	57.4

Source: Data from 1997 IFPRI/FOFIFA household survey

As rice constitutes the main crop for production and sales income (i.e. 45 per cent of total agricultural sales income) and given its importance in agricultural policy making, some separate specific analysis is done on it. The different rice harvests are aggregated and quantities are used instead of monetary values. Production levels are highest in the Majunga Plaines region with a production of 3.5 tons per household while they are lowest in the Fianarantsoa HT region (Table 7.3). In all the regions, the major part of the rice harvest is used for home consumption, even in major surplus regions such as Majunga Plaines. The net rice quantity sold represents only 14 per cent of total production in the survey region as a whole.[2] The Fianarantsoa HT region is a net deficit region in rice as the net quantity that is sold is negative over the year. All the other regions are, on average, surplus regions. Again, the biggest surplus region is Majunga Plaines where an agricultural household sells, on average, more than 1,200 kg of rice. While the rice sales in big production regions and the purchases in lower production regions reduce differences between regions in consumption levels, the variation in household rice consumption is still quite significant. Further analysis of more precise consumption level data will show to what extent the lower rice consumption is offset by other products and to what extent it results in effective lower consumption of calories (see chapter 10).

The low overall net quantity of rice sold per household does not imply that households do not engage in rice trade; most households do as only 5 per cent of the households reported that they neither bought nor sold rice over the year. While almost 60 per cent of the rural households are net buyers, 36 per cent are net sellers. While there is significant variability over the year and between regions in selling and buying patterns, there are also significant differences between households within a particular region.[3] Although Majunga Plaines has the highest rice surplus of all the regions, still almost 25 per cent of the households did not sell rice over the previous year and 20 per cent of the households were net buyers of rice. In constrast, while almost 80 per cent of the households were net buyers of rice in the Fianarantsoa HT region, 17 per cent were net sellers.

There is often a seasonal component to the selling or buying decision of a household. This can be seen by the fact that a significant number of farmers who are net sellers of rice over the year still buy rice during the lean season, and that more than 50 per cent of households sell and buy rice. Almost 80 per cent of the rural households bought rice at one point during the 1995/1996 agricultural year in the survey region as a whole (Table 7.3). This figure reaches 93 per cent of the households in the Fianarantsoa C/F region. While these numbers deal with rice quantities only, it can be assumed that the number of people who are net buyers in value terms over the year is higher than in quantity terms as there are significant variations in rice prices over the agricultural year. This is illustrated by the fact that rice prices in rural areas are on average twice as high during the lean season as during the harvest season (see Minten, 1999).

Seasonal Variability

Agriculture in Madagascar is characterized by significant seasonal variations in production, prices, and marketing decisions. In this section, we document the seasonality of total agricultural sales and expenditures. Figures 7.1 through 7.6 illustrate the seasonal patterns for those two variables in Malagasy francs (FMG). They show the significant seasonal variation in agricultural expenditures and sales over the year. As expected, average expenditures are higher when sales are low and vice versa. The period when

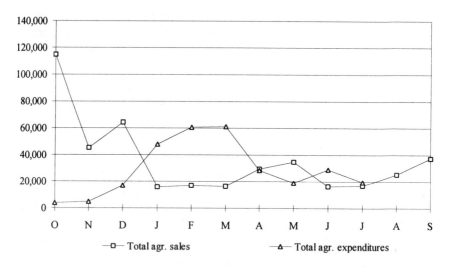

Figure 7.1   Cash agricultural income (Oct. 1995-Sept. 1996) and expenditures (Oct. 1996-July 1997) in Majunga Plaines, FMG per month per household

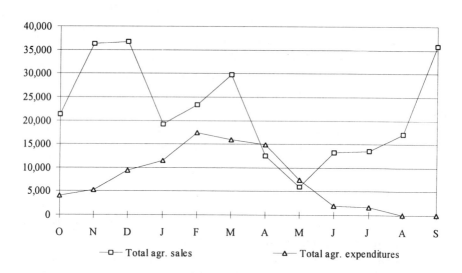

Figure 7.2   Cash agricultural income (Oct. 1995-Sept. 1996) and expenditures (Oct. 1996-Aug. 1997) in Majunga HT, FMG per month per household

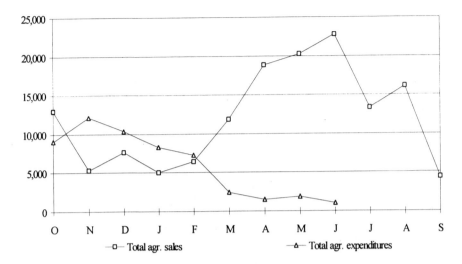

Figure 7.3   Cash agricultural income (Oct. 1995-Sept. 1996) and expenditures (Oct. 1996-Jun. 1997) in Fianarantsoa HT, FMG per month per household

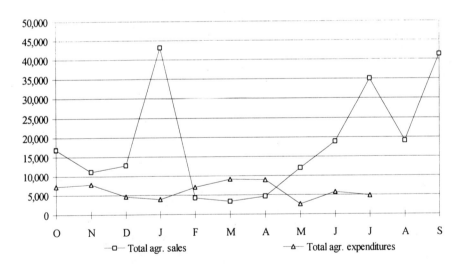

Figure 7.4   Cash agricultural income (Oct. 1995-Sept. 1996) and expenditures (Oct. 1996-Jul. 1997) in Fianarantsoa C/F, FMG per month per household

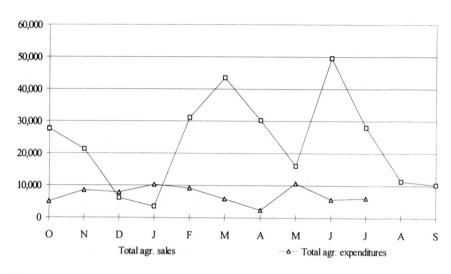

Figure 7.5 **Cash agricultural income (Oct. 1995-Sept. 1996) and expenditures (Oct. 1996-Jul. 1997) in Vakinankaratra, FMG per month per household**

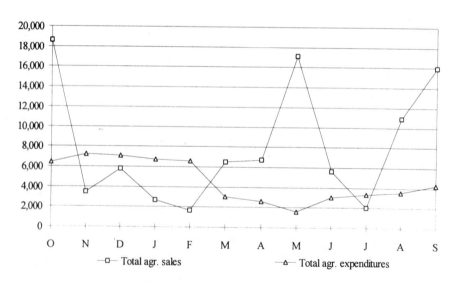

Figure 7.6 **Cash agricultural income (Oct. 1995-Sept. 1996) and expenditures (Oct. 1996-Sept. 1997) in Ranomafana, FMG per month per household**

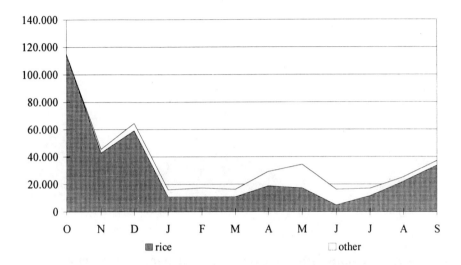

Figure 7.7 **Composition of cash agricultural income in Majunga Plaines, FMG per month per household (Oct. 1995-Sept. 1996)**

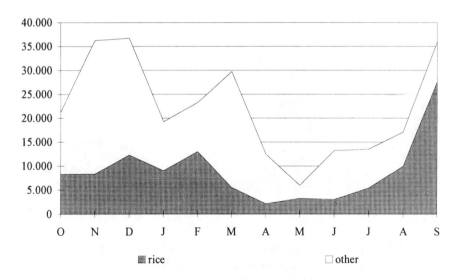

Figure 7.8 **Composition of cash agricultural income in Majunga HT, FMG per month per household (Oct. 1995-Sept. 1996)**

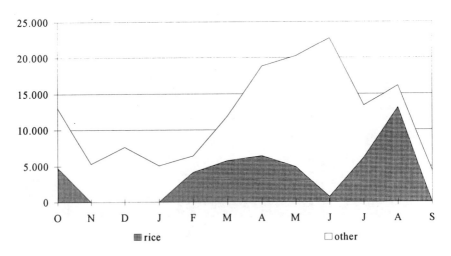

**Figure 7.9   Composition of cash agricultural income in Fianarantsoa
HT, FMG per month per household
(Oct. 1995-Sept. 1996)**

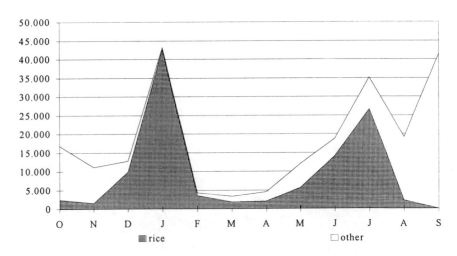

**Figure 7.10   Composition of cash agricultural income in Fianarantsoa
C/F, FMG per month per household
(Oct. 1995-Sept. 1996)**

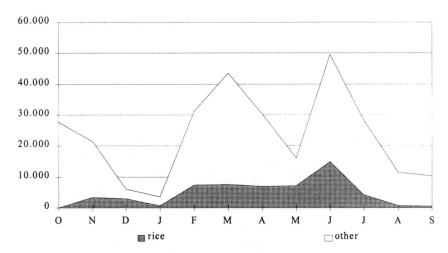

Figure 7.11   Composition of cash agricultural income in
Vakinankaratra, FMG per month per household
(Oct. 1995-Sept. 1996)

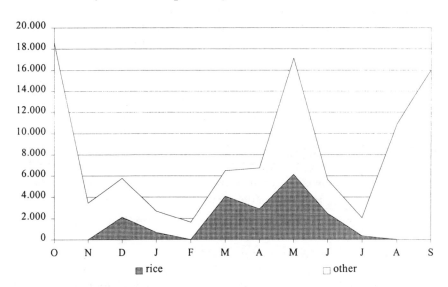

Figure 7.12   Composition of cash agricultural income in Ranomafana,
FMG per month per household
(Oct. 1995-Sept. 1996)

most households buy agricultural products, mostly rice, can be considered the lean period. The timing, length, and severity of this lean period differ among the different regions. Those are important findings as, for example, UNICEF estimated that in certain regions malnutrition rates average 15 per cent higher during the lean period than during the harvest period (SECALINE, 1997).

Seasonal patterns in agricultural income and expenditure are significantly different for the different regions. The composition of the agricultural income is also highly variable (Figures 7.7 through 7.12).

- Majunga Plaines: most agricultural income is received from October through December following the harvest of the 'vary jeby'[4]
- Majunga HT: the highest agricultural income is during the months of November and December, mostly from industrial crops; rice income is highest from December to February and in September
- Fianarantsoa HT: the highest income is during April through June, immediately after the harvest of the 'vary vakiambiaty'
- Fianarantsoa C/F: income peaks a little later than in the Fianarantsoa HT, i.e. from June to September with the harvest of 'vary vatomandry' and coffee, and in January following the harvest of the 'vary aloha'
- Vakinankaratra: highest income is received February through March, mainly from fruits and vegetables, and in June, from paddy vakiambiaty, beans, and vegetables

The high dependence on the vary jeby as its main source of income causes the highest seasonal variation in income and expenditures in the Majunga Plaines area. Through diversification of agricultural production, some regions are able to reduce the severity of the lean period. It seems to be that regions characterized by higher home consumption levels have longer lean periods as households' expenditures exceed agricultural income for four months in Fianarantsoa HT, but only two months in the Vakinankaratra region. In this last region, cash crop income seems to be used relatively successfully to smooth sales income and agricultural expenditures over the year.

To see how households use storage as a means to smooth income and consumption, we calculate some related statistics. Table 7.4 shows the main production periods for the different rice crops as reported by the households themselves. The main rice harvest runs from March through April in most regions, except in Majunga Plaines where it is during the month of September (indicated in that region by 'vary jeby'). Then, the average time between the main production month and the main sales month is calculated. On average, agricultural households store the majority of the rice that they put on the market for less than one month. Although there might be significant variability between storage behavior of the individual households (presumably based on their respective wealth and financial ability to store products) the overall results seem to indicate that the majority of the rural households in Madagascar limit storage of their agricultural products and seem to sell products immediately after harvest, forgoing higher prices later in the season. The percentages of rural households that hold their harvested rice for longer than three months are very low: 3 per cent for the main harvest and 4 per cent for the early harvest.

Table 7.4   Timing of main rice harvest and sales

Region	Main production month		Months between main selling and production		% of hhs that wait >3 months between main production/sales	
	Vary aloha/ asara	Vary vakiamb./ jeby	Vary aloha/ asara	Vary vakiamb./ jeby	Vary aloha/ asara	Vary vakiamb./ jeby
Majunga Plaines	May	October	0.04	0.49	0.0	0.0
Majunga HT	May	April	0.92	0.38	2.1	0.0
Fianar. HT	February	March	1.88	1.00	13.5	5.2
Fianar. C/F	February	March	0.67	0.83	1.0	0.0
Vakinankaratra	January	April	0.14	0.76	0.0	3.0
Ranomafana	January	March	0.00	0.29	0.0	0.0
Total			0.95	0.80	3.8	2.6

Source: Data from 1997 IFPRI/FOFIFA household survey

These results seem to confirm that most of the intertemporal rice trade (i.e. between harvest and lean periods) is not between different agricultural households in the same region, but rather with farmers of other regions or, more importantly, between farmers in rural areas and traders with storage activities based in urban centers.[5] Periods when expenditures exceed sales and vice versa seem to imply effective flows in and out of a region.[6] Hence, most rural regions seem to show rice deficits during the lean period. At that point, rice is brought in from local urban areas where it was stored or, alternatively, from other regions. In most regions a reversal of flows of rice is noticed between harvest and lean period. Because most of the rice seems not to be stored in the village, this means that transport costs are sometimes incurred twice for the same product causing significant seasonal price variations.7 This seasonal variation seems to be especially harmful for the net buyers, often the poorer households, as they buy rice at significantly higher prices in the lean season.

Market Conditions and Outlet Channels

In the questionnaire, questions were asked regarding where the produce was sold, the type of buyer, and the method of payment. The results indicate that most transactions are paid for in cash by the buyer (>95 per cent) and this does not seem to differ significantly between products. Hence, in output markets the use of credit relations between producer and consumer or assembler seems to be extremely low. Sales directly to other consumers represent the main part of total sales (43 per cent) (Table 7.5). Big local assemblers, small local assemblers, and assemblers coming from other regions represent, respectively, 12 per cent, 29 per cent, and 10 per cent of total sales. The minor importance of assembly by the large millers and farmer organizations is illustrated by their small percentage (respectively 5 per cent and 1 per cent) in purchases. However, given that millers often work with a network of small local assemblers that buy products for them on commission, it is difficult to deduct anything on marketing flows except at the primary level.8

While tubers are important for home consumption, their commercial surplus is rather low, and when they are sold they are often sold directly to other consumers. Tubers seem to be disadvantaged as a marketing crop because of their high per unit processing and transportation costs. The percentage of sales of medium or late lowland rice and industrial crops to other consumers is lowest of all products. This is self-explanatory for industrial crops; for rice it again seems to reflect the system in which rice goes through the whole marketing chain to be stored by big or small traders that are less constrained by opportunity costs of capital than rural households. While the trade of most agricultural products seems to be local with assemblers from other regions playing a small role, this is less so in the case of rice where their percentage varies between 12 per cent and 21 per cent.

Sales through regular or irregular local markets seem to be important in Madagascar. Table 7.6 shows that most of the products are sold at local markets. The exception is rice and other cereals where quite a significant part is sold in the village itself, mostly to assemblers and not to consumers. Given the importance of markets and of sales directly to other consumers, it seems that markets serve as a meeting place for local assemblers as well as local consumers. Some producers travel to further markets to sell their products; markets that are not the nearest market make up a non-negligible 6 per cent of total sales income.

Table 7.5   Importance of different type of buyers for different products, % of value of total sales (agr. year 1995/1996)

	Consumer	Large local assembler	Small local assembler	Miller assembler	Assembler from another region	Farmer organization
Tubers	59.8	7.1	26.1	1.3	4.5	0.2
Legumes, beans	51.1	7.4	30.3	-	9.8	0.5
Other cereals	40.7	20.5	22.2	4.3	6.7	5.6
Sugar cane and industrial crops	25.3	20.5	39.7	11.3	2.8	0.4
Fruit	54.0	10.6	27.8	1.9	4.6	-
Vegetables	57.8	4.4	27.4	-	7.4	-
Early lowland rice	51.7	13.3	12.6	2.8	19.5	-
Medium or late lowland rice	27.6	16.4	31.7	11.1	12.3	-
Upland rice	35.9	15.8	11.4	-	21.0	15.8
All crops combined	42.9	11.7	29.3	4.7	10.3	1.2

Source: Data from 1997 IFPRI/FOFIFA household survey

Net Buyers and Sellers of Rice

In this section we look specifically at the rice trade and at the characteristics of households selling and buying rice. In this analysis on rice we will only use data from the 1995/1996 agricultural season to ensure that we cover the harvest period and the lean season as to correctly incorporate net selling and net buying behavior. It can be that households are net buyers for two reasons: they are poor and do not have enough assets to cultivate for their own needs, or they have diversified into other, more lucrative activities. Initially it seems that the first reason is more prevalent than the second.

Table 7.6   Importance of sales by point of sale, in % of value terms (agr. year 1995/1996)

	Village/ at farm	Nearest market	Other markets	Miller	Others
Tubers	34.2	61.6	4.3	-	-
Legumes, beans	25.4	67.3	6.3	-	-
Other cereals	42.2	49.9	6.1	1.7	-
Sugar cane and industrial crops	27.3	67.9	2.3	1.5	-
Fruit	42.2	47.4	7.4	1.0	1.0
Vegetables	20.0	73.2	6.7	-	0.1
Early lowland rice	42.2	47.7	10.2	-	-
Medium or late lowland rice	41.5	49.7	5.3	3.0	0.5
Upland rice	63.8	17.1	19.1	-	-
All crops combined	35.8	56.0	6.5	1.2	0.4

Source: Data from 1997 IFPRI/FOFIFA household survey

Table 7.7 shows descriptive statistics for net sellers compared to net buyers, which include net buyers and households that do not participate in rice markets. Net sellers of rice are clearly better off. They have more assets and their expenditures, for food and nonfood items, are significantly higher than of the households that are net buyers of rice. On average, net sellers own almost three times more lowland than the other households. While it might have been the case that the net buyers of rice produce other agricultural products to pay for their rice purchases, this seems not to be the case. The net sellers of rice own also more upland than the other households and the net value of the upland production is higher for net sellers. The differences in quantities of rice sold are striking. The net buyers buy on average over 200 kg of rice while the net sellers sell just over 800 kg. The seasonal 'switching' component in selling and buying behavior is again illustrated by the fact that at one point 53 per cent of the net sellers bought rice over the previous year while 35 per cent of the net buyers sold rice.

While the income per adult-equivalent is twice as high for the net sellers, the composition of this income is also quite different for the two groups. For the net buyers, income from agricultural products is significantly lower while wage income and income from livestock is higher. Hence, it seems that net buyers pay for rice through income from wage labor and livestock. It is also clear from the table that there is a strong regional dimension to rice buying and selling behavior. While more households are net sellers than net buyers in the Majunga area, the reverse is true in the Fianarantsoa area.

Table 7.7   Characteristics of households that are net sellers of rice compared to net buyers (agr. year 1995/1996)

| | Net sellers | | |
	No	Yes	Total
Value of asset, in 1,000 ariary	1,236.87	2,640.51	1,737.37
Total area of lowland cultivated in ares	72.65	194.15	115.97
Total area of upland cultivated in ares	93.68	117.41	102.50
Net upland income, ariary/month	16,296.56	18,050.50	16,921.97
Net lowland income, ariary/month	12,307.17	44,710.36	23,861.29
Quantity of rice sold, kg/year	34.94	917.69	350.06
Quantity of rice bought, kg/year	247.81	94.67	193.21
% of households that bought rice during previous year	92.13	53.74	77.44
% of households that sold rice during the previous year	35.40	100.00	57.43
Total monthly food expenditures per capita, ariary	6,995.18	9,740.57	7,974.12
Total monthly nonfood expenditures per capita, ariary	1,724.39	3,157.99	2,235.57
% of crop income in total income	53.45	73.48	60.59
% of wage income in total income	19.52	11.38	16.61
% of gifts in total income	1.34	1.34	1.34
% of rental income in total income	0.96	2.38	1.47
% of hunting, gathering in total income	1.76	2.51	2.03
% of entrepreneurial income in total income	7.70	5.93	7.07
% of livestock income in total income	15.26	2.98	10.88
% of households in Fianar. HT	42.34	16.05	32.97
% of households in Fianar. C/F	21.48	17.70	20.49
% of households in Vakinankaratra	19.77	22.73	20.82
% of households in Majunga HT	12.77	26.53	17.67
% of households in Majunga Plaines	3.65	15.98	7.05
Number of households	317	176	495

Source: Data from 1997 IFPRI/FOFIFA household survey

Determinants of Commercial Surplus

After the presentation of the descriptive statistics, we now turn to the discussion of the determinants of commercial surplus. The level of commercial surplus is determined by agricultural production and consumption decisions of the household. A reduced form marketable surplus equation is estimated where commercial surplus is modeled as the difference between household supply (production) and demand (consumption) choices. This implies that variables that explain consumption and production decisions are included as explanatory variables. A similar analytical framework was used for example in Strauss (1984), Renkow (1990), Goetz (1992), and Zong and Davis (1998). The commercial surplus, measured in value terms, per adult-equivalent is used as the dependent variable. The definition of the variables, their respective means and variation, and the results of the regression are shown in Tables 7.8 and 7.9. To illustrate the differences between poor and rich households and to test the robustness of the results, the regression is split along the median of wealth of households.

An important determinant for commercial surplus, as for total agricultural income, is access to land. The lowland and upland area possessed per adult-equivalent are both significant determinants for commercial surplus per adult-equivalent. Their respective elasticities are of similar magnitude, i.e. respectively 0.13 and 0.09, in the overall regression. However, lowland and upland area affect the commercial surplus of poor and rich households differently. For the poorer households, the coefficient on upland area is significant while the one on lowland area is not. In addition, the price of the upland crops mostly shows a positive influence on total marketed surplus while the effect of rice prices is negative, although neither is significant. Descriptive statistics confirm the importance of upland crops as a source of income for the poor as the share of upland crops in total commercial surplus amounts to 73 per cent for the poorer households, but only 49 per cent for the rich households. For richer households, both the coefficients on lowland and upland area are significant although the coefficient on lowland area is slightly bigger than on upland area. In their case, the effect of rice prices is also positive and significant.

Hence, it seems that access to more lowlands for poorer households does not increase their commercial surplus but probably does increase their home consumption of rice. It might also be that the wealth effect is more important than the production effect for poorer households; while production might increase with increased prices, poorer households might increase their own consumption of rice as the value of commercial surplus goes up due to higher prices even though the quantity sold might be lower. For richer households, given that they are mostly net sellers, rice prices clearly have a positive effect on total marketed surplus, with an elasticity of 0.41, ceteris paribus. For the overall sample, this elasticity amounts to only 0.27.

Access to credit is not a significant determinant for commercial surplus for wealthier households. This variable turns out to be more significant for the poorer households with a coefficient two times larger than for wealthier households. Three reasons might explain this phenomenon. On the production side, access to credit improves the potential to buy agricultural inputs and therefore increases production (as seen in the previous chapter). On the consumption side, access to credit allows households to take advantage of seasonal price variation through storage, or early sales and purchases in the lean period. Third, access to credit increases the risk-bearing capacity of households, thus enabling them to better integrate into the market economy by moving out of subsistence and into commercial production.

Infrastructure also turns out to be a significant determinant of the total value of commercial surplus. On average for all households, a one hour distance from a paved road decreases the value of commercial surplus by 13 per cent. The infrastructure effect is insignificant for poorer households but slightly larger for richer households (a 15 per cent reduction for one hour distance). The impact of roads on the value of commercial surplus might work through two ways: an increase of the price that the product is sold for and an increase in the actual quantities sold.[9] As we control for price effects through their inclusion as separate variables, most of the measured effects are indeed increased quantities sold. The extent of the decrease diminishes the further one is from a paved road as the quadratic term shows a positive sign. However, the magnitude of this quadratic term is small. There is no correction for the potential endogeneity of road placement as roads might be constructed in areas that have a higher commercial surplus as shown in for example Binswanger et al., (1993) and Rosenzweig and Wolpin (1985). So, caution in interpretation is warranted.

If households have the choice between traders when selling agricultural produce, the commercial surplus is quite higher than for households that have no choice.[10] However, this effect is not statistically significant. The composition of the household seems in most cases not to have a significant effect on the commercial surplus per adult-equivalent. As shown in the previous chapter, the dependency ratio is an important variable for area allocation, crop choice, and agricultural production, but it seems that most of this effect is offset by consumption decisions and consequently, does not affect the commercial surplus. The number of adult-equivalents reduces the

Table 7.8 Mean and variation of variables used in regression analysis

Variables	Overall		Poor households*		Rich households	
	Mean	Std. Dev.	Mean	Std. Dev.	Mean	Std. Dev.
Value of commercial surplus per adult-equivalent (ariary)	4,027.99	7,040.45	2,237.12	3,239.97	5,820.52	9,076.68
Lowland area owned per adult-equivalent in ares	23.35	49.80	11.47	37.04	35.24	56.91
Upland area owned per adult-equivalent in ares	21.59	35.60	14.09	15.24	29.09	46.85
Price of rice, ariary/kg	214.08	127.72	219.05	129.86	209.12	125.61
Price of maize, ariary/kg	223.19	163.51	211.21	147.71	235.17	177.40
Price of beans, ariary/kg	515.01	327.55	559.92	359.76	470.12	285.56
Price of cassava, ariary/kg	87.54	20.83	87.41	20.79	86.67	20.87
Total credit available to the household, 1,000 ariary	553.57	451.06	492.58	347.51	614.55	527.67
Education level of household head (from 1=no education to 6=university)	2.30	0.96	2.18	0.91	2.42	1.00
Dummy gender household chief (1=male)	0.87	0.33	0.84	0.36	0.91	0.29
Number of adult-equivalents	5.26	2.15	4.83	1.98	5.70	2.23
Dependency ratio	0.52	0.20	0.53	0.20	0.52	0.21
Average wage at the village level, ariary/day	642.25	467.71	602.27	464.72	682.23	467.20
Choice between output traders (1=yes)	0.63	0.48	0.63	0.48	0.62	0.49
Travel time to a paved road (hours)	2.86	3.39	3.12	3.71	2.59	3.03
Travel time to a paved road (hours) - squared	19.65	57.33	23.44	63.96	15.87	49.69
Dummy Majunga Plaines	0.08	0.27	0.06	0.24	0.10	0.30
Dummy Majunga HT	0.18	0.38	0.13	0.34	0.22	0.42
Dummy Fianarantsoa HT	0.33	0.47	0.37	0.48	0.29	0.45
Dummy Fianarantsoa C/F	0.20	0.40	0.28	0.45	0.13	0.34
Number of observations	495		247		248	

* Division between poor and rich households along the median of asset value

Source: Data from 1997 IFPRI/FOFIFA household survey

Table 7.9 Determinants of the commercial surplus per adult-equivalent, in ariary

	All Households		Poor Households*		Rich Households	
	Coefficient	t-value	Coefficient	t-value	Coefficient	t-value
Intercept	811.75	0.32	1,684.73	1.00	-113.59	-0.02
Lowland area owned per adult-equivalent in ares	26.39	3.41	1.79	0.30	29.16	2.05
Upland area owned per adult-equivalent in ares	27.97	3.09	46.20	3.31	25.34	1.85
Price of rice, ariary/kg	5.32	1.92	-0.92	-0.51	11.46	2.11
Price of maize, ariary/kg	2.50	0.63	0.71	0.23	3.24	0.47
Price of beans, ariary/kg	-1.09	-0.78	0.85	0.87	-2.66	-0.97
Price of cassava, ariary/kg	-11.21	-0.54	6.90	0.45	-26.63	-0.74
Total credit available to the household	0.0009	1.24	0.0012	1.68	0.0006	0.54
Education level of household head	864.87	2.73	-1.77	-0.01	1,305.22	2.29
Dummy gender household head (1=male)	2,400.20	2.59	1,207.54	2.07	3,156.55	1.58
Number of adult-equivalents	-309.34	-1.93	-340.30	-2.94	-495.16	-1.63
Dependency ratio	-167.86	-0.11	54.31	0.05	1,255.86	0.46
Average wage at the village level (ariary/day)	-2.63	-1.69	-1.06	-0.77	-3.25	-1.23
Choice between output traders (1=yes)	2,086.37	1.54	-207.17	-0.22	3,924.48	1.57
Travel time to a paved road (hours)	-544.21	-2.43	-129.69	-0.81	-840.99	-2.03
Travel time to a paved road (hours) - squared	17.57	1.61	5.20	0.68	24.93	1.11
Dummy Majunga Plaines	2,070.58	1.10	-60.35	-0.05	4,307.40	1.27
Dummy Majunga HT	2,719.73	1.27	1,034.69	0.54	4,352.82	1.19
Dummy Fianarantsoa HT	-914.03	-0.61	-1,246.01	-1.05	551.76	0.21
Dummy Fianarantsoa C/F	635.19	0.61	823.03	1.14	2,487.93	1.20
Number of observations	495		247		248	
F-value	4.70		2.06		2.69	
Ajusted R2	0.125		0.076		0.115	

* Division between poor and rich households along the median of asset value

Source: Data from 1997 IFPRI/FOFIFA household survey

commercial surplus.[11]   Male-headed households and better-educated households sell more.   It was also previously shown that the former households produce significantly more.

The village wage level might influence commercial surplus in two ways. Higher wages might induce people to work as salaried labor and therefore reduce their own commercial surplus or it might reduce the labor employed by households and thus reduce production and marketed surplus.   Wages show the expected negative sign in the overall and the rich household regressions.   Hence, it seems that the second effect is the most important as it can be assumed that richer households are more likely to employ labor than to hire out labor.

Conclusions

In this chapter, we focused explicitly on cash agricultural income and commercial surplus and its determinants.   The main conclusions that emerge from the analysis are the following:

- Commercial agricultural surplus makes up 50 per cent of total net agricultural income in the survey region.   The value of commercial surplus amounts to $25 US per household per month or equivalently around $50 US per capita per year.   Agricultural income is highly variable over the year.   Storage of agricultural products in the village is not used as a means to smooth income.   Regions that are able to diversify their agricultural production show shorter and less severe lean periods.
- It is estimated that 60 per cent of rural households in the survey region are net rice buyers while almost 80 per cent are occasional rice buyers.   Most purchases of rice by rural households occur in the lean period.   Poorer households are more likely to be buyers than richer households.   Hence, changes in agricultural prices, and more in particular rice prices, have major and different consequences on rural households in Madagascar.   A reduction of variability and seasonality in rice prices through, for example, community storage schemes can induce significant welfare-increasing effects, especially for poorer households.
- Higher wages are important and significant determinants for commercial surplus.   It seems that they induce employing households to employ less labor and households that hire out labor to sell part of their produce immediately after harvest and buy agricultural products back in the lean

period through wage income. While the first effect is important for the total commercial surplus, the second is important in rice production.

- Distance to a main road and having a choice among traders are significant determinants of commercial surplus. While one has to be careful with assuming causality, it is estimated that one additional hour of travel time from a paved road decreases the value of commercial surplus by 13 per cent. These variables are also important determinants for an increase in the number of households that are net sellers of rice. Hence, infrastructure and measures to increase competition among traders or alternative marketing channels indeed increase rural cash income, seemingly through both price and supply effects.

- Poorer households seem to more often sell because of liquidity constraints and distress. Richer households are more responsive to market conditions such as product prices, distance to a main road, and choice among traders. It is also found that commercial surplus from upland crops is relatively much more important for the poorer households than for the richer households. If increased agricultural income for the poor is the goal, increased production in upland crops seems necessary. Limiting access to upland areas, as through the establishment of protected areas, might take income sources away from the poorer households. This might, for example, be an explanation for the higher malnutrition levels that were found around protected areas in the IFPRI/FOFIFA study (see chapter 10).

Notes

1   As salaries are often paid partly in cash and partly in kind, the full cost of hired labor compared to total production is higher as cash salaries are not included in this calculation.
2   The commercial surplus seems considerably lower than the number mentioned in Table 7.2. However, food purchases were not taken into consideration in that analysis.
3   A net seller is defined as a household that sells more quantities of rice than it buys while a net buyer household buys more than it sells.
4   Vary jeby, vary vakiambiaty, vary vatomandry, and vary aloha are local names in Madagascar that are widely used in specific rural areas to identify rice harvests at specific dates.
5   There is ample evidence that the majority of the storage is by large firms in rural towns (see Barrett, 1997a).
6   If similar purchase and sales prices are assumed.
7   The observation of this phenomenon has pushed some NGOs to start communal storage schemes, often with mixed results.

8   For a more detailed discussion on marketing flows and margins, see Mendoza and Randrianarisao (1998) and Fafchamps and Minten (1998).

9   The effect of distance to paved roads on price levels is discussed in Minten (1999) who estimates the price effect on rice of a one-hour distance from the paved road to be between 2 and 3 per cent. It can be assumed that this will be higher for more perishable products, e.g. fruits, vegetables, and cassava.

10   At the community level, respondents were asked if the households had a choice between different traders for selling the majority of their agricultural products always, occasionally, or never. This was converted to a choice dummy (1 for always or occasionally, and 0 for never); 51 per cent, 22 per cent, and 27 per cent of households reported, respectively, that they always, occasionally, or never had a choice between different traders. The choice between traders is of course, related to access to infrastructure (see Minten, 1999).

11   Particular caution in interpretation is warranted as there might be spurious correlation due to the inclusion as a enumerator in the dependent variable.

8 Non-agricultural and Total Incomes

CÉCILE LAPENU and MANFRED ZELLER

Equitable and sustained economic growth in Madagascar seems to mainly depend on the development of the agricultural sector which represents 29.5 per cent of GDP (1996), employs 85 per cent of the population, and accounts for 47 per cent of exports (Ramarokoto, 1997). Since the beginning of the 1980s, reforms were initiated to liberalize internal and external trade and to adjust prices to the market (Razafimandimby, 1997). These reforms directly affect rural households as agriculture represents their main activity.

Previously agricultural incomes were analyzed (chapter 6). The determinants of the other sources of income (wages, microenterprises, renting, gathering food or firewood, gifts) and the total income of the households will now be studied. Income diversification aims to increase total income, reduce fluctuations over the year, and minimize risk by relying on different sources of income. Moreover, due to the constraints on land extension and the low productivity in agriculture, rural households, particularly young ones without much land, must find sources of income other than agriculture.

We will identify these sources of income, the characteristics of the households that diversify, and the constraints or favorable conditions for diversification, in order to better understand the strategies of the households. During the two rounds of the survey, the household head, spouse, and any children over 14 years of age were questioned on sources of income other than agriculture and income levels. These incomes were aggregated over the whole year.

Wage Income

Wage income is defined as compensation directly from another party in exchange for labor. As shown in Table 8.1, 42.9 per cent of the sample individuals over 14 years of age and 56.2 per cent of the households are involved in wage-earning activities. Nearly two-thirds of the wage earners work in agriculture; microenterprises for handicraft and trade employ

143

18.9 per cent of them; administration (employment with state or parastatal institution), 5.5 per cent; and the industrial sector, less than 1 per cent. In terms of volume of income, wages in agriculture only account for 47.5 per cent of the total wages while administration represents nearly 30 per cent and the industrial sector, 3 per cent. For the period between October 1996 and the first survey round (seven months on average), the average monthly income for the people with wage-earning activities corresponds to 3,000 ariary for agricultural wages, 16,000 ariary for the industrial sector, and 24,000 ariary for administration.[1]

Table 8.1   Distribution of people and income by wage-earning activity

	No. of workers	Workers (%)	Income (%)	Average income (in ariary)[a]	St. dev.
Crop and livestock prod.	520	73.40	47.50	3,030	3,
Handicrafts, small trade	134	18.90	19.60	4,926	5,
Administration	39	5.50	29.60	24,382	14,
Industry	6	0.90	2.90	16,238	14,
Other	9	1.30	0.40	1,288	1,
Total	708	100.00	100.00	4,650	7,
Total of the sample[b]	1,6	42.90			

[a] If income was received
[b] Over 14 years of age

Source: Data from 1997 IFPRI/FOFIFA survey

Wages, particularly in agriculture, are commonplace and women take an active role in salaries (40 per cent of the individuals are women). Yet, for men wages are on average 30 per cent higher than those of the women. All age groups are involved; wages increase with age until 45 years and then decrease; they also vary with the level of education increasing from 2,500 ariary for the people who never went to school to more than 20,000 for those with a 'baccalauréat' (Table 8.2).

There is also significant regional variation in wage income. Wages are more frequent in the Fianarantsoa regions where agriculture, handicrafts, and trade involve around 50 per cent of the adult population (Table 8.3). In contrast, wages are less developed in the Majunga districts despite the number of workers in the industrial sector.

Table 8.2   Share of wage-earning activities, by sex, age, and level of education

	No. of workers	Workers (%)	Income (%)	Average income (in ariary)	St. dev.
Gender					
Males	422	59.60	67.70	5,280	7,785
Females	286	40.40	32.30	3,720	6,517
Age					
<15 years	30	4.20	1.80	2,000	2,856
15-24	231	32.60	17.70	2,532	3,414
25-34	175	24.70	25.10	4,720	6,064
35-44	138	19.50	33.00	7,894	10,916
45-54	94	13.30	18.70	6,575	9,496
>=55	41	5.70	3.60	2,928	4,821
Education					
No school	106	15.00	8.00	2,494	3,324
< 6 years	415	58.60	48.20	3,829	5,107
6 years	128	18.10	19.40	4,990	6,702
9 years	50	7.10	17.50	11,663	16,063
Bac	7	1.00	4.90	24,455	10,309
University	3	0.20	1.90	19,933	18,534
Total	**708**	**100.00**	**100.00**	**4,650**	**7,334**

Source: Data from 1997 IFPRI/FOFIFA survey

Table 8.3   Wages by region

Region	No. of wage-earners	Total of sample*	Wage earners (%)
Majunga Plaines	48	134	35.80
Majunga HT	46	284	16.20
Fianar. HT	296	558	53.00
Fianar. C/F	171	351	48.70
Vakinankaratra	148	323	45.80
Ranomafana	153	338	45.30
Total (except Ranom.)	708	1,650	42.90

* Individuals over 14 years

Source: Data from 1997 IFPRI/FOFIFA survey, first survey round

Except for Majunga HT where less than 10 per cent of the population is engaged in paid agricultural work, 30 to 40 per cent of the individuals in the other regions earn agricultural wages (Table 8.4). In terms of the monthly average income, wage incomes in the Vakinankaratra are twice those of the Majunga regions. Fianarantsoa regions have the lowest agricultural wages. Nevertheless, the community surveys showed that wages are the highest in the Majunga regions (1,160 ariary a day on average over the year in Majunga Plaines; 1,560 ariary in Majunga HT); wages are lower for Fianarantsoa C/F (660 ariary), Vakinankaratra (570 ariary), and Fianarantsoa HT (420 ariary). These different results could be explained by a more regular and stable labor demand in the Vakinankaratra.

Table 8.4   Agricultural wages by region, in ariary

Region	No. of wage-earners	Wage earners (%)	Average income (in ariary)	St. dev.
Majunga Plaines	37	27.60	2,677	2,746
Majunga HT	28	9.80	3,104	4,727
Fianar. HT	206	36.90	2,252	3,130
Fianar. C/F	130	37.00	2,271	2,261
Vakinankaratra	120	37.10	5,274	5,671
Ranomafana	134	39.60	3,988	7,616
Total (except Ranom.)	520	31.50	3,030	3,969

Source: Data from 1997 IFPRI/FOFIFA survey

Incomes from Off-farm Self-employment Activities

Incomes from off-farm self-employment activities are now analyzed. They are represented by incomes from microenterprises, gathering (hunting, fishing, gathering products from the forest), and renting. Table 8.5 shows that 24.7 per cent of the individuals over 14 years of age and 41.7 per cent of the households are involved in these activities. Trade and handicrafts are the two main sources of income (35.4 per cent and 28.3 per cent respectively); incomes from gathering follow.

We can see that the main source of self-employed off-farm incomes after renting (which involves only a few families) is trade and that the volume of income from handicrafts remains low. The monthly income for those involved in those activities is 2,300 ariary for handicrafts, 9,700 ariary for trade, 4,800 ariary for gathering, and 16,800 ariary for renting.[2] The high variability of microenterprise income, in particular for trade, indicates the risks and different scales of these activities between the households.

Table 8.5   Employment and incomes, off-farm self-employment activities, by activity

	No. of workers	Workers (%)	Income (%)	Average income (in ariary)	St. dev.
Gathering	76	18.60	8.60	4,809	5,846
Enterprise	303	74.00	50.40	6,922	24,402
Handicrafts	116	28.30	6.40	2,301	2,575
Small trade	145	35.40	33.80	9,689	33,804
Renting	29	7.40	41.00	16,832	115,146
Total	408	100.00	100.00	7,271	37,995
Total of the sample	1650	24.70			

Source: Data from 1997 IFPRI/FOFIFA survey

The differences between incomes earned in off-farm self-employment activities by males and females are even stronger for these activities than for wages in general. In 46 per cent of the cases, women are involved but on average their incomes are 50 per cent lower than those of men (Table 8.6). Women are more frequently conducting microenterprise activities; of the sample, 93 women work in handicrafts compared to 22 men and there are 74 male and 69 female traders. On average, incomes are similar for people between 25 and 44 years of age (around 8,000 ariary per month). For people above 45 years of age, off-farm self-employment incomes average around 110,000 ariary; incomes from microenterprises decrease but incomes from renting increase, as people seem to have accumulated some capital. The impact of the level of education seems only to be important for income from microenterprise, with an average income five times higher for people with nine years of schooling in comparison with people who never attended school.

Gathering generates the more important monthly income in the Vakinankaratra and Majunga Plaines but occupies only a small part of the population whereas in Ranomafana 11.8 per cent of people are involved in this type of activity (Table 8.7).[3] In Fianarantsoa C/F and Majunga HT, microenterprise incomes are the largest self-employment income source; in the Majunga Plaines renting is the source of the largest incomes. In the second survey round, fewer people were involved in off-farm self-employment activities than in the first survey round (20.5 per cent compared to 24.8 per cent). Trade is the dominant self-employment activity reported in the second round (47.5 per cent of survey population); certainly this is due to the commercial transactions carried out following the harvests. Consequently there was a decline both in the numbers of people engaged in gathering or handicrafts and in their income levels.

Table 8.6   Share of off-farm self-employment activities by sex, age, and level of education

	Gathering		Microenterprise		Renting	
	No.	Av. income	No.	Av. income	No.	Av. income
Gender						
Men	64	5,243	128	10,745	24	16,521
Women	11	2,600	167	4,062	4	22,844
Age						
<15 years	3	831	4	2,299	0	-
15-24	29	4,768	84	2,704	1	6,288
25-34	11	5,820	67	7,143	8	19,083
35-44	9	5,827	73	8,671	6	2,718
45-54	12	4,218	48	13,358	8	3,502
>=55	11	5,152	18	3,020	6	51,568
Education						
No school	7	2,195	48	3,677	3	2,156
< 6 years	41	5,914	161	4,631	14	10,003
6 years	14	5,144	59	10,526	11	30,649
9 years	13	2,634	20	18,550	1	2,500
Bac	0	-	6	20,998	0	-
University	0	-	1	16,026	0	-

Source: Data from 1997 IFPRI/FOFIFA survey

Analysis of the Total Household Income

The main source of household income is crops (Table 8.8). The three main sources of noncrop income are wages, microenterprise, and cattle. Gifts (transfers between households, village-level social organizations, etc.) seem to remain low indicating that solidarity mechanisms and informal insurance through safety nets are weak. Income from cattle can be important, but on the other hand, seems rather risky, as the income generated is on average negative in some regions.

Table 8.7   Off-farm activities and income, by region

		Gathering			Microenterprise			Renting	
	No.	% of the sample	Average income	No.	% of the sample	Average income	No.	% of the sample	Average income
Maj. Plaines	8	6.0	6,370	29	21.6	6,340	8	6.0	60,717
Maj. HT	12	4.2	4,647	64	22.5	8,520	6	2.1	2,825
Fianar. HT	36	6.4	3,761	96	17.2	4,989	4	1.0	2,218
Fianar. C/F	12	3.4	5,006	45	12.8	9,140	0	0.0	0
Vakinan.	7	2.2	8,390	63	19.5	6,921	12	3.7	3,267
Ranomafana	18	11.8	4,022	74	48.4	7,382	2	1.3	4,997
Total (except Ranom.)	75	4.5	4,854	294	17.8	6,952	29	1.7	16,832

Source: Data from 1997 IFPRI/FOFIFA survey

The poverty line has been set at 10,400 ariary which represents the cost of 2,100 calories (minimum requirement) and a minimum of nonfood expenditures. Table 8.9 shows the numbers of survey households with incomes below the povery line in each region. Overall, 67 per cent of the households are estimated to be below the poverty line. The total average monthly income of 65,000 ariary per household or 11,000 ariary per capita corresponds to a daily income of 2,100 ariary per household or 370 ariary per capita. In general, incomes obtained from household surveys are slightly underestimated. Nevertheless, these results underscore the difficult situation of rural survey households who live on an average of $130 US per capita per year. This is less than the $250 US GDP per capita calculated by the World Bank for 1996. This may be an indicator of a greater poverty in the survey regions and a strong differentiation between urban and rural areas.

In 1993, the World Bank estimated that 70 per cent of the total population of Madagascar was under the poverty line of 248,400 FMG per capita. The situation seems to be the same in 1997. Nevertheless, our poverty analysis does not take into account regional differences in consumer prices and can be biased by fluctuations in income over years. Availability of calories can also be used as an indicator of poverty (von Braun and

Table 8.8   Average monthly income, by activity and region, in ariary

Region	Crops	Small livestock	Cattle	Wages	Enterprise	Renting	Interest	Gifts	Gathering
Majunga Plaines	55,162	2,064	12,855	5,299	6,164	16,341	0	1,595	4,648
Majunga HT	39,270	21	-3,371	2,428	6,197	439	3	336	633
Fianar. HT	38,295	2,628	2,531	6,663	3,897	61	18	521	646
Fianar. C/F	38,176	1,647	-607	8,760	5,811	0	0	284	580
Vakinankaratra	43,017	-1,011	20,989	10,778	10,452	750	3	568	739
Ranomafana	25,909	2,316	482	11,974	8,508	47	1	230	908
Total	40,783	1,163	5,519	7,091	6,243	1,545	7	536	972

Source: Data from 1997 IFPRI/FOFIFA survey

Table 8.9   Total average household monthly income by region, in ariary

Region	Crops and livestock	Off-farm income	Household total income	Total per capita income	% of total population below poverty line	Tot. income per adult-equiv.
Majunga Plaines	70,082	33,623	101,403	22,815	42.50	24,930
Majunga HT	35,921	10,038	45,958	9,104	80.40	10,458
Fianar. HT	43,453	11,806	55,259	9,059	70.50	10,394
Fianar. C/F	39,217	15,435	54,652	9,210	75.20	10,505
Vakinankaratra	62,995	23,290	86,286	14,122	51.40	16,303
Ranomafana	28,708	21,836	50,692	9,690	78.80	10,981
Total	47,466	17,637	65,103	11,356	67.00	12,933

Source: Data from 1997 IFPRI/FOFIFA survey

Table 8.10 Comparison of monthly average income from the panel households, by activity (1991–1997)[a]

Region	Crop	Livestock	Wages	Micro enterprise	Renting	Interest	Gifts	Total income
Majunga Pl. 1991 No.38	52,274	7,703	3,194	13,666	12,884	255	2,373	88,850
Vakinan. 1991 No.112	41,560	9,152	9,730	12,963	131	276	2,808	73,676
Total 1991 No.150	44,274	8,785	8,074	13,141	3,298	270	2,698	77,520
Majunga Pl. 1997 No.38	60,602	11,335	3,497	6,172	19,370	–	1,085	122,337
Vakinan. 1997 No.112	40,319	13,133	11,613	16,118	837	–	554	82,574
Total 1997 No.150	45,457	12,678	9,557	13,598	5,439	–	689	86,463
Evolution 1991-1997	2.70%	44.30%	18.40%	3.50%	64.9%[b]	–	- 74.50%	11.50%

a The comparison is based on the ratio of the average consumer price index in Antananarivo over the period Oct. 1990-Sept. 1991 and the period Oct. 1995-Sept. 1996. A monthly average of the 12 months was calculated and then a ratio of the two periods was made. The result gives a ratio of 3.0895. This index is calculated with urban data, but data on inflation in rural areas are not available

b Not directly comparable as in 1992 only lands were taken into account; in 1997, land and agricultural material renting are included

Source: Data from 1997 IFPRI/FOFIFA survey

Pandya-Lorch, 1991). A more detailed analysis of poverty is made using data on consumption (food and total expenditures, caloric consumption, nutritional status of children) in chapters 9 and 10.

A comparison on income of the available panel households was made. On average, total incomes of 150 panel households have increased by 11.5 per cent over the 6 year period (1991-1996) corresponding to an annual rate of growth of 1.9 per cent (Table 8.10). Agricultural and microenterprise incomes have remained stable while incomes from cattle and wages have increased, but it seems that transfers between households have declined. Incomes per capita have progressed only slightly between 1991 and 1997 seemingly due to the rate of growth of the households (births, new household members). The increase is more important in Majunga (2.3 per cent a year) compared to the Vakinankaratra (0.1 per cent a year).

Household Characteristics by Level of Income

The Determinants of Total Household Income

Now we turn to the types and determinants of income (Table 8.11: descriptive statistics of variables; Table 8.12: results). Household incomes evolve with the age and the life cycle of the household: young and old households have lower incomes than middle-aged households. On average, the maximum incomes are earned by households with a head aged fifty years. Female-headed households earn significantly lower incomes: income from a female-headed household is 13,500 ariary a month below average, ceteris paribus. Incomes increase with the level of education in the household. All other factors remaining constant, an average increase of three years of education for the adults of the households leads to a 8,000 ariary increase in monthly income. Migration, contrary to what one might expect, favors incomes ceteris paribus as a significantly higher income is reported for migrants compared to natives. This could be explained by the fact that migrants settle in areas with higher potential. They can also benefit from broader experience and be more open-minded, characteristics which increase adaptability and the adoption of more efficient technologies.

Higher incomes for migrants may also be explained by the possibility of extending cultivated and grazing land. This observation underscores the continuing pressure put on forest and grasslands. On the other hand, in villages where constraints on land extension are strong, migrants develop microenterprise activities which can compensate for lower income from agriculture and livestock. A close family network (brother, sisters, or children in the same village) also favors incomes, as this provides additional labor in time of need.

Table 8.11 Descriptive statistics of the variables in the total household income regression model

	No.	Minimum	Maximum	Average	St. dev.
Tot. hh monthly income, except gifts (in ariary)	488	-107,203	426,667.9	55,934.05	57,721.37
Max. formal loan (predicted value, in ariary)	488	0	23,1458	26,094	33884
Dummy Region 1 (Majunga Plaines)	488	0	1	0.078	0.26
Dummy Region 2 (Majunga HT)	488	0	1	0.177	0.38
Dummy Region 3 (Fianar. HT)	488	0	1	0.330	0.47
Dummy Region 4 (Fianar. C/F)	488	0	1	0.206	0.40
Age of head	488	20	84	44.803	12.86
Age head*age head	488	400	7,056	2,172.592	1,258.66
Sex of the HH head (1 = man)	488	0	1	0.874	0.33
Index level of educ. of the adults[a]	488	1	5	2.214	0.70
Index 'degree' of migration[b]	488	1	3	1.461	0.77
No. of brothers/sisters, sons/daughters in same village	488	0	21	3.506	3.31
Value of assets, in ariary	488	0	59,039,185	1,640,489	336,0318
Index quality irrigation of tanimbary possessed[c]	488	0	3	2.142	0.91
Price of rice, ariary/kg	488	60	856.53	212.040	126.19
Distance to tarred road	488	0	129.00	26.999	26.81
Distance*index soft infrastructure[d]	488	0	645.00	125.72	145.06
Visit of extension services	488	0	1	0.118	0.32

a Index for education level of the adults calculated as an average of each adults score: 1=never attended school, 2=attended school, did not receive CEPE, 3=CEPE or attestation; 4=9 years of school; 5=12 years of school; 6=university, CAP, BTS
b Degree of migration: 1=from the village; 2=migrant family but born in the village; 3=not born in the village
c Quality of irrigation: 0=none, 1=poor; 2=average, 3=good
d Soft infrastructure is the village existence (1) or absence (0) of the following: Fivondronana office, Firaisana office, bank branch, savings bank, primary and secondary schools, post office, public phone, link via radio contact, electricity, police station

Source: Data from 1997 IFPRI/FOFIFA survey

Logically, the value of the household assets (rice land, upland, forest, cattle, house and buildings, productive assets, consumption durables, monetary savings, harvest stock, loans) is positively correlated with the level of total income; a 1,000 ariary increase of the value of total assets leads to a 5.3 ariary increase in monthly income (63.6 ariary increase in annual income).[4] The quality of irrigation on rice land positively influences the level of income. However, it is difficult to quantify this effect as the measures of irrigation quality only roughly distinguish bad, average, or good quality irrigation.

Table 8.12   Results of regression of total household income (2SLS)*

Variables	Coefficient B	t-score	Signific.
Constant	-101,601.3	-3.099	0.0021
Max. formal loan (predicted value), ariary	0.268	4.653	0.0000
Dummy Region 1 (Majunga Plaines)	20,476.3	2.096	0.0366
Dummy Region 2 (Majunga HT)	-7,108.3	-0.756	0.4501
Dummy Region 3 (Fianar. HT)	631.520	0.080	0.9364
Dummy Region 4 (Fianar. C/F)	11,036.9	1.370	0.1714
Age of hh head	3,014.4	2.488	0.0132
Age head*age head	-30.397	-2.458	0.0144
Sex of hh head	13,526.0	1.896	0.0586
Index level of educ. of the adults	7,989.5	2.147	0.0323
Index 'degree' of migration	8,560.9	2.607	0.0094
No. of brothers/sisters, sons/daughters in same village	919.958	1.289	0.1981
Value of assets, ariary	0.005	6.599	0.0000
Index quality irrigation	6,100.4	2.305	0.0216
Price of rice, ariary/kg	53.999	2.584	0.0101
Distance from village to tarred road	-255.582	-1.452	0.1472
Distance*index soft infrastructure	52.684	1.908	0.0570
Visit of extension services	16,231.0	2.105	0.0359

Adjusted R square = 0.36217; F = 15.02165 (signif F = 0.0000)
* Indexes for education, migration, irrigation, and soft infrastructure calculated as in Table 8.11

Source: Data from 1997 IFPRI/FOFIFA survey

Access to external capital, through the formal financial system positively influences total income. One can see that a 1,000 ariary increase of the formal maximum limit leads to a 268 ariary increase of the monthly income.

In terms of elasticity, when the formal financial institutions relax the liquidity constraint by 1 per cent, incomes rise by 0.125 per cent. This variable expresses in fact, not only the household's access to credit, but also the possibility to save, or even to have access to technical assistance and a social network when participating in the formal financial system.

As for the price of rice, when the producer price increases by 1 ariary, total income can increase by 54 ariary, which corresponds to an income elasticity of 0.205. It seems that greater distance to a tarred road has a negative impact on income but, as it creates a favorable environment for economic transactions access to markets, education, and other services, it may be counter balanced by the presence of soft infrastructures. Access to extension services also significantly favors income growth. Finally, by region, the Majunga Plaines is again found to be the most favorable in terms of total income.

These results clearly underscore the necessity of access to education and extension services, of rehabilitation and development of irrigation systems, and of development of soft infrastructure and roads to improve households' incomes. Access to the financial system can alleviate the liquidity constraints of the households.

Characteristics of the Extremes

Negative annual incomes were recorded for 14 households in the sample. This is mainly due to negative income from livestock activities (illness, death, or theft of animals) and has not been compensated for by the non-agricultural incomes which are positive but low. The level of transfer received by poor households is lower than the average. This observation was already made from the EPM data (Dorosh et al., 1998) and can also be found in the analysis of household expenditures (see chapter 9). Compared to the average household in the sample, these households are characterized by a lower level of education, lower quality of lands, fewer total assets, and a higher frequency of social events which have involved expenses during the previous three years.

At the other extreme, 23 households earned monthly incomes over 200,000 ariary. They have household heads above the average age and their family network in the village is more developed. They inherited more valuable land and other assets. Moreover, they have better access to credit and have received larger transfers from other households.

Income Inequalities

The analysis of income inequalities shows that in the sample, 20 per cent of the poorer households earn 4.3 per cent of the total incomes while 20 per cent of the richer drew 55 per cent (Figure 8.1). When the three regions are looked at separately, the highest income inequalities are seen in the Majunga regions and the most egalitarian income distribution is in the Fianarantsoa areas. However, the differences are small.

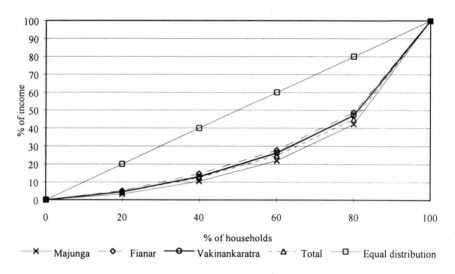

Figure 8.1   Lorenz curve of total income

The calculation of the Gini coefficient gives a value of 0.496 for the whole sample, 0.537 for the Majunga regions, 0.479 for the Vakinankaratra, and 0.456 for the Fianarantsoa areas. To compare, one can note that the Gini coefficient ranges between 0 (perfect equal distribution) and 1 (perfect inequality); the coefficient for highly inegalitarian countries typically varies between 0.5 (Mexico) and 0.7 (Jamaica) while more egalitarian countries have coefficients around 0.4 (India) and 0.3 (Indonesia) (Sadoulet and de Janvry, 1995). For Madagascar, a Gini coefficient of 0.4 has been calculated for consumption at the national level with a lower concentration of incomes in the Fianarantsoa regions (Ravelosoa, 1996).

As 150 households were surveyed in 1992 and 1997, the evolution of the inequalities can be followed over time; the coefficient was 0.411 in 1992 and is 0.492 in 1997 which means that a further concentration of incomes occurred. If the two regions of the panel are distinguished, Vakinankaratra sees a slight decrease of the coefficient (0.432 in 1992 against 0.426 in 1997), but the concentration of income in the Majunga Plaines with a coefficient which increases from 0.380 in 1992 to 0.545 in 1997 offsets this.

When the Gini coefficient is followed over time, there is a natural trend towards more concentration (Deaton, 1997); households with more capital at the beginning have more capacity to rapidly increase their incomes in comparison with poorer households. If there is no active policy of redistribution (taxation, allocation of resources according to income, etc.), a concentration of incomes is generally observed but this does not necessarily mean that markets are inefficient.

Diversification of Incomes

On average, households have four sources of income among the following possibilities: agriculture, small livestock, cattle, wages, renting, gathering, enterprises, and transfers. This corresponds to 1.7 sources of income per adult in the household which shows a high level of diversification.

Diversification outside agriculture is more important in the Majunga Plaines and Vakinankaratra (Table 8.13). These are also the two regions where total income is relatively higher. On the other hand, diversification by quartile of income decreases as income increases: the poorer earn an average of 35.6 per cent of their total income outside agriculture compared to 23.9 per cent for the richer quartile. In fact, the poorer households rely more on income from agricultural wages (Table 8.14).

For the three main groups of activities (agricultural income, agricultural wages, and income from microenterprise), some determinant elements can be identified (Table 8.15 through 8.18). Agricultural income (crops and livestock) increases with access to formal credit. There is no significant impact made by the age of the household head, education level, or region. Agricultural income increases when households have valuable assets (especially land), when the price of rice is high, when households can extend their area of land cultivated, or when they receive extension services. The impact of good quality rice land irrigation is positive but not significant. Hence, agricultural income can be improved through intensification (credit for inputs such as labor or fertilizer, household capital, irrigation) or extensification (increase of cultivated land). In order to move towards sustainable agriculture and to protect natural resources, efforts can be made to develop irrigation systems and access to credit, fertilizers, and advice from extension services, all of which favor intensification over extensification (see chapter 11).

Table 8.13 Percentage of different sources of income in total household income, by region

Region	Crops	Livestock	Wages	Microenterprise
Majunga Plaines	49.6	13.9	8.0	9.9
Majunga HT	50.9	38.7	5.6	0.2
Fianar. HT	63.0	6.0	18.1	9.7
Fianar. C/F	71.7	0.0	20.4	5.5
Vakinankaratra	58.3	4.5	23.1	9.2
Ranomafana	62.2	2.7	19.4	11.3
Total	60.6	10.9	16.6	7.1

Region	Gathering	Renting	Gifts	Off-farm income*
Majunga Plaines	3.6	12.3	2.6	36.4
Majunga HT	2.1	1.4	1.1	10.4
Fianar. HT	1.5	0.1	1.4	30.9
Fianar. C/F	1.4	0.0	1.1	28.4
Vakinankaratra	2.9	0.8	1.2	37.2
Ranomafana	3.3	0.1	0.8	35.0
Total	2.0	1.5	1.3	28.5

* Off-farm income includes income from wages, microenterprises, gathering, renting, and gifts

Source: Data from 1997 IFPRI/FOFIFA survey

Agricultural wages decrease with the age of the household head and with the education level of the adults in the household. Agricultural wages are negatively correlated to access to formal credit, but positively correlated to the number of adult men in the household and the 'degree' of migration. Agricultural wages typically represent the main income source for households that own few resources apart from their labor. Regional differences are significant with income from wages higher in the Vakinankaratra.

The income from microenterprises increases with the age of the household and reaches a maximum for rather old households (around 60 years of age). It is positively correlated with the number of women in the household. Income significatively depends on the level of education; it also increases with the percentage of households in the village with more than 2 hectares of lowland and upland combined. This latter variable expresses the inequality of land distribution and it indicates that part of the population has sufficient purchasing power to create a viable demand for the services and products of off-farm microenterprises.

Table 8.14 Percentage of different sources of income in total household income, by income quartile

Income quartile	Crops	Livestock	Wages	Microenterprise
1 (poor)	46.3	18.0	26.6	2.5
2	68.8	0.0	17.2	9.8
3	67.0	9.2	14.0	7.3
4 (rich)	59.9	16.3	9.1	8.6
Total	60.6	10.9	16.6	7.1

Income quartile	Gathering	Renting	Gifts	Off-farm income*
1 (poor)	3.2	0.8	2.5	35.6
2	2.4	0.5	1.3	31.2
3	1.2	0.5	0.7	23.7
4 (rich)	1.4	4.0	0.9	23.9
Total	2.0	1.5	1.3	28.5

* Off-farm income includes income from wages, microenterprises, gathering, renting, and gifts

Source: Data from 1997 IFPRI/FOFIFA survey

The value of assets remains insignificant and access to credit seems to have a low influence on the microenterprise incomes; in general, these activities are implemented with a low level of capital investment. This result indicates that further potential for microenterprises exists if access to credit and households' capacity to bear risks is improved.

Table 8.15 Descriptive statistics on the variables of the regressions

Variable	No.	Minimum	Maximum	Mean	St. dev.
Monthly agricultural income (crops and livestock) by hh, in ariary	495	-118,779	623,936.4	47,465.57	74,464.93
Monthly hh agricultural wage, in ariary	495	0	43,686.39	2,860.14	4,829.09
Monthly hh income from enterprise, in ariary	495	-30,428.5	465,350.9	6,243.19	26,933.42
Max. formal credit limit	495	0	1,000,000	19,385.61	97,835.17
Max. informal credit limit	475	0	3,500,000	135,207.11	297,256.45
Region 1	495	0	1	0.08	0.27
Region 2	495	0	1	0.17	0.38
Region 3	495	0	1	0.33	0.47
Region 4	495	0	1	0.20	0.40
Age of the hh head	495	20	87	45.02	13.00
Age of the hh head – squared	495	400	7,569	2,196.22	1,281.28
Sex of the hh head (1=male)	495	0	1	0.87	0.33
No. of children in the hh (LE 14)	495	0	11	2.99	1.89
No. of adult women in the hh	495	0	6	1.43	0.83
No. of adult men in the hh	495	0	6	1.73	1.097
Index aver. level of education of hh members	495	1	4.5	1.88	0.49
Index aver. level of education of the adults in the hh	495	1	5	2.21	0.70
'Degree' of migration	495	1	3	1.46	0.77
Visit from extension services	495	0	1	0.12	0.32
Price of rice, ariary/kg	495	60	856.5333	214.08	127.72
Area-weighted irrigation quality of tanimbary possessed	495	0	3	2.15	0.90
Value of assets, in ariary	495	0	59,039,185	1,737,371.99	3,524,338.89
Dummy possibility of extension of the cultivable lands	471	0	1	0.33	0.47
% of village hhs with more than 2 ha land	495	0	0.8	0.33	0.22

Source: Data from 1997 IFPRI/FOFIFA survey

Table 8.16 Determinants of agricultural income (2SLS)

Variables	Coefficient B	t-score	Signific.
Constant	-17,640.49	-1.006	0.3151
Max formal credit limit	0.237	4.101	0.0000
Max informal credit limit	0.040	0.420	0.6749
Region 1	4,748.23	0.498	0.6188
Region 2	-5,378.12	-0.527	0.5982
Region 3	-3,493.26	-0.439	0.6608
Region 4	7,604.05	0.882	0.3784
Age of the hh head	167.557	0.719	0.4727
Sex of the hh head	6,654.14	0.599	0.5498
Index aver. level of education of all hh members	4.966	0.001	0.9994
'Degree' of migration	4,270.38	0.941	0.3473
Visit from extension services	13,056.00	1.797	0.0730
Price of rice, ariary/kg	76.880	3.817	0.0002
Area-weighted irrigation quality of tanimbary possessed	3,149.48	1.016	0.3100
Value of assets, in ariary	0.004	2.646	0.0084
Dummy possibility of extension of the cultivable lands	13,240.50	2.204	0.0281

Adj. R square = 0.245, F = 10.037 (Signif F = 0.0000)

Source: Data from 1997 IFPRI/FOFIFA survey

Table 8.17   Determinants of agricultural wages (2SLS)

Variable	Coefficient B	t-score	Signific.
Constant	6,504.699	3.960	0.0001
Max. formal credit limit	-.011	-1.527	0.1274
Region 1	-2,748.753	-2.676	0.0077
Region 2	-4,373.213	-5.113	0.0000
Region 3	-3,644.718	-4.720	0.0000
Region 4	-3,673.673	-4.605	0.0000
Age of the hh head	-44.326	-2.247	0.0252
Sex of the hh head	828.937	1.210	0.2271
No. of children in the hh (LE 14)	-213.737	-1.844	0.0658
No. of adult women in the hh	382.311	1.417	0.1572
No. of adult men in the hh	860.871	3.734	0.0002
Index aver. level of education of the adults of the hh	-482.923	-1.391	0.1648
'Degree' of migration	661.003	2.156	0.0316
Price of rice, ariary/kg	1.810	0.972	0.3315
Value of assets, in ariary	-3.78E-05	-0.521	0.6026
Dummy possibility of extension of the cultivable lands	609.048	1.234	0.2177
% of hh in village with more than 2 ha of land	-3,248.781	-2.156	0.0316

Adj. R square = 0.126, F = 5.173 (Signif F = 0.0000)

Source: Data from 1997 IFPRI/FOFIFA survey

Table 8.18   Determinants of microenterprise income (2SLS)

Variable	Coefficient B	t-score	Signific.
Constant	-11,248.694	-2.145	0.0325
Max. formal credit limit	0.017	1.279	0.2014
Region 1	-1,403.451	-0.735	0.4626
Region 2	-1,906.063	-1.202	0.2301
Region 3	348.759	0.248	0.8041
Region 4	-857.714	-0.598	0.5501
Age of the hh head	480.586	2.254	0.0247
Age*age	-4.942	-2.283	0.0229
Sex of the hh head	-14.905	-0.012	0.9903
No. of children in the hh (LE 14)	-265.611	-1.194	0.2329
No. of adult women in the hh	840.734	1.637	0.1023
No. of adult men in the hh	-443.287	-1.010	0.3132
Index aver. level of education of the adults of the hh members	1,536.678	2.420	0.0159
Price of rice, ariary/kg	-5.303	-1.502	0.1338
Value of assets, in ariary	9.168E-05	0.661	0.5092
% of hh in village with more than 2 ha land	7,801.987	2.733	0.0065

Adj. R square = 0.051, F = 2.721 (Signif F = 0.0005)

Source: Data from 1997 IFPRI/FOFIFA survey

Conclusions

The results of this section may be thus summarized:

- In terms of non-agricultural income, a large number of the rural households is involved in wage activities, mainly in the agricultural sector. The number of people employed in the industrial or public sector remains very limited. Due to the high level of wages and to the nonseasonality of this type of employment, wages in administration are very high for the household involved. Off-farm self-employment incomes are earned by 42 per cent of the households, in particular in trade and handicrafts. However, handicrafts seem to not fetch much income. Trading and handicraft activities rely on a low level of capital (not a significant coefficient for the variables expressing access to capital or value of the assets). Women significantly diversify household income sources, but their wages remain much lower than those of men. They could be targeted by loan programs that wish to diversify their portfolios towards non-agricultural credit.

- The average total survey household income reaches 65,000 ariary a month or, in an average household with 6 members, an annual income of 650,000 FMG ($130 US) per capita. Monthly household incomes are highest in the Majunga Plaines (101,000 ariary), followed by the Vakinankaratra (86,000 ariary). Incomes are the lowest in Majunga HT (46,000 ariary) underscoring the high disparities that can exist within the same administrative region. Sixty-seven per cent of the sample remains under the poverty line of 10,400 ariary per capita per month. This corresponds to World Bank figures in 1993 which found 70 per cent of the population failing to earn the minimum income. Between 1992 and 1997, households in the panel data set had slightly increasing incomes thanks to the increase in incomes from livestock activities. The disparities between households are high and increasing over time, in particular in the Majunga areas.
- The level of diversification outside agriculture is important (28.5 per cent of total income). Non-agricultural income is more important for the poor (35.6 per cent in the poorest quartile of income compared to 23.9 per cent in the richest). The vast majority of observed diversification is 'unhealthy' (as it is focused on earning income from agricultural wages) and seems to be driven by poverty and a lack of other profitable opportunities.
- The analysis of the determinant factors for income generation underscores the importance of the socioeconomic environment of the households including their access to credit, infrastructure, and extension services; the quality of irrigation; and variations in the price of rice. At the household level, education and migration positively influence income and diversification outside agriculture.

Notes

1   To calculate the monthly average income, the total of wages earned between October 1996 and the first round was divided by the number of months for this period (7 months on average). Average monthly income then depends on the regularity of the activities during this period and cannot be analyzed as a wage for a full-time job.

2   For renting, few households earned a very high income which explains the very high standard deviation (115,146 ariary); if the three households from the Majunga regions

with rent income above 100,000 ariary are excluded from the sample, rent incomes decrease to an average of 3,000 ariary.

3   Ten people are involved in hunting and fishing for a monthly income of 1,000 ariary; 6 people produce charcoal for 9,000 ariary a month.

4   The regression takes into account production factor incomes (agriculture, livestock, wages, microenterprise, renting, gathering) without transfers and gifts.

9 Consumption Expenditures

BART MINTEN, CLAUDE RANDRIANARISOA, and MANFRED ZELLER

Introduction

An understanding of consumer behavior is important when discussing a wide range of development policy questions. First, better knowledge of consumer behavior might help in the guidance of policy interventions to improve the nutritional status of particular individuals (pregnant women, infants) or households. Second, consumption expenditure parameters are useful for policy analysis in a country's strategy of food subsidies and taxes in order to minimize the cost and maximize the benefits of such schemes. Third, these consumption expenditure parameters are essential inputs for sectoral and macroeconomic policy simulations through models such as General Equilibrium and multimarket models.

In Madagascar, there are different dimensions to food and nonfood consumption expenditures such as regional influences, seasonality, and income level. We discuss some of these dimensions in the descriptive section. Then, we analyze the determinants of expenditures using an estimation of a complete demand system through an Almost Ideal Demand System (AIDS) model. The results of this estimation will provide insights into the impact of prices and income on the level and composition of total food and nonfood consumption expenditures of rural households.[1] We conclude by highlighting the main results.

Descriptive Statistics

Total food and nonfood expenditures in the survey area amount to just over 56,000 ariary per household per month or equivalently, 550,000 FMG or $110 US per capita per year (Table 9.1).[2] This level is similar to the estimate of the average for rural households of the national household survey (EPM) of 1994 and it is reassuring to note that average per capita expenditures are very close to per capita income levels (estimated at $130 US).[3] The difference can easily be explained by different time periods and methodologies. In accordance with the distribution pattern of income, expenditures for food and nonfood consumption items are highest in the Majunga area and lowest in the

Fianarantsoa area.   The share of food in total expenditures amounts to 80 per cent, varying between 67 per cent in the Majunga Plaines and 83 per cent in the two Fianarantsoa areas.   The fluctuations between regions in the share of rice, other cereals, and tubers basically result from the differences in cropping patterns and cropping calendars among the regions which influence production and acquisition costs for different foods.   Rice is more important in the Majunga area than in the Fianarantsoa HT and C/F and vice versa for tubers.   Meat and fish expenditures make up 15 per cent of total food expenditures.   The most important category in nonfood expenditures is domestic utensils and clothing.   It is remarkable that health and education are of relatively minor importance making up only 4 per cent and 1 per cent respectively of the total nonfood budget.   This is especially surprising given the fact that a significant proportion of the population reported illnesses in the two days prior to the survey (see Ralison and Lapenu, 1998).   Gifts, social obligations, and events represent 14 per cent of the total nonfood budget.

In further analysis, statistics are presented by per capita expenditure quartiles to allow comparison of characteristics of poorer and richer households.   Table 9.2 presents some relevant statistics of the respondent households.   Household composition varies significantly among the quartiles as measured by household size, dependency ratio, and gender of the household head.   On average, richer households have smaller families (5.1 members) compared to poorer households (7.0 members).   The dependency ratio, defined as the number of elderly and children per number of adults, is significantly higher for the lower quartile than for the upper quartile.   Female-headed households are disproportionally represented among the poorest households; one-quarter of the households in the lower quartile are female headed compared to only 7 per cent in the upper quartile.   While the change of household composition with expenditure levels is straightforward, human capital in the household also shows a clear change. The number of household heads who finished at least primary school is significantly higher in the upper quartile (35 per cent) than in the lower quartile (22 per cent).

The level of food and nonfood expenditure is, by definition, higher in the upper quartile.   This is also the case, as expected, for the value of total assets. The amount of cultivated land between the different categories differs significantly; the upper quartile cultivates 3.5 times more lowland area and almost two times as much upland per household as the lower quartile.[4] However, this variation in area of land cultivated surprisingly does not cause a relative difference in crop income compared to total income across the quartiles indicating that noncrop income is (relatively) as important for poor as for rich households. However, the composition of the other sources of income compared to total income is different, as, for example, the part of salary income for the lower quartile represents 24 per cent of total income compared to only 11 per cent for the upper quartile (the same trends are also shown in the previous chapter). We again see the regional dimension in expenditure levels as the households in the Fianarantsoa areas are more represented in the lower expenditure quartile while there are proportionately more Majunga households in the upper quartile.

While income sources differ between quartiles, so does the composition of expenditures. Table 9.3 shows the shares of the different categories in total food and nonfood expenditures, disaggregated by expenditure quartiles. The share of food in total expenditures declines from 85 per cent for poorer households to 74 per cent for the richer ones. Disaggregation by crop between the different quartiles reveal some noteworthy trends. The relative importance of rice declines from poorer to richer households. However, given the smaller change in shares than the changes in total expenditures, absolute rice expenditures actually go up. This might be due to two reasons: increased quantities of rice consumed and increased rice quality. In further regression analysis in the consecutive chapter, we will shed some light on the relative importance of those phenomena.

Other agricultural products show similar patterns as seen in previous studies based on the EPM (SECALINE, 1996; Dorosh et al., 1998; Ravelosoa, 1996). Tubers are clearly an economically inferior food. They represent 13 per cent of the food expenditures of the poor compared to 5 per cent for the rich households. Vegetables show a similar pattern but to a smaller extent. The most dramatic change across income groups is shown for meat, animal products, and fish. Combined, they represent 6 per cent of the food budget for poorer households compared to 26 per cent for richer ones. In absolute values this difference is even more striking as total food expenditures are four times as high for the upper quartile as for the lower quartile.

For nonfood expenditures, a relative decline is seen for domestic utensils and clothing from the poorer to the richer households. Energy expenditures show a similar decline. However, the most dramatic change is seen in the gifts, social obligations, and events section which represents 19 per cent of household expenditures for richer households compared with 7 per cent for

Table 9.1 Household expenditure shares of food and nonfood items for the different survey regions, in %

	Majunga Plaines	Majunga HT	Fianar. HT	Fianar. C/F	Vakinankaratra	Ranomafana	All areas
Rice	48.57	52.68	46.93	43.93	38.53	46.91	45.71
Other cereals	3.52	1.47	0.92	0.30	5.25	0.40	2.00
Tubers	4.33	4.76	8.05	18.69	8.16	13.15	9.37
Legumes, beans	2.04	2.31	6.02	1.41	9.22	2.96	4.35
Meat and animal products	8.66	8.12	8.94	6.67	12.19	13.91	8.99
Fruit	2.55	4.30	2.56	9.47	3.92	1.58	4.16
Vegetables	5.62	10.27	13.24	6.57	6.32	9.23	9.29
Fish	14.70	9.59	4.09	1.37	9.12	1.69	5.99
Purchased products (sugar, bread, etc.)	5.15	2.25	3.30	3.72	5.93	3.08	3.90
Cooking oils	2.50	1.03	1.18	0.54	2.65	0.42	1.44
Alcohol, coffee	2.06	1.96	4.54	8.43	2.60	9.65	4.27
Miscellaneous purchased snacks and soups	0.31	1.26	0.21	0.90	0.11	1.02	0.52
Share of food in total expenditures	69.38	79.69	83.10	83.81	79.69	85.60	80.25
Cigarettes	10.04	3.90	10.72	13.74	14.53	19.06	10.87
Education	1.66	3.08	4.11	3.04	5.26	2.52	3.75

Domestic utensils, clothing	31.78	46.19	39.83	49.50	34.03	45.32	40.67
Energy	16.61	14.71	14.14	15.18	15.94	15.26	15.03
Building and agricultural material	3.82	3.57	1.70	1.28	2.87	1.10	2.36
Taxes, household help, rent	11.42	2.83	8.22	4.50	4.09	5.06	5.90
Gifts, social obligations/events	19.18	15.25	13.77	9.61	18.04	9.31	13.93
Health	1.23	1.51	1.15	0.84	0.77	0.73	1.07
Other nonfood	0.04	0.10	0.09	0.23	0.06	0.10	0.11
Share of nonfood in total expenditures	32.62	20.31	16.90	16.19	22.31	14.40	19.75
Value of total household monthly expenditures, in ariary	81,488	71,193	44,202	49,752	59,414	45,096	56,277

Source: Data from 1997 IFPRI/FOFIFA survey

the poorest ones.   This confirms sociological evidence that for richer households there is significant value in active participation and in contribution to social events.   On the other hand, there is no significant change between income groups in education and health expenditures.

Table 9.2   Household and income characteristics, by per capita expenditure quartile

	Quartile				All
	1	2	3	4	quartiles
Household size	6.98	6.31	6.29	5.07	6.16
Dependency ratio	0.58	0.55	0.50	0.47	0.52
% of male-headed households	74.61	89.77	94.25	93.19	89.46
Household head finished at least primary school, %	22.17	30.70	29.91	34.98	28.93
Total monthly food expenditures per capita, in ariary	4109	5900	8054	13820	7974
Total monthly nonfood expenditures per capita, in ariary	730	1297	1989	4921	2236
Value of assets, 1,000 ariary	1098	1259	1391	3200	1737
Riceland total area cultivated, in ares	53	89	134	189	116
Upland total area cultivated, in ares	65	110	117	118	102
% of crop income in total income	62.25	60.85	55.19	64.11	60.59
% of salary income in total income	23.74	14.06	19.44	11.18	16.61
% of gifts in total income	1.10	0.63	1.60	2.04	1.34
% of loans and rental income in total income	0.34	1.59	1.28	2.66	1.47
% of income from hunting, gathering, etc. in total income	1.24	2.03	3.08	1.77	2.03
% of enterprise income in total income	4.52	5.69	11.96	6.07	9.07
% of income from livestock in total income	6.80	15.17	9.44	12.17	10.88
% of households from Fianar. HT	46.40	43.09	32.73	9.72	32.97
% of households from Fianar. C/F	25.36	19.95	22.41	14.21	20.49
% of households from Vakinankaratra	18.24	19.61	18.58	26.87	20.82
% of households from Majunga HT	8.95	13.03	16.07	32.63	19.67
% of households from Majunga Plaines	1.04	4.33	10.21	16.57	8.05

Source: Data from 1997 IFPRI/FOFIFA survey

Table 9.4 shows how households obtained the food they consumed.   As only 36 per cent of food consumed is paid for in cash and the food obtained through salaries (1 per cent), barter (0.3 per cent), gifts (2 per cent), and credit

Table 9.3   Household expenditures and expenditure shares for different product categories, in %

	Per capita expenditure quartile				All quartiles
	1	2	3	4	
Rice	50.65	49.11	46.05	39.05	45.71
Other cereals	1.61	1.53	2.73	2.14	2.00
Tubers	13.31	10.65	8.07	5.47	9.37
Legumes, beans	4.62	5.15	4.80	2.84	4.35
Meat and animal products	3.97	5.52	10.72	15.71	8.99
Fruit	2.19	4.37	4.21	5.85	4.16
Vegetables	10.64	10.26	9.62	8.67	9.29
Fish	2.54	5.57	6.08	9.78	5.99
Purchased products (sugar, bread, etc.)	4.47	3.68	3.58	3.86	3.90
Cooking oils	1.12	1.25	1.04	2.34	1.44
Alcohol, coffee	4.42	4.28	4.56	3.83	4.27
Miscellaneous purchased snacks and soups	0.47	0.63	0.54	0.45	0.52
Share of food in total expenditures	84.68	81.82	80.09	74.43	80.25
Cigarettes	13.74	12.47	9.60	9.69	10.87
Education	5.04	3.45	3.27	3.24	3.75
Domestic utensils, clothing	43.21	43.49	39.13	36.87	40.67
Energy	19.15	12.59	14.44	15.91	15.03
Building and agricultural material	1.53	1.91	2.00	4.00	2.36
Taxes, household help, rent	4.76	9.31	6.09	5.46	5.90
Gifts, social obligations/events	6.85	12.81	19.02	19.04	13.93
Health	1.19	0.83	1.17	1.12	1.07
Other nonfood	0.01	0.15	0.18	0.11	0.11
Share of nonfood in total expenditures	15.32	18.18	19.91	25.57	19.75
Expenditures per capita, in ariary	4,839	7,197	10,044	18,742	10,210

Source: Data from 1997 IFPRI/FOFIFA survey

(0.3 per cent) are of minor importance, it follows that the majority of a household's food is produced by the household. There are some differences between income quartiles as food gifts are more important for richer households (5 per cent) while food received as salary matters for poorer households (3.5 per cent). It is interesting to see that the richer and poorer households rely equally on markets to obtain food. However, the types of foods purchased vary as shown by the figures for rice. In this case, poor households rely significantly more on the market, i.e. 41 per cent of the rice consumed by households in the lowest quartile is purchased compared to only 28 per cent for those in the highest quartile.

Table 9.4   Food sources, % of total household consumption

| | Per capita expenditure quartile | | | | All |
	1	2	3	4	quartiles
Food purchased [a]	35.76	32.96	36.02	38.04	35.69
Rice purchased [b]	40.83	31.51	33.76	28.14	33.55
Food received as salary	3.45	0.69	0.83	1.15	1.53
Food received through barter	0.48	0.50	0.22	0.13	0.33
Food received as a gift	0.87	1.51	2.58	4.68	2.41
Food obtained through credit	0.37	0.01	0.25	0.56	0.30
Food from own production	59.07	64.33	60.09	55.45	59.74

[a] Purchased during the three days prior to the survey
[b] % of total rice consumption

Source: Data from 1997 IFPRI/FOFIFA survey

Determinants

While the previous section presented the level and nature of food and nonfood expenditures, this section will discuss the determinants of the total level of expenditures as well as the determinants of the allocation of expenditures. To this end, a complete demand system for different food categories and one aggregated nonfood category was estimated using the AIDS methodology developed by Deaton and Muellbauer (1980). This methodology is widely used in empirical demand research as the estimation satisfies the requirements of demand theory and allows one to easily obtain a complete matrix of own price, cross-price, and expenditure elasticities.

Total household expenditures are assumed to be determined by household characteristics, assets, community characteristics, and consumer prices of products. Table 9.5 shows the results of this regression using the logarithm of total household expenditures as dependent variable. Except for prices, all variables show an expected and significant sign.[5] One more adult household member in the family increases household expenditures by

Table 9.5 Determinants of total household expenditures*

	Coefficient	t-value
Intercept	9.065	59.680
Log (total area of lowland area possessed, in ares)	0.043	3.552
Log (total area of upland area possessed, in ares)	0.043	3.702
Dependency ratio	-0.236	-3.000
Total adult-equivalent	0.132	16.992
Education level of household head	0.079	4.681
Gender of household head (1=man)	0.258	5.192
Time to get to a paved road (in hours)	-0.023	-1.966
Time to get to a paved road (in hours) - squared	0.001	2.159
Average wage level, ariary/day	0.000	3.124
Rice price, ariary/kg	0.331	5.647
Cereals price, ariary/kg	0.011	0.270
Tuber price, ariary/kg	0.035	0.852
Legumes price, ariary/kg	0.002	0.222
Meat and animal products price, ariary/kg	0.069	1.593
Fruit price, ariary/kg	0.047	3.381
Vegetable price, ariary/kg	0.011	0.664
Fish price, ariary/kg	-0.082	-4.193
Other food, ariary/kg	0.000	0.001
Dummy Fianar. HT	-0.266	-5.563
Dummy Fianar. C/F	-0.275	-4.811
Dummy Majunga HT	-0.103	-1.176
Dummy Majunga Plaines	0.091	1.122
Dummy round 2	-0.019	-0.428

* Dependent variable: log (monthly household expenditures in ariary)

Source: Data from 1997 IFPRI/FOFIFA survey

13 per cent. An increase in the dependency ratio decreases expenditures as the more time spent on care of children and the elderly, the lower the household's productive activities. Female-headed households show 25 per cent less expenditures ceteris paribus, while better educated household heads show higher expenditures. A 10 per cent increase in household land area, lowland or upland, increases household expenditures by 0.4 per cent. Distance to the paved road decreases household expenditures by 2 per cent for every extra hour of traveling time. This effect diminishes the further one is from the paved road as shown by a significant quadratic term. The higher the wage

levels, the higher the expenditures level for the household. The positive sign overall seems to suggest that the extra income generating effect from wages for the poorer households is more important than the extra input costs of these higher wages for the richer households who employ laborers. This might be due to the higher number of households in the former category compared to the latter.

The determinants of the allocation of expenditures within the household budget are evaluated through the estimation of a system of budget shares for different types of commodities.[6]   The resulting elasticities of these estimations are shown in Table 9.6. The income (expenditure) elasticity of demand is interpreted as the percentage change in the quantity demanded when income changes by one per cent, other factors held constant. Those products that show an expenditure elasticity significantly above one are 'luxury' goods; those with elasticity significantly below one are 'necessity' goods. The expenditure elasticities for the different categories show that when income increases, households will consume relatively more meat and animal products (2.16), fish (1.71), and nonfood items (1.46). On the other hand, households consume relatively less tubers (0.42) and vegetables (0.44) when income increases. Rice and cereals show an expenditure elasticity of 0.75. Rural households in Madagascar spend less on rice and cereals, in relative terms, the richer they become.[7]

Table 9.6 also shows all the own- and cross-price elasticities for the different categories. Rice shows an own-price elasticity of -0.66 meaning that an increase of the rice price by 10 per cent would decrease rice consumption by almost 7 per cent. To compensate for such a price increase and lowered consumption, households would increase tuber and cereal (mostly maize) consumption by 4.6 per cent and 4.7 per cent respectively as shown by the magnitude of their respective cross-price elasticities. While changes of rice price have significant relative repercussions on the quantities of other products consumed due to the importance of rice in the budget share, this is less the case for the impact of price changes of other products on rice consumption. For example, an increase of the tuber price by 10 per cent would decrease tuber consumption by 5.6 per cent while it would increase rice consumption only by 0.7 per cent.

As expected, own price elasticities show a negative sign for all product categories. They tend to be lower (in absolute value) for the goods that show low expenditure elasticities, such as tubers and vegetables, and higher for goods with high expenditure elasticities, such as beans, fish, meat/animal

Table 9.6 Expenditure and price elasticities*

	Budget share	Expenditure elasticities	Uncompensated price elasticities (Marshallian)									
			Rice	Cereals	Tubers	Legumes	Meat	Fruit	Vegetables	Fish	Other food	Nonfood
Rice	0.371	0.752	-0.663	0.475	0.464	-0.620	-0.189	-0.329	0.249	-0.401	-0.131	-0.677
Cereals	0.016	0.752	0.020	-0.372	-0.119	0.092	-0.004	-0.018	-0.092	-0.013	0.006	-0.035
Tubers	0.077	0.424	0.071	-0.603	-0.562	-0.097	-0.307	-0.057	-0.182	-0.047	-0.021	-0.141
Legumes, beans	0.034	1.250	-0.040	0.214	-0.015	-0.928	0.052	0.253	-0.095	0.285	0.022	0.083
Meat/animal products	0.068	2.163	0.061	0.076	-0.151	0.165	-0.851	-0.374	-0.098	0.051	-0.025	-0.123
Fruit	0.032	1.026	-0.020	-0.028	-0.004	0.231	-0.215	-0.075	-0.075	-0.032	-0.061	0.012
Vegetables	0.074	0.445	0.027	-0.452	-0.174	-0.267	-0.235	-0.216	-0.409	0.037	-0.059	-0.074
Fish	0.046	1.715	-0.005	0.007	0.031	0.402	0.014	-0.014	0.081	-1.057	0.016	0.017
Other food	0.082	1.008	-0.008	0.053	0.026	0.032	-0.125	-0.156	-0.019	-0.029	-0.931	0.043
Nonfood	0.200	1.461	-0.195	-0.122	0.080	-0.258	-0.304	-0.039	0.195	-0.508	0.176	-0.567

* Changes in relative consumption with respect to relative price changes

Source: Data from 1997 IFPRI/FOFIFA survey

products, and other food. Hence, it seems, on average, that price changes of the luxury goods have more impact on the quantities consumed than do price changes of necessities. This seems self-evident as necessary goods have to be bought, no matter the price. However, while this is often the case, it has also been observed in previous studies that low income households often respond to price changes in a manner that differs from that of the general population (Alderman, 1986).

Table 9.7   Expenditure and uncompensated price elasticities, by income group

| | Expenditure elasticity | | | Uncompensated own-price elasticity | | |
	All	Upper quartile	Lower quartile	All	Upper quartile	Lower quartile
Rice	0.75	0.71	1.13	-0.66	-0.31	-0.82
Cereals	0.75	0.42	1.25	-0.37	0.16	-2.50
Tubers	0.42	0.78	0.21	-0.56	-0.66	-0.55
Legumes, beans	1.25	0.47	2.47	-0.93	-0.40	-1.15
Meat/animal products	2.16	1.54	2.21	-0.85	-0.71	-1.21
Fruit	1.03	0.07	1.85	-0.08	0.48	-1.10
Vegetables	0.45	0.90	0.96	-0.41	-0.39	-0.53
Fish	1.71	1.63	0.81	-1.06	-0.97	-1.16
Other food	1.01	1.14	0.83	-0.93	-0.83	-0.96
Nonfood	1.46	1.31	0.51	-0.57	-0.53	-0.23

Source: Data from 1997 IFPRI/FOFIFA survey

To investigate this in the Malagasy context, demand elasticities of the different products were reestimated for all the survey households and for the sample in the first and fourth per capita expenditure quartile, reflecting the poorest and the richest households. The estimates of price and expenditure elasticities suggest that the low income households are more price responsive than the high income households (Table 9.7). In the case of rice, low income households are highly responsive to own-price and income. In contrast, high income households respond more moderately to income and, especially, price changes. This indicates that the demand for rice by high income rural households is almost insensitive to the market price of rice, probably because a majority of these households meet their rice consumption from their own production. These same trends seem to hold for most other food categories. The most striking exceptions are fish and tubers. This might be explained by the low fish consumption in the lower quartile (2 per cent of the budget share). In the case of tubers, the composition of this group changes between income quartiles. While cassava is the main tuber product for the lower quartile group, potatoes are more important in the upper quartile.

Conclusions

In this chapter, the descriptive statistics and the determinants of food and nonfood expenditures are discussed. The results can be summarized as follows:

- Poorer households are more likely to have a female head, to be larger, to have a higher dependency ratio, and to have a head who did not complete primary school. They have less access to land and they rely relatively more on wage labor for their income than do richer households. They are also located further away from paved roads.
- Total expenditures in the survey area amount to $110 US per capita per year on average. The low income level is also illustrated by relatively high food expenditures which make up 80 per cent of total expenditures of rural households. Within the food budget, rice represents almost half of the expenditures.
- Expenditures on tubers and vegetables decrease relatively strongly with increases in income; expenditures on meat and animal products, fish, and nonfood items increase with income. Rice shows an expenditure elasticity of 0.75 implying a 75 per cent increase in rice expenditures for a doubling of total expenditures. Own-price elasticities tend to be lower (in absolute value) for the goods that show low expenditure elasticities and higher for goods with high expenditure elasticities.
- Tubers and maize are found to be the most important substitutes of rice. An increase of the rice price by 10 per cent would decrease rice consumption by 6.6 per cent and increase tuber and maize consumption by 4.7 per cent.
- While price effects are more important for the rich than the poor in the determination of supply and commercial surplus (see chapter 6), the reverse is seen on the demand side. On average, the poor show higher responses to price and income changes than rich households. One

explanation is that the poor rely more on the market for their food purchases of staple products than do richer households. On the other hand, the poor might also be more responsive as marginal changes in prices have bigger marginal effects on their consumption due to their lower income levels.

Notes

1   Although household income data are available from the IFPRI/FOFIFA survey, household consumption expenditures are used in the analysis as a proxy for income as based on the permanent income hypothesis, expenditures are likely to reflect permanent income and therefore are a better determinant of consumption behavior.

2   Food expenditures and consumption are calculated based on a three day recall period during two survey rounds for the same households (round 1: March/April 1997; round 2: July/August 1997). Nonfood expenditures are based on all expenditures in the period July 1996/June 1997. A whole year was taken into consideration to ensure that all, and often highly seasonal nonfood expenditures during the year were captured. Nonfood expenditures exclude any investment in consumer or producer durables and any payment of interest. Food and nonfood expenditures were all converted to monthly figures. Food from own production was valued at village price levels if available. Otherwise regional prices are used. In the descriptive analysis of food and nonfood expenditures, the average of the two rounds was used while each round observation was a different entry in the regression analysis.

3   Based on the EPM, total expenditures were estimated at 322,000 FMG/capita/year in 1994 (Dorosh et al., 1998). Between those time periods, the urban price index (INSTAT) rose from an average of 2,200 in 1994 to 4,200 during the survey period in 1997.

4   The differences between quartiles are similar to the ones obtained by Dorosh et al., (1998). Given that richer households are relatively smaller, this difference is even more pronounced at the per capita level.

5   As prices are also indirectly included in the dependent variable (for example, if prices for rice are higher, expenditures on rice are higher), no further discussion is done here. Price effects are discussed in more detail in the demand system analysis.

6   The estimated regressions look like:

$$w_i = \alpha_i + \sum_j \gamma_{ij} \log P_j + \beta_i \log(\frac{X}{P*})$$

where w_i is the budget share of the ith good, P_j is the price of the jth good, and X is total expenditure. P* is the Stone price index where prices are normalized to one before the index is computed. In this case, the linear approximation of the AIDS model is equivalent to the AIDS model (Asche and Wessels, 1997). Slutsky symmetry and homogeneity conditions were imposed upon the system. Unit prices were obtained through a division of values by quantities. The logarithm of the number of adult-equivalents was included as an extra regressor in the model to allow for scale effects (see Sadoulet and de Janvry, 1995).

7   However, there are substitutions between the quantity of calories and the quality of food as income increases, leading to a shift to higher nutrient-cost foods. As a result, the income elasticity of quantity intake is usually smaller than the income elasticity of food expenditures.

10 Nutritional Status and Caloric and Protein Consumption

CÉCILE LAPENU, MANFRED ZELLER, and ELIANE RALISON

The level of food consumption and the nutritional status of households expresses the satisfaction of a number of basic human needs. They can be used as a direct indicator of welfare and as an indirect indicator of the socioeconomic development of a country. A good understanding of the living conditions of the households can help to define economic policies for the improvement of the food and nutritional security of the population. The interest in measuring the level of food consumption and nutrition comes from the fact that precise methodologies and objective thresholds have been defined by nutritionists that allow for a clear distinction of households in difficulty. There are fewer methodological issues to be resolved with these indicators than with the definition of a poverty line based on household income. A poverty line can be drawn at calorie consumption of 80 per cent of the recommended level for an active and healthy life; extreme poverty is defined as 60 per cent of the recommended consumption (von Braun and Pandya-Lorch, 1991).

Survey Methodology

During the two rounds of the 1997 IFPRI/FOFIFA survey, the consumption for each household was recorded for the three days prior to the survey. The person mainly responsible for cooking and serving the meals was asked to recall the nature and the quantity of the food consumed during the previous three days. The number of men, women, and boys and girls aged from 1 to 6 and from 7 to 13 years participating in each meal was carefully recorded. Participants were members of the household or occasional visitors. A list of 94 local food items was established; the quantity consumed during the previous three days was measured in kilograms, liters, pieces, or 'kapoaka', a local unit of measure. Then all quantities were converted into grams. A quantity of available calories and proteins corresponds to each gram of food item. The caloric and protein consumption is expressed per capita or by adult-equivalent in order to take into account specific needs by gender and by

183

age. The calculation of the adult-equivalent fixes, by age and gender, the daily quantity of calories required for a normal life. As the 1997 IFPRI/FOFIFA data do not provide sufficient age details, the required quantities have been weighted according to the proportion of people in each age group in the sample. An adult-equivalent corresponds to a man over 13 years of age with a required consumption of 2,837 calories per day. Therefore a woman over 13 represents 0.747 adult-equivalent (2,119/2,837), a young boy from 7 to 13 years represents 0.767 adult-equivalent (2,181/2,837) and so on (Table 10.1). The daily dietary minimum needs per capita for normal life with a normal professional activity are fixed at 2,133 calories and 56 g of protein (SECALINE, 1997).

Table 10.1 Methodology for the calculation of adult-equivalent

Age (in years)	Sex	Calorie Needs	% in the sample	Weighted average consumption
1	Child	820	14.7	
1-2	Child	1,150	16.3	
2-3	Child	1,350	11.1	1,443.1
3-5	Child	1,550	28.1	
5-7	Child	1,800	29.8	
7-10	Boy	2,100	49.5	
10-12	Boy	2,200	33.8	
12-13	Boy	2,400	16.6	2,181.5
13-14	Boy	2,400	4.6	
14-16	Boy	2,650	8.6	
16-18	Boy	2,850	11.1	
18-30	Man	3,000	27.7	
30-60	Man	2,900	39	2,837.1
>60	Man	2,450	9	
7-10	Girl	1,800	57.5	
10-12	Girl	1,950	30.4	1,881.9
12-13	Girl	2,100	12.1	
13-14	Girl	2,100	5.5	
14-16	Girl	2,150	10.3	
16-18	Girl	2,150	6.2	
18-30	Woman	2,100	30.6	
30-60	Woman	2,150	42.1	2,119.4
>60	Woman	1,950	5.2	

Source: 1997 IFPRI/FOFIFA household survey

The Caloric and Protein Consumption of the Survey Households

On average for all the regions, the total caloric and protein consumption of the households by adult-equivalent or per capita nearly corresponds to the daily minimum required (2,695 against 2,837 and 2,094 against 2,133 respectively) as shown in Table 10.2. These results are similar to those of SECALINE (1997) which found an average consumption per capita of 2,115 calories, but with considerable regional disparities. By region, the average level of consumption is high in Majunga HT with more than 3,200 calories per adult-equivalent; Majunga Plaines, Fianarantsoa HT, Vakinankaratra, and Ranomafana are situated around the required consumption. At the other extreme, the Fianarantsoa C/F records an average consumption well below the minimum required expressing a very difficult situation for the majority of households in terms of food security. Indeed, the first round of surveys in Fianarantsoa C/F (March/April) corresponded to the worst period of the lean season.

Table 10.2   The caloric and protein consumption of the households by region, round 1*

Region	No.	Calories per adult-equivalent	Calories per capita	Protein per adult-equivalent	Protein per capita
Majunga Plaines	37	2,906	2,295	107	85
Majunga HT	77	3,240	2,496	90	70
Fianar. HT	159	2,738	2,130	69	53
Fianar. C/F	97	2,145	1,683	38	30
Vakinankaratra	95	2,661	2,051	70	54
Ranom.	97	2,613	2,017	56	43
Total (except Ranom.)	465	2,695	2,094	69	54

* Extreme values under 600 calories per adult-equivalent (1 household) or above 5,000 (28 households) per adult-equivalent have not been integrated in the analysis

Source: 1997 IFPRI/FOFIFA household survey

In the second round, average consumption slightly decreased (see Table 10.3). In fact, an important drop was experienced in Fianarantsoa HT and Ranomafana placing these regions, on average, under the required level of daily consumption. The two Fianarantsoa areas are in a difficult situation in the second round while the Majunga Plaines and Vakinankaratra maintain a reasonable consumption level. Consumption is the highest in Majunga HT. For per capita protein consumption, three levels can be seen: Majunga areas with a high average of around 60 g, Vakinankaratra around 50 g, and the Fianarantsoa areas and Ranomafana with less than 40 g.

Table 10.3   The caloric and protein consumption of the households, by region, round 2*

Region	No.	Calories per adult-equivalent	Calories per capita	Protein per adult-equivalent	Protein per capita
Majunga Plaines	35	2,782	2,174	82	65
Majunga HT	72	3,172	2,459	81	63
Fianar. HT	149	2,357	1,828	51	40
Fianar. C/F	92	2,312	1,806	44	34
Vakinankaratra	93	2,763	2,128	64	49
Ranom.	86	2,353	1,843	46	36
Total (except Ranom.)	440	2,600	2,017	60	46

* Extreme values under 600 calories (2 households) or above 5,000 (23 households) per adult-equivalent have not been integrated

Source: 1997 IFPRI/FOFIFA household survey

The survey period can be related to the sales period for agricultural products as a proxy for the harvest season and for an evaluation of agricultural income flows. For the Majunga areas, the two survey rounds (February/April and July/September) were conducted before the main sales periods (September/December), and thus reflect more difficult periods in terms of food security. As on average the level of consumption remains reasonable, the majority of Majunga area households do not seem to face major food consumption problems. In Fianarantsoa C/F, the first round corresponded with the lean season and a very low level of consumption was indeed observed. In Fianarantsoa HT, the surveys were conducted during the sales period (March and July) and did not take place during the lean season (January/February). The situation however is already critical although it does not correspond to the worst period. Similarly in the Vakinankaratra, where even if average consumption is high, it was registered during the sales period and does not express the level of consumption during the lean season.

From these observations, the regional means indicate that the Majunga areas, in particular the HT, are relatively secure in terms of food consumption; in the Vakinankaratra, the level of consumption is reasonable but there are likely to be some difficulties during the lean season. Similar results had already been found in these areas in 1992 (Zeller, 1993). However, the lean season in Vakinankaratra seems to be shorter than in the other regions (see chapter 7). On the other hand, the Fianarantsoa regions are in a much more difficult situation, even outside the lean season.

The disparities among the households are taken into account with an analysis of the households with a low (less than 80 per cent of the minimum) or a very low (less than 60 per cent of the minimum) level of consumption. Table 10.4 confirms the worrying situation in the Fianarantsoa areas, with more than 50 per cent of the households under the threshold of 80 per cent of the required daily food intake and nearly one-third under 60 per cent for the second round. Moreover, even in the regions with a reasonable average, a significant portion of the households remain under the required quantities. In Ranomafana in particular, 50 per cent of the households are in a difficult situation, and 30 per cent are in a critical situation. However, regional means can hide high inequalities among households. Therefore characteristics of the households according to their level of consumption will be examined in more detail based on the daily caloric intake.

Table 10.5 shows calorie consumption levels by adult-equivalent differentiated both by food type and by region. By food type, rice is the most important food in all the regions, followed by tubers. The 'other cereals' (essentially corn and wheat) are only significant in the Majunga regions (first round) and in the Vakinankaratra. Food intake is mainly vegetarian. However, high fish consumption is observed in the Majunga areas.

In the Majunga HT where the total caloric consumption is the highest, rice consumption during the second round is nearly 50 per cent higher than the average of the sample (2,362 calories compared to 1,632); fish, fruits, and vegetables are also consumed in more important quantities. The food intake in the Majunga HT is higher and more diverse than the average, but remains dependent on rice. The Fianarantsoa regions are characterized by a higher consumption of tubers, fruits, and vegetables, but by low quantities of the other food types, rice in particular. The drop in the caloric consumption in the Fianarantsoa HT and the Ranomafana areas for the second round can be explained by the strong decrease in rice consumption (-28.9 and -26.5 per cent respectively) which is only partly compensated by an increase in tuber consumption. For the second round, the Fianarantsoa areas and Ranomafana highly depend on tubers.

Table 10.4   Households in which adult-equivalents consume less than 80 per cent or 60 per cent of daily caloric requirement

| | Less than 80 % | | | |
| | Round 1 | | Round 2 | |
	No.	%	No.	%
Majunga Plaines	9	22.1	11	29.5
Majunga HT	12	13.8	15	18.8
Fianar. HT	43	26.6	79	51.4
Fianar. C/F	59	57.8	52	54.2
Vakinankaratra	31	29.8	28	28.4
Ranomafana	40	40.4	45	51.1
Total	154	31.0	185	39.7

| | Less than 60 % | | | |
| | Round 1 | | Round 2 | |
	No.	%	No.	%
Majunga Plaines	5	12.3	5	14.3
Majunga HT	4	4.2	4	5.1
Fianar. HT	10	5.9	42	27.7
Fianar. C/F	34	33.7	27	28.4
Vakinankaratra	18	17.7	8	8.1
Ranomafana	14	14.1	27	30.7
Total	71	14.3	86	18.7

Source: 1997 IFPRI/FOFIFA household survey

The results underscore the importance of rice, in particular in the Majunga HT.[1] Rice constitutes from 50 to 75 per cent of the calorie intake for the surveyed areas.   When the total caloric consumption decreases (e.g. Fianarantsoa HT, round 1 to round 2), the share of rice decreases in favor of the share of tubers.   Animal products and fish contribute on average 6 per cent of calorie intake.   They are a less important source of calories with the exception of the Majunga areas for fish and the Vakinankaratra in the second round for meat. In terms of protein, however, animal products supply 18 per cent of the daily intake.

By quartile of total expenditures, rice remains important, at around 60 to 65 per cent of total calorie intake, whatever the level of household wealth (Table 10.6). This demonstrates the sociocultural importance of rice in Madagascar. For the first round however, the poorest quartile consumes 65 per cent of rice against 60 per cent for the richest. The households classified at low wealth levels are more distinctly characterized by a higher consumption of tubers, mainly cassava (around 15 per cent in the first round, 21 per cent for the second). Higher consumption of animal products is seen for the rich: 9.7 per cent and 11.8 per cent for the two rounds respectively compared to 2.4 per cent and 2.2 per cent for the poor. These observations confirm the size of the expenditure elasticities of the previous chapter.

The evolution of household food consumption between 1992 and 1997 can be evaluated from the panel data on 150 households (Table 10.7). In 1992, three survey rounds were conducted (mid-January to early April; end of April to early June; mid-August to mid-September). In 1997, the two survey rounds were conducted in March/April and July/August. As food consumption can vary over the year according to the agricultural seasons, it is important to compare equivalent periods. Thus Table 10.7 compares the first rounds of the 1992 and 1997 surveys. The level of consumption is evaluated in adult-equivalents thus compensating for the evolution in the composition of the households (e.g. age, number of members) over the 6 year period.[2] Caloric consumption appears to be relatively stable over the 5 year period. The differences between 1992 and 1997 are not significant for caloric consumption (t-tests for the comparisons of means were nonsignificant). Protein consumption improved slightly, which suggests an increase in products with a high protein content, such as meat or fish, consumed by the households.

Cost of Calories

The prices for food items are derived from the 1997 survey data on households' food expenditures. For home-comsumed food items, prices could not been obtained from the respondents, therefore some products only have few observations for prices, and in general the price of calories can be slightly overestimated. The following observations can be derived from Table 10.8. Calories from cassava are in general less expensive than calories

Table 10.5   Household caloric consumption by adult-equivalent, by food type and region

Region	Rice	Other cereals	Tuber	Beans	Fruits & veg.	Animal products	Fish	Other sources	Total per ad.-equiv.
Round 1									
Majunga Plaines	1,718	353	80	51	28	94	376	206	2,906
Majunga HT	2,249	153	231	41	140	73	191	162	3,240
Fianar. HT	2,027	29	98	199	80	46	59	200	2,738
Fianar. C/F	1,058	17	627	22	219	40	17	145	2,145
Vakinankaratra	1,422	157	360	292	114	52	66	198	2,661
Ranomafana	1,728	10	505	89	60	119	12	90	2,613
Total	1,713	99	283	143	122	54	99	182	2,695
Round 2									
Majunga Plaines	1,874	8	261	24	141	98	221	155	2,782
Majunga HT	2,362	11	197	66	144	119	129	144	3,172
Fianar. HT	1,442	50	565	107	50	89	12	42	2,357
Fianar. C/F	1,291	19	638	42	94	81	15	132	2,312
Vakinankaratra	1,619	262	261	91	81	222	26	201	2,763
Ranomafana	1,270	35	682	40	90	124	9	103	2,353
Total	1,632	79	432	77	88	121	51	120	2,600

Source: 1997 IFPRI/FOFIFA household survey

Table 10.6 Share of calories, by food type and quartile of total expenditures

Expenditure quartile	Rice	Other cereals	Tuber	Beans	Fruits & veg.	Animal products	Fish	Other sources
Round 1								
1 (poor)	65.0	1.7	14.7	5.0	4.7	0.6	1.8	6.5
2	64.5	2.2	11.0	6.5	4.7	1.4	2.6	7.0
3	61.6	4.3	10.2	6.5	4.8	2.3	3.6	6.7
4 (rich)	59.8	4.7	8.6	3.5	6.1	3.4	6.3	7.6
Total	62.8	3.2	11.2	5.4	5.1	1.9	3.5	7.0
Round 2								
1 (poor)	62.9	3.0	210	3.8	2.8	1.8	0.4	4.2
2	62.8	2.8	18.7	3.9	3.6	2.2	1.2	4.7
3	64.9	2.4	16.2	2.9	2.8	4.0	2.1	4.6
4 (rich)	62.2	2.9	9.6	2.9	4.5	8.2	3.6	6.1
Total	63.2	2.8	16.4	3.4	3.4	4.0	1.8	4.9

Source: 1997 IFPRI/FOFIFA household survey

from rice; where this is not the case, cassava consumption remains low (Majunga Plaines, round 1). Fianarantsoa C/F is an exception but the period of the survey corresponds to the lean season and both rice and cassava prices are high. In the second survey round, the regions where the consumption of tubers is high (the Fianarantsoa areas, Ranomafana) correspond to the regions where the price of tubers is lower than the price of rice. These observations confirm the idea that tubers are substituted for rice when its price increases relative to the price of tubers. Calories from beans are, on average, expensive, particularly in the second round. The two exceptions are the Vakinankaratra (first round) and Fianarantsoa HT (second round) which are also the regions where the consumption of beans is higher than average.

Table 10.7   Caloric and protein consumption by adult-equivalent, 1992 and 1997

Region	1992, Round 1		1997, Round 1	
	calorie	protein	calorie	protein
Majunga Plaines no.=38	3,032	81	2,850	99
Vakinankaratra no.=111	2,588	60	2,769	76
Total no.=149	2,701	66	2,789	82

Source: 1992 IFPRI/DSE/CNRE household survey; 1997 IFPRI/FOFIFA household survey

The differences in the quality of food consumed by households of different wealth levels (the poorest are in the first quartile) can be evaluated from the price of the products under the assumption that higher prices denote higher quality. In fact, in the first round, the richer households buy rice of better quality; quality differences attenuate in the second round. This may be a result of the lower number of observations. Moreover, consumption of own production is not taken into account although it can be important at harvest season (the second round). For tubers, the two rounds show price differences between the quartiles. Richer households buy more expensive tubers; they seem to replace cassava with potatoes (Table 10.9).

The Determinant Factors of Household Food Consumption

The determinant factors of the level of food consumption can be evaluated from the following standard model:[3]

Caloric consumption = f (income, prices, household characteristics, and village characteristics).

One can distinguish total caloric consumption per capita that expresses the total energy of the daily food intake from consumption of calories derived from animal products (meat and fish). The latter indicator reflects the nutritional quality of the diet. In terms of endogeneity of the variables, a test between income and caloric consumption shows that these variables are endogenous.[4] Hence, the use of OLS would give biased coefficients. A 2SLS model has therefore been used.

From a methodological point of view, Bouis and Haddad (1992) have shown that the high variations found in the literature for results on the elasticity of caloric consumption with regard to income came from the variables used and the method of analysis. The use of the calories available measured by food expenditure can distort the results due to measurement errors which generally increase with household income. By measuring effective consumption for a three day recall period, the IFPRI/FOFIFA survey tried to avoid this bias. Moreover, Bouis and Haddad (1992) show that total household expenditures are a good proxy for total income and that they give better results in the calculation of elasticities. However, in the IFPRI/FOFIFA survey, the level of income has been measured in great detail. It therefore seems more effective to directly use the data on monthly per capita income.

Energy Supply

Total caloric consumption is significantly higher in young households, where the head of the household is a man, and where the average level of education is higher (Tables 10.10 and 10.11). Table 10.1 showed that young households can have higher calorie needs; moreover, the level of education as well as the age of the household can favor a better awareness of the notion of improved diet leading to a positive impact on caloric consumption. In particular, one can expect young and educated households to be more flexible in view of traditions and taboos 'fady' which limit consumption of some types of food. SECALINE (1997) noted some typical problems in Madagascar: ignorance

Table 10.8   Price of 1,000 calories, by region and food type, in ariary

Round 1		Rice	Other cereals	Cassava	Beans	Fruit	Veg.	Animal prod.	Fish	Oil
Majunga Pl.	No.	21	11	2	8	3	37	16	36	28
	Mean.	113	68	142	165	618	3,072	426	257	251
	St. dev.	65	17	87	144	812	5,666	211	340	323
Majunga HT	No.	23	2	8	6	5	15	17	56	16
	Mean.	115	41	82	129	171	1,546	488	627	457
	St. dev.	41	18	39	104	119	1,704	407	823	790
Fianar. HT	No.	18	0	6	24	51	52	44	46	81
	Mean.	83	-	52	130	247	760	526	361	233
	St. dev.	62	-	15	81	308	473	198	309	391
Fianar. C/F	No.	85	3	33	15	14	21	8	22	14
	Mean.	119	45	104	135	156	464	397	291	143
	St. dev.	56	11	69	41	124	407	339	93	41
Vakinan.	No.	42	5	5	5	27	68	21	31	59
	Mean.	108	113	39	75	315	934	369	536	202
	St. dev.	123	74	24	18	201	1,971	112	400	335
Ranom.	No.	14	0	2	16	1	10	21	13	10
	Mean.	78	-	48	136	106	462	414	306	194
	St. dev.	10	-	29	56	-	323	92	101	107
Total	No.	190	21	54	57	101	192	106	191	198
	Mean.	112	73	90	131	260	1,291	464	439	238
	St. dev.	76	43	63	83	286	2,905	250	536	403

Round 2

Majunga Pl.	No.	20	0	16	12	26	61	10	43	17
	Mean.	80	-	92	869	364	3,645	543	895	603
	St. dev.	36	-	36	1,673	472	6,458	238	1,357	644
Majunga HT	No.	8	1	5	15	14	65	16	57	16
	Mean.	60	85	77	720	160	2,455	400	738	899
	St. dev.	25	0	37	2,347	139	3,678	141	992	992
Fianar. HT	No.	30	0	4	10	7	30	43	10	15
	Mean.	77	-	67	91	68	612	450	534	271
	St. dev.	18	-	65	20	45	437	128	274	320
Fianar. C/F	No.	46	0	10	13	0	34	37	8	14
	Mean.	102	-	69	122	-	638	439	485	231
	St. dev.	12	-	28	49	-	382	73	300	185
Vakinan.	No.	36	3	10	5	39	104	59	27	47
	Mean.	74	34	24	122	359	684	454	362	145
	St. dev.	16	4	11	60	319	651	169	184	71
Ranom.	No.	76	4	14	14	2	17	23	5	9
	Mean.	121	40	40	133	138	1,026	465	582	200
	St. dev.	117	18	21	26	105	682	79	385	30
Total	No.	140	4	41	55	86	294	164	144	109
	Mean.	84	41	69	442	302	1,679	449	686	357
	St. dev.	24	20	39	1,447	352	3,640	146	985	544

Source: 1997 IFPRI/FOFIFA household survey

of the nutritional value of food products; social and religious taboos, in particular for meat; sharing food between household members without taking into account the physiological needs of each member, etc.

Table 10.9   Price of calories, by quartile of total household expenditures (round 1), in ariary

Expenses quartile	Rice round 1		Rice round 2	
	No.	**Price**	**No.**	**Price**
1 (poor)	52	109	44	85
2	49	94	35	83
3	53	123	35	82
4 (rich)	35	126	25	82
Total	190	112	139	83

Expenses quartile	Tubers round 1		Tubers round 2	
	No.	**Price**	**No.**	**Price**
1 (poor)	16	85	12	76
2	23	110	14	78
3	12	170	13	108
4 (rich)	19	127	20	88
Total	70	119	60	88

Source: 1997 IFPRI/FOFIFA household survey

In terms of consumption of food within the household, children have a significantly lower level compared to adults. This seems logical, but the level of the difference is higher than the difference that corresponds to the consumption by adult-equivalent (see Table 10.1), which could mean that children suffer more than adults from food shortage.[5] These results could confirm the observation made by SECALINE (1997): 'given a tradition that still exists in some regions, adult men, who represent the labor force and who earn incomes, are served in priority in quantity and quality, often to the detriment of the women and children.' The presence of a family network in the village, instead of favoring a smoothing of consumption, seems to reduce the quantity of calories consumed but the result is not significant. On the other hand, special occasions with more visitors have a positive impact on the level of consumption.[6] Total caloric consumption increases with income, but at a decreasing rate (through the use of the natural logarithm). The elasticity of consumption with regard to income is estimated to be 0.09.[7] This elasticity expresses a low impact of the increase of income on the total consumption. It corresponds however to results obtained in other countries when problems of endogeneity and measurement error have been taken into account (for more discussion, see Bouis and Haddad, 1992), as was done in our analysis.

Table 10.10 Descriptive statistics for the variables of the regressions

Variables	No.	Minimum	Maximum	Mean	St.Dev
Animal calorie consumption per capita	908	0	1,609.15	127.58	208.69
Total caloric consumption per capita	908	335.58	4,594.99	2,050.46	807.67
Natural log for monthly per capita income (predicted value) (ariary)	908	5.5	11.71	8.86	1.04
Sex of the hh head (0=wom; 1=men)	908	0	1	0.88	0.32
Age of the hh head	908	20	87	45.12	12.98
Index aver. level of educ. in the hh	908	1	4.5	1.88	0.48
Dummy region 1 (region 1=Maj. Plaines)	908	0	1	0.08	0.27
Dummy region 2 (Maj. HT)	908	0	1	0.16	0.37
Dummy region 3 (Fian. HT)	908	0	1	0.34	0.47
Dummy region 4 (Fian. C/F)	908	0	1	0.21	0.41
Dummy round 1	908	0	1	0.51	0.5
Dummy Reg1 x Dummy Rd 1	908	0	1	0.04	0.2
Dummy Reg2 x Dummy Rd 1	908	0	1	0.08	0.28
Dummy Reg3 x Dummy Rd 1	908	0	1	0.17	0.38
Dummy Reg4 x Dummy Rd 1	908	0	1	0.11	0.31
% of children (0 to 5 years) in the hh	908	0	0.67	0.17	0.15
% of children (6 to14 years) in the hh	908	0	0.8	0.28	0.19
% of adult women in the hh	908	0	1	0.25	0.15
No. of brothers/sisters, sons/daughters in the village	908	0	21	3.58	3.48
Dummy visitors for the meals (0=absence; 1=presence)	908	0	1	0.23	0.42
Dummy occasion (1=special event or more than 5 visitors)	908	0	1	0.07	0.26
Price of rice, ar/kg	908	0	1,244.02	316.96	78.71
Price of cassav, ar/kg	908	20	400	79.55	26.13
Prix of beef, ar/kg	908	600	4,000	1,126.77	165.31
Prix fresh fish, ar/kg	908	100	2,800	972.89	263.25
Distance of village from a tarred road, km	908	0	129	26.68	26.4

Source: 1997 IFPRI/FOFIFA household survey

Table 10.11 Results of regressions

Variables	Total caloric consumption per capita			Animal calorie consumption per capita		
	Coefficients	t	Sig.	Coefficients	t	Sig.
Natural log for monthly per capita income (predicted value), in ariary	184.66	2.436	0.015	61.55	3.033	0.002
Sex of the hh head (0=wom; 1=men)	254.67	3.101	0.002	35.52	1.621	0.105
Age of the hh head	-6.83	-3.323	0.001	-1.9	-3.46	0
Index aver. level of educ. in the hh	168.36	2.66	0.008	34.26	2.027	0.043
Dummy region 1 (Maj. Plaines)	-11.52	-0.078	0.938	31.29	0.795	0.427
Dummy region 2 (Maj. HT)	403.14	2.84	0.005	91.76	2.416	0.016
Dummy region 3 (Fianar. HT)	-234.69	-2.392	0.017	-95.31	-3.623	0
Dummy region 4 (Fianar. C/F)	-137.12	-1.245	0.213	-73.35	-2.518	0.012
Dummy round 1	65.44	0.598	0.55	-92.37	-3.253	0.001
Dummy Reg1 x Dummy Rd 1	162.43	0.822	0.412	215.18	4.082	0
Dummy Reg2 x Dummy Rd 1	143.62	0.93	0.353	102.16	2.472	0.013
Dummy Reg3 x Dummy Rd 1	353.91	2.726	0.006	88.89	2.554	0.011
Dummy Reg4 x Dummy Rd 1	-90.52	-0.624	0.533	60.6	1.567	0.117
% of children (0 to 5 years) in the hh	-1,658.34	-7.889	0	-111.91	-1.986	0.047
% of children (6 to14 years) in the hh	-983.7	-5.333	0	-85.98	-1.74	0.082
% of adult women in the hh	-393.36	-1.82	0.069	7.65	0.132	0.895
No. of brothers/sisters, sons/daughters in the village	-9.05	-1.254	0.21	-1.31	-0.677	0.499
Dummy visitors for the meals (0=absence; 1=presence)	-32.51	-0.569	0.569	14.21	0.929	0.353
Dummy occasion (1=special event or more than 5 visitors)	147.06	1.598	0.11	78.46	3.188	0.001
Price of rice, ar/kg	-1.41	-3.867	0			
Price of Cassava, ar/kg	-1	-1.065	0.287			
Prix of beef, ar/kg	0.18	1.164	0.245	0.1	2.313	0.021
Prix fresh fish, ar/kg	-0.06	-0.57	0.569	-0.04	-1.481	0.139
Distance of village from the tarred road, km	3.31	2.882	0.004	-0.63	-2.063	0.039
(Constant)	1106.33	1.484	0.138	-400.05	-2.021	0.043
	Adjusted R2 = 0.261			Adjusted R2 = 0.227		
	F = 14.337 (sig = 0.000)			F = 13.098 (sig = 0.000)		

Source: 1997 IFPRI/FOFIFA household survey

In terms of the direct influence of consumer food product prices, different impacts are observed. The variations in the price of rice have a negative and significant influence on food consumption. The calculation of the elasticity shows that an increase of 1 per cent of the price of rice for the consumer decreases the total caloric consumption by 0.22 per cent; this high decrease can be explained by the major role of rice in the daily diet. However, this elasticity is calculated at mean values and probably does not hold for larger variations. The magnitude of this elasticity could also confirm the difficulties faced by households during the lean season: if the price of rice is twice the average price (100 per cent increase), total consumption will drop by 22 per cent. On the other hand, we saw that the price of rice positively influences household incomes (elasticity of 0.257, see chapter 8). This gives an indirect effect of the price with an elasticity of 0.023.[8] The direct effect remains more important.

The results on the price of cassava are not significant, but the negative sign seems to suggest that when the price of cassava increases, aggregate food consumption decreases (elasticity of -0.039). This characterizes a product of substitution which will be consumed when its price is low compared to the price of other products. The influence of the variation of beef or fish prices remains nonsignificant due to the low share of animal products in the household diet. By region (dummy region), the level of consumption is lower in the Fianarantsoa areas and more important in the Majunga HT. The comparison between the two rounds generally gives an insignificant coefficient, except for the Fianarantsoa HT where consumption drops for the second round.

The distance of the villages to a tarred road is positively correlated with the level of the total consumption. A priori, opposite results were expected to express difficulties of transport and costs of supply. However, the high level of home consumption in the villages (SECALINE, 1997) can compensate for the effects of distance. The coefficient of 3.31 underscores that the impact is low (1 km closer to the tarred road increases consumption by 3.31 calories or 0.16 per cent of the average consumption). Here again, the indirect effects of distance on income can interfere, but they are relatively low and differ from one region to the other one (see chapter 8).

Quality of the Diet

Well-educated, young, and male-headed households have a more diversified diet, certainly for the same reasons explained for total consumption. However, animal consumption varies a lot over the year with a drop for the second round for the Majunga and Fianarantsoa areas but an improvement for the Vakinankaratra. Animal consumption also increases with the occurrence of social events. The results on prices are not easily interpreted as we try to see the impact of the increase in the price of beef on overall animal consumption (meat, fish, dairy). However, it seems that an increase in the price of beef does not directly impede animal calorie consumption due to substitution effects or an increase in expenses; on the other hand, an increase in the price of fish causes a decrease in the animal calories in the household diet.

The impact of income on animal consumption is very large and significant, with an elasticity of 0.482. Finally, the effect of the distance to a tarred road is negative: each additional km from the village to a tarred road, ceteris paribus, leads to a decrease of 0.63 animal calories in the daily diet, or a decrease of 0.5 per cent from the average consumption. Households in remote areas seem to better ensure their needed quantity of calories but they face more difficulties in ensuring the quality of their diet.

The Nutritional Status of Children

Survey Methodology

Anthropometric measures were conducted during the second round on children aged from 6 months to 6 years. As the correct measurement of age is crucial, the age of the children was certified by an official document in 70 per cent of the cases. In the remaining cases, it was verified as far as was possible, with both the mother and the father. Height and weight of the children were registered as well as any illness (malaria, cough, diarrhea, etc.) in the previous week.

The following ratios are usually used by nutritionists (see von Braun et al., 1989):
- Weight for height (WHZ) is usually considered the measurement that best expresses the child's present nutritional situation. The thin or 'wasted' child is regarded as showing evidence of recent nutritional deprivation.

- Weight for age (WAZ) reflects the total growth history of the child, but since weight can be rapidly lost or gained, it is also influenced by the child's recent nutrition and health experience.
- Height for age (HAZ) is a long term measure of a child's nutrition and health experience, since it represents the total growth achieved. It identifies 'stunted' children.

These anthropometric measures are compared to those of a reference population where food is freely available in quantity and quality and where the health status of the children is satisfactory.

The concept of z-score is used to express the extent to which a child's anthropometric measurement deviates from median or average age-specific measures in the reference population. The z-score is computed as follows for each child's observation:

$$\frac{\text{Child's actual measure - Reference value}}{\text{Standard deviation of reference population}}$$

A z-score of zero is 'normal', although one must allow for normal individual variation around that norm. Conventionally, a z-score value below minus 2 is considered as significant malnutrition, a z-score value below minus 3 is severe malnutrition. Five hundred seventy-five children were surveyed, including children in the Ranomafana. When extreme values of the z-score are omitted (the values were imposed to be within the following range: $-4<WHZ<5$; $-5<WAZ<5$; $-6<HAZ<5$), the total sample concerns 447 children.

The nutritional status of children is determined by a complex set of factors e.g. seasonality, sanitary environment, water quality, accessibility to health services, maternal activities, household incomes, etc. The IFPRI/FOFIFA surveys could not take into account all these factors as more specific nutrition questions would have been necessary. Therefore the determinant factors of malnutrition will not be determined through an in-depth analysis (econometric model).[9] However, the description of the situation by region, sex, or level of households income can give some important insights.

Nutritional Status Results

For the whole sample of children, only 5 per cent of the children are 'wasted', 1.6 per cent severely, according to their weight for height (WHZ) (Table 10.12). This is relatively low, but it must be noted that the second survey round does not correspond to the lean season in any of the regions. 28 per cent of the sample have a low weight for their age (WAZ) and 6 per cent are severely underweight. The most worrying figures relate to long term nutritional status (HAZ), with nearly 50 per cent of the children stunted, 21 per cent severely so.   These figures are similar to those found by SECALINE (1997). In fact, long term malnutrition must be a consequence of the difficulties faced by the households during the lean seasons.

Table 10.12 Percentage of the population importantly (z<-2) and severely (z<-3) malnourished, by region

	No.	Imp.	No.	Severe
		Weight/Height (WHZ)		
Majunga Plaines	4	13.6	1	4.4
Majunga HT	1	1.8	1	0.9
Fianar. HT	9	6.1	4	2.5
Fianar. C/F	2	2.6	1	1.1
Vakinankaratra	5	4.7	1	0.8
Ranomafana	4	4.9	3	3.7
Total	22	4.6	8	1.6
		Weight/Age (WAZ)		
Majunga Plaines	14	45.2	3	9.2
Majunga HT	13	17.2	1	0.5
Fianar. HT	43	28.9	9	6.2
Fianar. C/F	23	25.7	7	7.8
Vakinankaratra	41	37.6	10	9.4
Ranomafana	30	36.6	14	17.1
Total	134	28.1	30	6.2
		Height/Age (HAZ)		
Majunga Plaines	13	41.8	3	9.2
Majunga HT	35	44.4	14	18.4
Fianar. HT	75	49.1	31	20.6
Fianar. C/F	43	51.7	28	33.1
Vakinankaratra	61	55.7	25	22.7
Ranomafana	56	68.3	38	46.3
Total	227	47.4	101	21.1

Source: 1997 FPRI/FOFIFA household survey

By region, Majunga HT is the region where malnutrition is less severe; the good level of food consumption recorded by the survey seems rather consistent, noted through consumption as well as malnutrition measures. The situation in the Majunga Plaines reveals more contrasts, with a low occurrence of chronic severe malnutrition (HAZ), but a high frequency of low WAZ and WHZ. Yet, the per capita caloric consumption is among the highest in the sample: these results can come from the high disparities of the Majunga region (see discussion of income inequality, chapter 8) or they can illustrate the hypothesis put forward in the food consumption section that children can be more directly stricken by food shortages than adults. The situation in Ranomafana seems to be particularly difficult, with two-thirds of the children stunted.

Table 10.13 Percentage of important and severe malnutrition, by quartile of monthly food expenditures

		Weight/Height (WHZ)		
Quartile	No.	Imp.	No.	Severe
1	6	6.3	2	1.7
2	8	7.7	3	2.8
3	6	4.9	2	1.6
4	1	0.9	1	0.7

		Weight/Age (WAZ)		
Quartile	No.	Imp.	No.	Severe
1	38	37.0	5	4.7
2	30	27.9	10	9.0
3	33	24.8	5	3.4
4	33	29.5	11	9.3

		Height/Age (HAZ)		
Quartile	No.	Imp.	No.	Severe
1	45	45.9	22	21.9
2	55	50.2	22	19.9
3	71	53.5	31	23.7
4	56	48.7	26	23.0

Source: 1997 IFPRI/FOFIFA household survey

Table 10.13 shows that the level of food expenditure has a short term impact on reducing the number of wasted children; however, the long term impact on chronic malnutrition remains unclear. On the one hand, this could reflect the evolving situation of households; on the other hand more complex factors may interfere to determine the nutritional status of the children.

As in the case of income level and food expenditures, the level of education of the household head alone does not improve the nutritional status of the children (in a cross-tabulation not shown here), except that it is perhaps slightly related to improved long term nutrition.

The gender of the household head seems to have a clear influence on the nutritional status of the children (Table 10.14). Even if women are more sensitive to the nutritional needs of their children, this cannot compensate for the more difficult economic situation of the female-headed household.

Table 10.14 Percentage of important and severe malnutrition, by gender of the head of the household

	No.	Weight/Height (WHZ) Imp.	No.	Severe
F	6	16.8	4	11.0
M	17	4.0	4	0.9
	No.	Weight/Age (WAZ) Imp.	No.	Severe
F	11	33.7	2	4.9
M	123	29.3	28	6.7
	No.	Height/Age (HAZ) Imp.	No.	Severe
F	19	57.8	9	26.6
M	207	49.6	92	22.0

Source: 1997 IFPRI/FOFIFA household survey

Table 10.15 shows that significant differences also exist along gender lines: in the long run the girls are in better condition than the boys. This can perhaps be explained by the fact that they spend more time with their mothers, in particular during meal preparation so they may have better access to food. The surveys from EPM also recorded a more favorable situation for girls (INSTAT, 1995).

Table 10.15 Percentage of important and severe malnutrition, by gender of the children

	Weight/Height (WHZ)			
	No.	**Imp.**	**No.**	**Severe**
F	10	4.2	6	2.4
M	12	5.9	2	0.8
	Weight/Age (WAZ)			
	No.	**Imp.**	**No.**	**Severe**
F	59	23.9	11	4.6
M	75	36.7	18	8.9
	Height/Age (HAZ)			
	No.	**Imp.**	**No.**	**Severe**
F	109	43.9	42	17.1
M	118	57.8	59	28.8

Source: 1997 IFPRI/FOFIFA household survey

By age, no specific group could really be distinguished from one another in terms of nutritional status. Yet, some trends could be detected: average WHZ and WAZ scores seem to decline with the age of the children and chronic malnutrition seems to be more frequent in 2 to 3 year old children which may correspond to the consequences of weaning.

Conclusions

In terms of food consumption and nutritional status of the survey households, the main results can be summarized as follows:
- On average, the daily caloric consumption of the households is around 2,695 calories per adult-equivalent, 2,094 calories per capita, and

54 grams of proteins per capita. These values are approximately the minimum quantities required for a normal life set at 2,837 calories per adult-equivalent, 2,133 calories per capita, and 56 grams of proteins per capita. However, these means hide considerable regional and household disparities. The nutritional status of the children shows a rather critical situation as nearly 5 per cent of the children are 'wasted', 28 per cent have low height for age scores, but most worrisomely, nearly half of them are 'stunted'. The dominance of vegetables in the rural household diet, the large number of food-insecure households, and the prevalence of child malnutrition underscore the difficulties in ensuring the food security of the rural population of Madagascar.

- By region, the highest level of food consumption is recorded in the Majunga HT, certainly due to the important role of home production. Fianarantsoa C/F is the region with the lowest level of consumption. When the timing of the surveys are compared with the harvest and lean seasons, it can be concluded that on average, Majunga has a reasonable year-round level of consumption; some difficulties can be recorded in the Vakinankaratra during the lean season, but this period does not last long (2 months); Fianarantsoa faces a critical situation even outside the lean season.

- Although the level of consumption is, on average, acceptable for the Majunga Plaines, many children are found to be 'wasted'; this underscores the role of information campaigns targeted towards child nutrition. Moreover, average results (income, level of food consumption, etc.) often hide high regional disparities, in particular for the nutritional status of the children. Local interventions in rural areas should have the means to individually target malnourished children.

- Rice remains the basis of the diet, whatever the wealth level of the households. However, the caloric consumption strongly varies with variations in the price of rice. The elasticity of the total consumption related to income is 0.09. This result suggests that an increase of income is not sufficient to greatly improve the quantity of consumption of the households. Moreover, our analysis shows that the consumption of animal calories is more responsive to increases in income with an elasticity of 0.48. Therefore, an increase of income leads primarily to an improvement in the quality of the diet.

- As the level of education has a positive impact on consumption, educational programs concerning the nutritional value of foods and the diversity of the diet can be an efficient policy, complementary to efforts leading to increased incomes. It seems that female-headed households with young children are the first to be affected by food shortages thus they should be given priority in targeting disaster and other relief programs.

Notes

1. SECALINE gives a figure of 49 per cent for the share of rice for the rural areas at the national level, but this figure takes Toliara into account (28 per cent of rice in the total calorie consumption); the share of rice is 48 per cent for Fianarantsoa and 64 per cent for Majunga; the share of cassava is 18 per cent at the national level and 25 per cent for Fianarantsoa.

2. In order to compare with the calculations made in 1992, the adult-equivalent taken corresponds to 1 for the adults and 0.7 for the children. To ensure compatibility, a kapoaka of rice has been set to 310 g of rice in 1992 and might therefore differ from estimations elsewhere.

3. This section has benefited from the advice of H. Bouis of the Food Consumption and Nutrition Division, IFPRI.

4. We used the Haussman test: identifier = SUMRICE (rice field area possessed by the household) and VALUE (value in ariary of household assets); the test of validity of the identifiers shows that they are highly correlated with income (F=38.688) and that they are not correlated to the error terms $R^2 = 0.000$; t=0.23; and -0.47 respectively). The correlations between the error term and income are significant (t=-4.851 and t=-7.530 for total consumption and animal consumption respectively).

5. Moreover, the same models run with the consumption by adult-equivalent and the number of children in the household also give a consumption significantly lower for the children compared to the minimum required intake.

6. Big ceremonies such as Famadina, the reburying of the dead, have not been considered.

7. The elasticity of Y related to X for a semilog equation of the form: $Y=a+b\ln X+u$ is equal to b/mean(Y).

8. Elasticity $_{income/price}$ * Elasticity $_{consumption/income}$ = 0.257*0.09 = 0.023.

9. Some precedent analysis by IFPRI and other research institutions with the same level of precision of this survey did not give significant and satisfying results as too many variables were omitted from the regressions, giving biased coefficients.

11 The Critical Triangle Between Environmental Sustainability, Economic Growth, and Poverty Alleviation

MANFRED ZELLER, CÉCILE LAPENU, BART MINTEN, ELIANE RALISON, DÉSIRÉ RANDRIANAIVO, and CLAUDE RANDRIANARISOA

Introduction

Most of the world's poor and food insecure depend directly or indirectly on agriculture for their livelihood. Much-needed increases in agricultural production can in principal come about through two pathways of rural development: expansion of cultivated area or increases in yields. We term the former the pathway of agricultural extensification since it does not require increases in agricultural productivity by using modern inputs, such as high-yielding seed varieties and mineral fertilizers. Shifting cultivation, by burning tropical forests to gain arable land, is a prime example of the first pathway. The second is called the pathway of agricultural intensification (Boserup, 1965; Pingali et al., 1987; Ruthenberg, 1980). Which factors induce rural communities to follow a certain pathway of land and forest resource use, and how can policy assist in achieving environmentally sustainable pathways of development while at the same time improving incomes and alleviating poverty? In this chapter, we seek to shed some light on this complex question, using a descriptive and econometric analysis of community level data from Madagascar.

Conceptual Framework

Induced Innovation Theory

Induced innovation theory suggests that environmental degradation can be self-correcting, as population growth, increasing resource scarcity, and environmental externalities induce new agricultural and resource management

209

practices (Boserup, 1965) and new forms of collective regulation of common property resources (Kikuchi and Hayami, 1980; Ruttan and Hayami, 1984). However, this early work on induced institutional innovation is overly optimistic, and tends to overlook the fact that evolution, including long term institutional equilibria and the corresponding pathways of development, is itself dependent on the initial stock of social capital, the actions by the state, and the distributive consequences of institutional change (Baland and Platteau, 1998).

Ruthenberg's (1980) survey of literature on farming systems in the tropics documents many agricultural innovations that were associated with increasing population growth and market integration in different agroecological zones. He explains the observed technical changes in crop and soil management with the occurrence of increased scarcity of land and declining soil fertility. More recent literature, reviewed by Scherr and Hazell (1994), has described similar endogenous processes leading to pathways of agricultural intensification.

The Critical Triangle of Rural Development: The Case of Madagascar

Vosti and Reardon (1997) conceptualize a critical triangle that links three development objectives: economic growth, poverty alleviation, and environmental sustainability. These authors emphasize the importance of a simultaneous consideration of all three development objectives, plus possible links between and trade-offs among them.

In recent years, Madagascar has become internationally known for its rich and unique biodiversity that is threatened by rapid deforestation (Jarosz, 1993). Since the mid-1980s, Madagascar has been a focus of international conservation efforts with international development organizations providing loan and assistance programs explicitly aimed at environmental objectives. In 1984, the government of Madagascar embarked on a National Strategy for Conservation and Development (Larson, 1994) that recognized the critical triangle by including environmental conservation, economic development, and human needs into the policy framework. However, as pointed out by Gezon (1997), a number of important environmental projects implemented during the early 1990s sought to address the links between poverty and environmental degradation, but failed to take into account their economic sustainability.

The national survey, 'Enquête Permanente auprès des Ménages', conducted in 1993 by INSTAT, had few questions that touched on the critical triangle. Apart from some in-depth surveys in or near protected areas, no statistically representative data on a national or regional scale exist to the knowledge of the authors that contain both agroecological and socioeconomic data and that can be meaningfully exploited for causal analysis. Yet, the existence of such combined databases is a precondition for in-depth analysis of the underlying determinants of rural development, economic growth, poverty alleviation, and environmental sustainability. One recent data set collected by the authors attempts to combine these topics, and is the basis for the analysis of this chapter.

Changes in Rural Development: a Descriptive Analysis

Major Trends Characterizing the Critical Triangle of Rural Development

Rice is the major crop and the staple food in Madagascar. For the nation as a whole, about half of calories consumed are from rice (Ravelosoa, 1998; SECALINE, 1997; chapter 10). Rice is mainly grown on irrigated lowland fields, or to a small extent on rainfed upland plots. In Table 11.1, irrigated rice yields are shown for the agroecological regions in the sample. For all regions, average rice yields declined from 1,765 kg per ha to about 1,540 kg per ha between 1987 and 1997. Yet, important differences across regions exist. In the Vakinankaratra region, the yields remained the same. Major declines in rice yields can be noticed for the Majunga regions (Minten et al., 1998). Insofar as rice yields can be viewed as a performance indicator for the agricultural sector as a whole, we conclude that there was either stagnation or decline in productivity.

In the community survey, we sought to ask about the changes in poverty over the ten years prior to the survey. Poverty encompasses many dimensions such as food insecurity, malnutrition, and illiteracy. Most of them are difficult to measure through community level surveys. Moreover, we were interested in the changes in poverty over the ten year period and, therefore, had to find variables that could be easily recalled by our respondents. One such variable, we believe, is the rural wage rate. In Madagascar, rural wages are often paid in rice and are commonly measured in 'kapoaka', a tin can used by the Nestlé Company for its condensed milk that holds 285 gm of white rice. Table 11.1 differentiates wage rates by agroecological regions. We note that wage rates have declined over the past ten years for all regions as a whole, but important differences exist among regions. The wage rate improved in the Vakinankaratra region, whereas the other regions experienced modest (Fianarantsoa) or severe declines in wage rates (Majunga HT). Insofar as wage rates determine the ability of the poorest of the rural poor in Madagascar to feed their families, we conclude that food insecurity and rural poverty increased.

Table 11.1 Indicators of economic growth, poverty, and resource degradation, by region and year

Region	Yield of irrigated rice kg per ha	Number of 'kapaoka' of rice paid per day worked	Index for change in fertility of upland soil*
Majunga Plaines			
1987	2,664.3	9.5	
1997	2,245.5	8.5	1.3
Majunga HT			
1987	1,927.1	14.7	
1997	1,469.7	8.0	1.2
Fianar. HT			
1987	1,704.6	4.2	
1997	1,611.4	3.7	0.3
Fianar. C/F			
1987	1,475.3	6.1	
1997	1,213.2	5.0	0.9
Vakinankaratra			
1987	1,853.7	6.5	
1997	1,851.9	6.7	0.9
All regions			
1987	1,765.3	7.6	
1997	1,539.5	5.7	0.8

* The soil fertility index: 3=improved, 2=no change, 1=reduced, 0=severely degraded

Source: Data from 1997 IFPRI/FOFIFA community survey

The change in soil fertility is the third indicator shown in Table 11.1, reflecting the environmental objective of the critical triangle. Community leaders were asked how the fertility of the upland in their community has changed. We find that soil fertility significantly decreased on average for all regions, with major degradation observed in the Fianarantsoa HT, the Vakinankaratra, and the coastal and escarpment area of the Fianarantsoa C/F. The rice yield, wage rate, and soil fertility variables in our analysis serve as indicators of the trends in agricultural growth, poverty, and environmental degradation, respectively. Overall, the data reveal quite disturbing trends. Only one of the five regions improved in two of the three criteria over the ten year period.

The Expansion of the Agricultural Frontier in Rural Madagascar

Rice yields have stagnated or declined in Madagascar during the ten year period covered by the survey. This is not evidence that an intensification strategy was chosen by the rural households and communities as shown in Table 11.2. While rice land area grew by about 5.3 per cent as an average for all regions, the area of cultivated upland increased by about 24.0 per cent. Considering that the population in the survey regions grew by about 3.5 per cent per year over this time, or by more than 35 per cent over the previous ten years, the rate of growth in arable area is actually below that of the growth in population.[1]

Table 11.2 Indices of change in area of grassland, forest, arable upland, and irrigated lowland, 1987-1997*

Index for change in	Majunga Plaines	Majunga HT	Fianar. HT	Fianar. C/F	Vakinan-karatra	All regions
bushland	79.22	86.70	67.50	86.48	84.33	79.91
primary forest	83.46	88.45	43.28	72.96	69.84	67.35
secondary forest	80.42	79.83	63.19	76.25	67.54	71.96
upland	131.58	129.63	134.19	107.26	119.79	123.96
lowland	112.60	104.58	105.66	104.04	105.66	105.32

* The figures are indices for which the value 100 was given for the area held in 1987 by the community; for example, an index of 120 implies a 20 % average increase in the area of the sample villages belonging to a particular region

Source: Data from 1997 IFPRI/FOFIFA community survey

The expansion of the agricultural frontier came at the expense of forest-, bush-, and grassland. These land types are usually held as common property resources but become, under Malagasy law, private property when cultivated by succesive generations of the same family.[2] On average for all regions, the largest losses were experienced for area under primary forests (Table 11.2). Indicating the level of primary forests as 100 for 1987, the index fell to 67.4 in 1997. The loss in secondary forest amounts to about 28 per cent, whereas the loss in grass- and bushland was about 20 per cent. If this rate of deforestation continues, the survey regions could be without primary forests in two to three decades.[3]

That the agricultural frontier can still be expanded in many Malagasy villages is evident from the survey data. On average for all regions, 59 per cent of villages report that there is additional land available for expanding upland cultivation; 50 per cent of villages for expanding irrigated land, and 35 per cent of villages for both types of land. Despite this, the average holding of upland per household declined from 1.74 ha in 1987 to 1.28 ha in 1997. Clearly, growth in population has outpaced growth of agricultural land in many communities and pressures for agricultural intensification have tended to increase over time.

The Three Major Pathways of Rural Development in Madagascar

We conclude from this analysis that about half of the villages in the survey regions will still be able to choose the extensification pathway in the near and distant future. These more land-abundant communities may maintain their living standards with their low input agriculture for some time, continuing to expand arable area and degrade soils. Yet, while such extensive expansion of agricultural production may meet subsistence needs in the short run, the continued degradation of forests, watersheds, and soils has implications for future agricultural productivity, health, and nutrition (von Braun, 1997). Current subsistence and food security are then likely to be at the expense of future generations. The households are most certainly aware of these trade-offs; however extreme poverty can lead to high time preference rates. For example, Lapenu et al., (1998) show that households in a significant number of sample villages needed more time to collect firewood in 1997 compared to ten years earlier. In these villages with increasing firewood shortages, the need for reforestation was perceived more frequently than in villages with below average time needed to collect firewood.

The remaining half of the villages no longer have the possibility of further expanding cultivated land. In order to maintain or improve their living standards, households in these land-constrained villages can in principal pursue two other generic development pathways: agricultural intensification (and related increased trade and diversification into off-farm enterprises) or migration. The main, and certainly most promising and viable strategy in the long run, is to intensify agriculture, thus making it more productive and environmentally sustainable.[4] The third strategic response to land scarcity is to migrate, i.e. leave the village seasonally or forever. Its consequences for poverty alleviation and the environment can be quite different from an agricultural intensification strategy, as shown later.

Trends in Access to Financial and Commodity Markets and to Public Services

A number of factors that are considered to have exogenously evolved during the period 1987-1997 are expected to have influenced the phenomenon that villages differ in their development pathways. These factors include access to financial and to agricultural input and output markets, and access to public services.

Access to microfinance institutions As in most low-income countries in Subsaharan Africa, the formal banking sector has barely penetrated rural Madagascar. Until 1986, the state-owned Banque pour le Développement Rural was the main institution providing loans to farmers. Apart from the requirement of tedious paperwork and collateral that poor households can neither understand nor provide, the one-way travel time of the average smallholder to the nearest bank branch is 4.75 hours. In other words, it takes an entire day to apply for a loan. The travel times to banks, post offices, and postal savings banks also increased during the ten year period (Table 11.3). In the early 1990s, a number of village bank programs and credit and savings cooperative societies were introduced and subsequently expanded to better reach rural smallholders, especially in the Vakinankaratra, the Fianarantsoa HT, at Lac Alaotra, and in Majunga Plaines (Fraslin, 1997). The survey obtained information on the existence and size of member owned financial institutions in the village that allowed the definition of a variable that measures the density of village-level participation in financial institutions. This information was only obtained for 1997, but it is safe to assume that none of the villages had access to similar organizations in 1987 because they were all formed after that year. Eleven per cent of households participated in member based financial institutions in 1997.

Access to agricultural input and output markets   Survey data not presented here for lack of space, show that access to markets for seed rice and farm equipment improved, while access to mineral fertilizer, pesticides, herbicides, vegetable seeds, and veterinary inputs worsened over the survey period. Particularly noteworthy is the large decline in access to fertilizer markets. On the other hand, the access to agricultural output markets improved somewhat, in particular for rice.

Table 11.3   Participation in microfinance programs and travel time to financial institutions

	All regions	
	1987	**1997**
Rainy season travel time to nearest bank, in hours	4.33	4.75
Rainy season travel time to nearest post office or postal savings bank, in hours	3.59	4.04
Percent of households participating in credit	0.00	11.37

Source: Data from 1997 IFPRI/FOFIFA community survey

Community access to public services   We asked about the travel time from the village to over fifteen public services that are provided by the central or local government. Travel time in the rainy season using the commonly used modes of transport in the village, ranges between two and four hours. Travel time to access a public phone is highest among all public services. It takes an average of two hours to travel to either the nearest primary and secondary school, or the nearest health post or hospital. For all regions taken as a whole average travel times are either the same or slightly higher in 1997 compared to 1987.

A Causal Diagram of the Critical Triangle

Three major pathways of development are distinguished in this analysis. The first is the extensification pathway, that is, the continuation of low input, low output agriculture by expanding cultivated land area and subsequently reducing fallow years until soil fertility is depleted. The second pathway is to intensify agricultural production and increase yields by exploiting access to financial and commodity markets, thus adopting more capital-intensive, higher yielding technology and reaping the benefits of interregional specialization. Migration is the third major pathway that we observe from the data. The migration pathway is similar to the extensification pathway; if migrants are attracted by the possibility of farming new land, as we will confirm in the econometric analysis, the pressure on natural resources is simply shifted from one region to another.

Hence, our conceptual framework stipulates four endogenous outcome variables: rice yield, wage rate, changes in soil fertility, and changes in the area of upland. These are influenced by three strategies leading to different pathways of rural development. The villagers' choice of strategy is, of course, endogenous, as it is influenced by the endogenous wage rate, rice yields, and soil fertility, by the socioeconomic and agroecological characteristics of the region, by access to financial and commodity markets and public services, and by the various institutional arrangements that regulate the use of common and privately owned forest, grassland, and arable land resources.

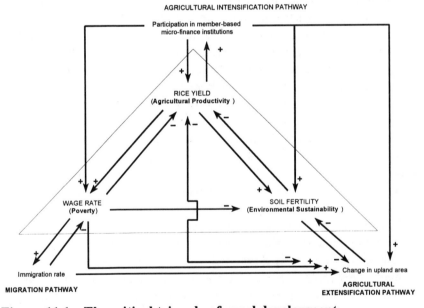

Figure 11.1   The critical triangle of rural development

Figure 11.1 presents a causal diagram of the critical triangle of rural development. Arrows between the variables represent relationships. A positive sign implies that an increase in the value of the variable from which the arrow originates is expected to induce an increase in the value of the other variable. For example, we hypothesize that higher lowland rice yields will decrease the incentives for further expansion of upland since the returns to lowland rice production become relatively higher. This relationship is reflected by an arrow with a negative sign.

Let us consider first the arrows that feed into the upland area from the other endogenous outcomes or strategies. These arrows come from access to financial markets, the wage rate, the soil fertility of upland, and the net immigration rate. First, improved access to financial markets (reflected either through lower interest rates, lower transaction costs for clients, or higher amounts available for borrowing) will make the capital used in rice production and in upland fields less costly. With the reduced cost of capital, the profitability of these enterprises rises, leading to increases in yields in both lowland and upland areas. Second, with increasing wage rates, farm households will tend to choose more labor-extensive crop production technologies. Since cultivation of irrigated rice is more labor intensive than most upland crops, higher wage rates are hypothesized to induce lower labor input and therefore lower yields of rice, but increased expansion of upland area. Third, the expansion of upland area is expected to be positively influenced by a higher net immigration into the village, since migrants are expected to cultivate new lands not already occupied by villagers. Fourth, and last, expansion of upland cultivation will have negative effects on soil fertility, due to shorter fallow periods for already cultivated land or increased cultivation of marginal or infertile land. The negative arrow from soil fertility to upland area change reflects the vicious, unsustainable cycle of extensification and soil degradation: lower soil fertility will induce farmers to abandon fields after only a few harvests and seek new farmland to cultivate.

Since most investments in conserving soil fertility are labor intensive (e.g. spreading manure, planting trees, or terracing land), rising labor costs will reduce the relative profitability of soil conservation investments. Moreover, we hypothesize that increased participation in member based financial institutions will improve soil fertility because it reduces the cost of capital and increases availabile investment for conservation.

In the causal model of Figure 11.1, the net immigration rate is perceived to be a function of the endogenous wage rate. We hypothesize that villages with high wage rates will attract migrants. As more migrants come into those high wage villages, they will increase the supply of labor and therefore push wage rates down, an effect that is expressed through a negative feedback loop. In addition to immigration, wage rates are hypothesized to be influenced by two other endogenous variables: access to financial markets and lowland rice yields. As access to financial markets improves, the cost of capital to the community and its households decreases, thus increasing the marginal return to labor and pushing wage rates up. Similarly, if yields of irrigated rice (a labor-intensive crop) increase, the marginal return to labor used in rice production increases, resulting in an increase in wages.

Lowland rice yields are influenced by four variables. Two of them, improved access to financial markets and wage rates, have already been discussed. We further expect that increases in crop production on upland will reduce incentives for households to intensify rice production, in particular if rice production is more capital and labor intensive than upland production and if ample opportunities to expand upland continue to exist. The same type of argument can be made for the expected effect of soil fertility of upland on lowland rice yields. If upland soils are fertile and productive, and one can get good harvests on upland, little economic incentive exists for increasing yields of irrigated rice.

We choose to model the access to member based financial institutions as an endogenous outcome variable for the following reasons. First, as mentioned above, financial institutions that reach smallholders in Madagascar were formed only during the ten year survey period. The placement of financial institutions is driven by a variety of factors that directly or indirectly determine loan repayment performance or transaction costs for the financial institution and the client (Sharma and Zeller, 1999). Second, as Pitt et al., (1995) demonstrate, failing to correct for the possible nonrandom placement of government programs can result in substantial biases in the estimates of the programs' effects. In the case of Madagascar, one can observe that placement of financial institutions was concentrated mostly in areas with high agricultural potential and above average infrastructure. More particularly, we hypothesize that lowland rice yields are a good indicator of agricultural productivity, and that financial institutions tend to place programs in villages with above average lowland rice yields in order to increase their performance. There are, as Pitt et al., (1995) argue, other, unobserved variables that determine the placement of programs. In this case, simple ordinary least squares of cross-sectional data may over- or underestimate the effect of access to credit on yields. In order to control for endogenous placement of programs, Pitt et al., (1995) use a fixed-effect model that sweeps out unobservable characteristics.

The causal diagram in Figure 11.1 could be further extended by including additional endogenous variables if one would wish to extend the time horizon of the analysis beyond the ten years considered in this analysis. In the very long run, everything is endogenous. We choose to conceive only the six variables shown in Figure 11.1 to be endogenous during the time span of our analysis. The main reason is that the ten year period is sufficiently short that access to public services and infrastructure is not likely to change much as a result of endogenous processes.

Econometric Model and its Results

With information on endogenous strategies and outcomes at two points in time, the potential biases resulting from unobservable characteristics can be avoided by using a fixed-effect model (Pitt et al., 1995). Figure 11.1 shows a total of six endogenous variables that depend on each other. To obtain consistent and unbiased estimates, we apply a two-stage least squares model with fixed effects (Greene, 1993).

The structural equations of the model are:

(1) Participation in financial institutions $(Y_1) = f(Y_2, X_i, BANK)$,
(2) Rice yield $(Y_2) = f(Y_1, Y_4, Y_6, X_i, TSTRIZ, PEREAU)$,
(3) Net immigration rate $(Y_3) = f(Y_1, Y_4, X_i, TRANHUMD, MONEYTRA)$,
(4) Wage rate $(Y_4) = f(Y_1, Y_2, X_i, SHARINCO)$,
(5) Change in upland $(Y_5) = f(Y_1, Y_2, Y_3, Y_4, Y_6, X_i, TSTPAT, A34BACC2, MARKMAN)$,
(6) Change in soil fertility $(Y_6) = f(Y_1, Y_2, Y_5, X_i, CONFLICT)$,

where X_i is a vector of exogenous variables, and Y_j is the vector containing the six endogenous variables. For brevity, the variables contained in X_i are only shown in the regression results itself. They have been included in the regression as hypothesized causal determinants of the dependent variables, following the conceptual framework outlined in the previous sections. The variables that are explicitly named in the above equations serve as instrumenting variables to identify the estimation.[5] The name, definition, mean, median, and standard deviation of all variables used in the regression model are shown in Table 11.4.[6]

Table 11.4 Descriptive statistics of variables used in regressions*

Name of variable	Definition	Mean	Median	St. dev.
OUTREACH	% of households participating in credit program	5.68	0.00	29.28
RNATPOP	Annual natural population growth rate, in %	3.56	3.45	3.33
RNETIMIG	Net annual immigration rate in village, in %	0.01	0.00	0.87
WAGERATE	Number of 'kapoaka' of rice per labor day	6.67	5.00	4.36
CHTAN	Index for increase in upland area, 1987=100	111.98	100.00	25.55
YLDRICI	Irrigated rice yield	1,652.40	1,500.00	760.22
SOILFERT	Soil fertility change, from 3=improved to 0=very degraded	1.40	2.00	0.80
ACCINPUT	Mean of indices of access to seven agriculture input markets, 100=1987	0.99	1.00	0.26
A34ACC1	Change in access to fertilizer dealers during past five years, from 2=improved to 0=worse	0.92	1.00	0.42
A34BACC2	Change in access to buyers of upland crops, from 2=improved to 0=worse	1.04	1.00	0.46
MARKRIZ	Interacted term: price of rice (PRIZ)* index of access to rice markets	89.43	59.52	78.44
BANK	Rainy season travel time in hours to nearest bank	4.54	3.00	6.19
BANKRISK	Interacted term: BANK times number of covariate risks in last ten years	33.00	0.00	75.13
MONEYTRA	Rainy season travel time in hours to nearest post office or postal savings bank	3.81	2.00	5.25
DELEC	Electricity in village, 1=yes, 0=no	0.05	0.00	0.21
EDUC	Rainy season travel time to educational institutions	2.09	1.33	2.67
HOSPITAL	Rainy season travel time to hospital or health post	2.11	1.50	2.86
PEREAU	% of irrigated rice land	50.01	60.00	37.81
FOODPOOR	Interacted term: LANDLT1*PRIZ	2,189.20	1,200.00	2,760.30
SHARINCO	Share of primary income source in village income	60.43	60.00	16.20
PRIZ	Consumer price of 1 'kapaoka' of white rice	63.30	60.00	38.85
PRICAUTR	Interacted term: price of rice (PRIZ)*rice	73.11	50.71	86.79

	self-sufficiency index (autoriz)			
FOKDENS	Number of people per square km in village	231.19	92.86	496.21
POPDENS	Number of people per square km in firaisana	67.43	34.83	103.26
LANDLT1	Number of households in village owning less than 1 ha of upland	29.59	20.00	29.93
LANDSCAP	Interacted term: social capital (SOCCAP) with LANDLT1	2,211.52	0.00	14,235.01
SOCCAP	Social capital: number of present informal groups* years of existence	68.24	0.00	360.96
PRICAUTR	Interacted term: price of rice (PRIZ) with LANDLT1	1,945.07	1,000.00	2,677.87
AUTORIZ	Index of rice self-sufficiency of village, 100 = 1987	1.07	1.00	0.41
TSTPAT	Possibility of extension of upland, 1=y, 0=n, 1987=1	0.79	1.00	0.41
TSTRIZ	Possibility of extension of rice land 1=y, 0=n, 1987=1	0.75	1.00	0.43
TSTRITA	Interacted term: tstpat*tstriz	0.67	1.00	0.47
CONFLICT	Number of conflicts about grassland/bushland	0.15	0.00	0.97
TRANHUMD	Distance in km to cattle grazing area	28.35	10.00	34.57
PRICEREL	Consumer price of rice divided by price of cassava	0.80	1.10	1.69
MARKMAN	Interacted term: price of cassava*index of access to nonrice agriculture output markets (A34BACC2)	50.91	96.90	109.64
WATPAT	Interacted term: WAGERATE TSTPAT	5.00	5.62	5.07
OUTRINPU	Interacted term: ACCINPUT OUTREACH	5.85	0	27.11
OUTRFERT	Interacted term: A34ACC1 OUTREACH	5.56	0	28.81

* No.=376 from 188 villages

Source: Data from 1997 IFPRI/FOFIFA community survey

Tables 11.5 through 11.10 list the results of the regressions for each of the six equations. With very few exceptions, all signs of regression coefficients are as hypothesized. In general, the models for participation in member based financial institutions (Table 11.5) and for net immigration (Table 11.7) have a low adjusted R^2 of 0.15 and 0.16, respectively. The other models have a higher explanatory power with a R^2 ranging from 0.34 (Table 11.9) for the change in upland to 0.68 for rice yield (Table 11.6).

Table 11.5 Determinants of participation in member-based financial institutions[a]

Variables	Coefficient	Standard error	t-value
YLDRICIR	0.12817E-01	0.71157E-02	1.801[c]
BANK	-0.21288	0.72728	-0.293
DELEC	15.190	22.492	0.675
SOCCAP	0.18258E-01	0.11007E-01	1.659[c]
FOKDENS	-0.10264E-01	0.13716E-01	-0.748
LANDLT1	0.20022	0.17806	1.124
LANDSCAP	-0.16480E-03	0.28227E-03	-0.584
Constant	-19.687	13.338	-1.476[b]

[a] Dependent variable is OUTREACH with mean of 5.68 and standard deviation of 29.28; number of observations: 376; degrees of freedom = 179; R-squared = 0.59 and adjusted R-squared = 0.15

[b], [c] Indicate significance at the 15 % and 10 % levels respectively

Source: Data from 1997 IFPRI/FOFIFA community survey

Determinants of Community Access to Member Based Financial Institutions

Participation in financial services can be perceived as the joint outcome of determinants of supply and demand for these services. The model estimates these determinants in a reduced form as here we are not interested in studying the formation of financial institutions (Table 11.5). The regression results indicate that formal market participation significantly increases with higher yields (YLDRICI) in the village and with higher social capital (SOCCAP). The former effect is likely to be a supply-driven one as program managers seek to place institutions in villages with high economic returns so as to improve loan repayment rates. As most credit programs target agricultural enterprises (Zeller, 1998), the yields of rice as the major crop can be a good predictor of such returns. The effect of social capital is interpreted as a demand-side effect: social capital encourages and promotes villagers' participation in semiformal credit groups or cooperative societies. Social capital is measured by the number of informal self-help groups, multiplied by the number of years of their existence during the previous ten years. Informal group action is expected to benefit participation in other groups since experiences gained in the formation and management of informal groups make it easier for community members to perform similar functions in member based microfinance institutions. The identifying variable in the regression is the travel time from the village to the nearest bank branch (BANK). Its coefficient has the expected negative sign but is highly insignificant. All credit programs in Madagascar rely to some extent on branches of commercial or agricultural banks for depositing savings, and, in many instances, for channeling lending funds from donor to village groups. Since the travel time from the village to the bank influences the transaction costs of the program, and since credit programs are presumably concerned with cost recovery, villages close to a bank branch are found to have a higher chance of having access to credit.

Table 11.6 Determinants of yields of irrigated rice[a]

Variables	Coefficient	Standard error	t-value
CHTAN	-0.47583	3.5631	-0.134
SOILFERT	-36.605	114.32	-0.320
WAGERATE	-30.095	32.101	-0.938
OUTREACH	20.107	7.6738	2.620[c]
OUTRFERT	-12.407	6.6113	-1.877[b]
PRIZ	-3.6858	2.7553	-1.338
MARKRIZ	0.39802	0.94583	0.421
MARKMAN	0.45386E-01	0.46810	0.097
TSTRIZI	-95.094	91.067	-1.044
A34ACC1	136.62	105.60	1.294
PEREAU	2.8289	2.6442	1.070
PRICEREL	83.247	21.707	3.835[c]
PRICAUTR	-1.1088	1.7382	-0.638
AUTORIZ	-269.62	256.21	-1.052
Constant	2177.7	588.08	3.703[c]

[a] Dependent variable is YLDRICIR with mean of 1,652.40 and standard deviation of 760.22; number of observations = 376; degrees of freedom = 172; R-squared = 0.86 and adjusted R-squared = 0.69

[b], [c] Indicate significance at the 10 % and 5 % levels respectively

Source: Data from 1997 IFPRI/FOFIFA community survey

We conclude from this regression that villages with higher agricultural productivity seem to be preferred by financial institutions since most of them lend for agricultural and food processing activities.

Determinants of Lowland Rice Yields

Table 11.6 shows the results of the regression concerning rice yields. Again, all signs are as expected. Yields significantly increase with improved access to credit (OUTREACH). The coefficient is very robust to alternative specifications of the model, and is significant at the 1 per cent level. The direct marginal effect of an increase of 1 per cent more households in the village being members of a microfinance institution raises average lowland rice yields at the community level by 20 kg per ha. This yields an elasticity of lowland rice yields with respect to credit access of 0.069. This positive and significant effect would not occur if capital were not a binding factor in the farm sector of Madagascar. As Zeller (1994) shows, informal and formal lenders alike frequently ration loans, and about half of the rural sample households have been subjected to credit rationing.

The access to fertilizer markets (A34ACC1) has the expected positive effect on lowland rice yields, but is insignificant. When multiplying access to fertilizer (A34ACC1) with access to financial markets (OUTREACH), the interaction term (OUTRFERT) has a negative coefficient significant at the 10 per cent level. This implies that the effect of access to credit on yields diminishes at the margin as access to fertilizer markets improves. Similar reasoning holds for the effect of fertilizer when the access to capital markets improves. This result suggests that access to fertilizer dealers acts as a substitute for access to financial institutions, and vice versa. Indeed, fertilizer dealers have been found to advance loans for fertilizer, and obtain repayment when buying the harvest.[7] Moreover, some microfinance programs provide credit in kind, mostly in the form of seed and fertilizer.

This finding is in line with the negative, though highly insignificant, coefficient of the change in upland area (CHTAN) and soil fertility of upland (SOILFERT). The higher the upland soil fertility (mostly found in the hillsides and slopes) and the greater the possibility of expanding upland, the lower the incentive to intensify rice production through, e.g. investments in improving existing irrigation and drainage systems. Similar results are obtained for the possibility of expanding irrigated lowlands (TSTRIZI). If a community still has additional area that can be terraced for irrigation, the yields of rice are, on average, 95 kg per ha lower than in land-constrained villages. Again, if further land expansion is possible, be it upland or lowland, less incentives for agricultural intensification exist. These results empirically confirm the Boserup induced innovation model: when land becomes scarce and its opportunity cost rises, rural households and communities seek to adopt technology and alter their institutional arrangements for the management of land in order to increase its productivity and return. As expected, higher wages (WAGERATE) reduce the yield of labor-intensive rice, although the coefficient is insignificant. The elasticity of rice yield with respect to wage rate is measured as 0.12. In summary, the most important determinants of rice yield are access to financial markets and availability of idle land that can be used for expanding cultivation.

Determinants of Migration

The dependent variable net immigration (RNETIMIG) is the average annual rate of net immigration into a village over the previous ten years. Table 11.7 shows the regression results. As expected, migrants respond to wage differentials, although this relationship is highly insignificant. The elasticity of immigration with respect to wage rates is measured at 1.74, that is, a 1 per cent increase in wage rates in a village increases the net immigration rate into the village by 1.74 per cent. In contrast, the net immigration rate (with a mean of 0.13 per cent per year for all villages) significantly increases by an absolute 0.66 per cent if a village has a possibility of expanding both upland and irrigated lowland (TSTRITA). In other words, villages with ample land have a five times higher net immigration rate compared to villages with constraints for future land expansion. The size of this coefficient shows that rural-to-rural migration is largely driven by the possibility of further expanding the agricultural frontier. The negative coefficient for the distance to grazing areas of cattle (TRANHUMD) supports this finding.

Migrants prefer villages that have lower travel time to institutions for transferring money or sending letters (MONEYTRA). As migrant families maintain their ties with their extended family in the home region, sending and receiving money and letters are important. Each additional hour of travel time to the post office or savings bank significantly reduces the net immigration rate by 0.12 per cent. This translates into an elasticity of 7. Controlling for all other factors, migrants seem to prefer villages with higher population density, either at the village (FOKDENS) or district (POPDENS) level. While the former is significant at the 20 per cent level, the latter is not. Social capital (SOCCAP) has a positive, but insignificant effect on the rate of immigration from the village. With an increasing percentage of households owning less than one hectare of upland, the positive effect of social capital on immigration diminishes (LANDSCAP). In other words, as more virtually landless households live in the village, pressure on idle land presumably increases and a countervailing power against further immigration may begin to gain strength, reducing the positive effect of social capital on immigration at the margin. Just as trade unions seek to protect the wages of their members, the landless class in rural villages may be able to form coalitions and exert a political voice that could perhaps undermine and work against the interests of the land-rich households that attempt to import cheap labor from other regions.

Table 11.7 Determinants of migration[a]

Variables	Coefficient	Standard error	t-value
WAGERATE	0.17356E-01	0.70694E-01	0.246
WATPAT	-0.87747E-01	0.52580E-01	-1.669[c]
TSTRITA	0.66022	0.39019	1.692[c]
HOSPITAL	0.12580	0.85311E-01	1.475[b]
EDUC	0.38938E-01	0.83788E-01	0.465
MONEYTRA	-0.12592	0.46989E-01	-2.680[d]
POPDENS	0.13163E-03	0.20789E-02	0.063
TRANHUMD	-0.58849E-03	0.29993E-02	-0.196
SOCCAP	0.36156E-03	0.45638E-03	0.792
LANDSCAP	-0.12310E-04	0.11700E-04	-1.052
FOKDENS	0.84745E-03	0.60349E-03	1.404
Constant	-0.25177	0.59452	-0.423

a Dependent variable is RNETIMIG with mean of -0.07 and standard deviation of 1.21; number of observations = 376; degrees of freedom = 175; R-squared = 0.61 and adjusted R-squared = 0.16

b, c, d Indicate significance at the 15 %, 10 %, and 5 % levels respectively

Source: Data from 1997 IFPRI/FOFIFA community survey

Determinants of Rural Wages

Improved community access to financial markets (OUTREACH) increases the wage rate, although the estimated coefficient is insignificant. Villages with higher population density (FOKDENS) and higher diversification of income sources (SHARINCO) have significantly higher wage rates. These results appear to be caused by the wage-enhancing effects of increased diversification of the rural economy that comes with higher population density and, linked with this, lower transaction costs in trade. As can be seen from the regression coefficient (RNETIMIG) in Table 11.8, rural migration depresses wages in villages that receive migrants and increases wages in villages that sent migrants. This result confirms the previous argument that the landless class in migrant-receiving villages may be negatively affected by migrants and has therefore built up political and social coalitions that dampen further immigration. As expected, since most wage laborers perform labor services for agricultural enterprises, improved agricultural productivity, measured by the yields of the major crop (YLDRICI), increases the wage rate (through the increase of the value of the marginal product from labor used in agriculture). The elasticity of the wage rate with respect to yields is measured at 0.33.

Table 11.8 Determinants of rural wage rate[a]

Variables	Coefficient	Standard error	t-value
RNETIMIG	-0.45322	0.38361	-1.181
YLDRICIR	0.13507E-02	0.12537E-02	1.077
OUTREACH	0.87814E-02	0.26850E-01	0.327
FOKDENS	0.27656E-02	0.15360E-02	1.801[c]
PRIZ	-0.21659E-02	0.17181E-01	-0.126
AUTORIZ	2.4720	1.6974	1.456[b]
PRICAUTR	-0.21634E-01	0.10671E-01	-2.027[d]
SHARINCO	-0.59400E-01	0.30764E-01	-1.931[c]
Constant	6.3875	3.5893	1.780[c]

[a] Dependent variable is WAGERATE with mean of 6.67 and standard deviation of 4.36; number of observations = 376; degrees of freedom = 178; R-squared = 0.7961 and adjusted R-squared = 0.56

[b, c, d] Indicate significance at the 15 %, 10 %, and 5 % levels respectively

Source: Data from 1997 IFPRI/FOFIFA community survey

As expected, the consumer price of rice has a negative effect on the wage rate. Since wages are paid in rice, an increase in the price of rice will result in paying a lower physical quantity of rice per labor day, if all other factors are held constant. Finally, with an increased self-sufficiency index of rice (a traditional indicator of prosperity of a village), the wage rate increases (see coefficient for variable AUTORIZ). This positive effect becomes smaller at the margin with an increasing price of rice (PRICAUTR).

Determinants of Expansion of Upland

Holding everything else constant, the agricultural extensification pathway gains in importance for villages with better access to financial institutions (OUTREACH), higher wage rates (WAGERATE), and higher net immigration (RNETIMIG). Less forestland and bushland is taken under cultivation if lowland rice yields are higher (YLDRICI) or if soil fertility of upland is higher (SOILFERT). While the direct effect of access to financial institutions (OUTREACH) on upland expansion is positive but insignificant (an absolute 1 per cent more of credit program participants increases upland area by 0.247 per cent), the indirect effects of improved credit access through other endogenous variables are negative, with the result that credit access actually reduces upland expansion. The indirect effects can be calculated from the regression coefficients for credit access (OUTREACH) on other endogenous variables, multiplied by the regression coefficient of the endogenous variable for upland in Table 11.9. As this has important policy implications, we discuss these results. From Table 11.6 we see that credit access improves rice yields. In turn, rice yields of one additional kilogram reduce upland expansion by 0.026 per cent. Assuming constant marginal returns, the indirect effect is a reduction of 0.52 per cent of upland area with an absolute 1 per cent increase in households participating in member based credit programs. The indirect effects of credit access on upland expansion, through higher wage rates and higher soil fertility, are 0.017 and -0.106, respectively. The combined effects, both direct and indirect, of a 1 per cent increase in the number of households participating in a credit program in the village is then a reduction of 0.36 per cent in upland area. Thus, improved access to credit markets promotes agricultural intensification and preserves soils and forests.

The effect of population growth (RNATPOP) on upland area is very small. A 1 per cent increase in the mean population growth rate increases upland by only 0.0092 per cent. This shows that other factors play a much more important role in explaining expansion. Research in other countries also shows that the effect of population growth on the expansion of cultivated area and resource degradation is mediated through and often overshadowed by pressures arising from changing market, policy, or institutional conditions (Cropper and Griffiths, 1994; Foster et al., 1997; Jodha, 1985).

Table 11.9   Determinants of expansion of arable upland[a]

Variables	Coefficient	Standard error	t-value
YLDRICIR	-0.26405E-01	0.14709E-01	-1.795c
SOILFERT	-14.013	6.3488	-2.207d
WAGERATE	2.0264	1.4973	1.353
RNETIMIG	1.4897	3.2619	0.457
OUTREACH	0.24726	0.24391	1.014
TSTPAT	16.705	5.4775	3.050d
DELEC	-28.826	23.325	-1.236
AUTORIZ	-21.228	14.796	-1.435
PRICAUTR	0.17182	0.87940E-01	1.954c
PRIZ	-0.25321	0.14753	-1.716c
MARKRIZ	0.37519E-01	0.48049E-01	0.781
MARKMAN	-0.12102	0.44332E-01	-2.730d
A34BACC2	19.863	9.5550	2.079d
RNATPOP	0.55790	0.70146	0.795
WATPAT	-0.41441	1.1443	-0.362
PRICEREL	2.0634	1.3793	1.496b
Constant	159.26	36.857	4.321d

[a] Dependent variable is CHTAN with mean of 111.98 and standard deviation of 25.55; number of observations = 376; degrees of freedom = 170; R-squared = 0.70 and adjusted R-squared = 0.34

[b, c, d] Indicate significance at the 15 %, 10 %, and 5 % levels respectively

Source: Data from 1997 IFPRI/FOFIFA community survey

More land is put under the spade 'angady' if the village still possesses the ability to extend its agricultural frontier (TSTPAT). The increase in upland is 16.7 per cent higher in such villages in comparison with those that cannot further expand. With improved access to markets for nonrice crops (A34BACC2) that are usually cultivated on upland, the villagers seek to expand their upland area; with an increase by one in the qualitative indicator for access to nonrice markets, the upland area increases by an absolute 19 per cent.   The positive effect of access to nonrice crop markets significantly diminishes at the margin with a higher consumer price of manioc

(MARKMAN). The results further suggest that the expansion of arable land can be slowed down by rural electrification (DELEC). Electricity provides an alternative energy source for the few that can currently afford it. More important, access to electricity enables a range of food processing, trading, and off-farm enterprises that increase the demand for labor and offer alternative employment for the poor.

Determinants of Soil Fertility of Upland

The descriptive analysis showed that soil fertility has declined over the past ten years. What caused this degradation? As shown in Table 11.10, holding all other determinants constant, an increase in upland (CHTAN) significantly reduces soil fertility (SOILFERT). Two effects explain this result. First, as more land is put into cultivation, more and more infertile soils are taken. Second, as the demand for land increases, the time for fallow is reduced, giving upland less and less time to regenerate.

As expected, improved lowland rice yields, that is, agricultural intensification, has a positive effect on soil fertility of upland as higher productivity of lowlands reduces the incentives to mine upland soils. An increase in the index for soil fertility of upland by 0.2 per cent is associated with a 1 per cent higher yield of lowland rice. The results show that soil fertility can also be enhanced by improving community access to financial markets (OUTREACH).[8] Given that rural households in Madagascar face credit constraints, improved access to credit reduces the opportunity costs of capital, leading to lower discount factors or time preference rates when valuing future income streams against current ones. A major hypothesized determinant of the decline in soil fertility is the high time preference rate that poor households use for discounting the value of future use of soils.

A third potential option to preserve soil fertility is to improve access to input markets (ACCINPUT). Yet, the coefficient on this variable is highly insignificant. As was the case for yields, the interaction term (OUTRINPU) between input and credit access is negative and significant, indicating that the two types of access can act as substitutes for each other. Population growth (RNATPOP) and its squared term (PSQRNAT), lead to improved soil fertility, perhaps indicating that as land gets scarcer through population growth, institutional arrangements and response mechanisms can be found to improve soil fertility. However, these results are highly insignificant. Increased conflicts over grassland and forest resources (CONFLICT) in the village during the previous ten years are used as an indicator of insecurity of land tenure. As tenure insecurity increases, investment in the maintenance of soils is reduced as the investor cannot be sure of his ability to reap the benefits of his or her investment. The sign of the regression coefficient confirms this hypothesis, although the result is not statistically significant. Lower access to school education, reflected by the travel time from the village to primary and secondary schools combined (EDUC), appears to have a negative influence on soil fertility.

Table 11.10 Determinants of soil fertility on upland[a]

Variables	Coefficient	Standard error	t-value
CHTAN	-0.82909E-02	0.39462E-02	-2.101
YLDRICIR	0.17701E-03	0.24547E-03	0.721
OUTREACH	0.76829E-02	0.13813E-01	0.556
OUTRINPU	-0.19943E-01	0.12347E-01	-1.615[c]
EDUC	-0.41241E-01	0.37853E-01	-1.090
ACCINPUT	0.59672E-02	0.21238	0.028
CONFLICT	-0.56723E-01	0.54192E-01	-1.047
AUTORIZ	0.35286	0.18792	1.878[c]
RNATPOP	0.23778E-02	0.18927E-01	0.126
PSQRNAT	0.75183E-03	0.15944E-02	0.472
LANDLT1	-0.59350E-02	0.42577E-02	-1.394[b]
FOODPOOR	0.16124E-04	0.28418E-04	0.567
LANDSCAP	-0.68352E-05	0.62478E-05	-1.094
SOCCAP	0.53611E-03	0.29026E-03	1.847[c]
Constant	1.9094	0.73036	2.614[d]

[a] Dependent variable is SOILFERT with mean of 1.40 and standard deviation of 0.80; number of observations = 376; degrees of freedom = 172; R-squared = 0.77 and adjusted R-squared = 0.50

[b, c, d] Indicate significance at the 15 %, 10 %, and 5 % levels respectively

Source: Data from 1997 IFPRI/FOFIFA community survey

Social capital of the village significantly contributes to the preservation and maintenance of soils (SOCCAP). The results confirm the notion that common property management requires collective action, and that collective action in turn necessitates social capital. It is further interesting to note that the rice self-sufficiency index in the village (AUTORIZ) has a significant and positive effect on soil fertility, confirming our hypothesis that a high dependency on highly seasonal markets for buying rice increases consumption and production risks that negatively impact on the overall investment capacity of households. In other words, if one has to rely on the uncertain provision of rice by the market, one wants to reduce this dependency by growing more food, even if this is at the expense of soil fertility and future food production. The results suggest that improved access to financial and agricultural input markets can help to preserve soil fertility, and, through the negative effect of soil fertility on the change in upland, to slow the expansion of agriculture into hillsides.

Conclusions

The critical triangle and its specific problems and ramifications in Madagascar point to one overarching issue that needs to be better understood: what makes households and individuals choose the environmentally more sustainable intensification pathway over the extensification pathway, and how can macroeconomic and sectoral policies and institutional and technological innovations in the financial, agricultural, health, and education sectors contribute to make the intensification pathway more attractive in both the short and long run.

The analysis in this chapter points to a number of implications for policy and further research. Access to member based financial institutions, such as credit groups, village banks, or savings and credit cooperative societies, seems to play an important role in enabling an agricultural intensification pathway in Madagascar. We find that access to financial institutions has significant positive effects on lowland rice yields and on soil fertility of upland. However, participation in member based financial institutions also led to the expansion of upland agriculture, as capital becomes cheaper and more available to farmers. The combined effect of access to financial institutions on changes in upland is the sum of the direct effect on upland change and the indirect effect of credit access bringing higher yields, higher soil fertility, and higher wages. The sum of all effects shows that increasing the percentage of households participating in a microfinance institution by 1 per cent reduces upland area by 0.36 per cent. We conclude therefore, that promoting microfinance institutions for rural households can have beneficial effects on agricultural productivity, poverty, and natural resources.

Our research further suggests a positive effect of improved access to markets for rice and agricultural inputs on rice yields, on soil fertility of upland, and on the reduction of newly cultivated hillsides. Yet, improved access to output markets for nonrice crops that are grown on upland seems to lead to an expansion of cultivated upland in the short run. As such market access increases, farmgate prices increase while farmers' transaction costs for selling and buying crops decrease, ultimately pushing up the value of land. Investments in soil conservation will consequently become more economical. Neglecting the buildup of rural infrastructure and markets would only condemn rural villages and households to continue with the low input, low output, but land-mining agricultural strategy.

We find that most migration is a search for villages where the expansion of the agricultural frontier is possible. Insofar as migrants search for better living conditions, poverty in the villages and regions sending migrants (namely the Faritany of Fianarantsoa) is a driving force for natural resource degradation elsewhere on the island. Thus, alleviation of poverty through improving access to public services, such as schools and health services, enhancement of domestic trade, and generation of off-farm income opportunities has beneficial effects on conservation of soils and natural resources. Our analysis weakly suggests that as land becomes scarcer, conflicts about common property may reduce investments in soil conservation because of tenure insecurity. On the other hand, social capital is found to significantly enhance soil fertility, presumably by enabling villagers to agree on more sustainable property rights regimes.

While the potential of generating employment and income opportunities in Madagascar's rural nonfarm sector should not be underrated, we note that most rural households will have to continue to depend either directly or indirectly on agriculture and related animal production. Agricultural intensification in the major food crops, i.e. rice, cassava, potatoes, and maize, is therefore in order. Madagascar is a country where the green revolution still needs to take place. The results strongly suggest a greater role for public policy in improving agricultural productivity on irrigated lowlands and hillside uplands through increasing investments in agricultural research and extension.

Because of a lack of data, the analysis could not properly include a number of factors that deserve further research. These include:

- the interdependence between food security, health and nutritional status, and related pathways of rural development

- the linkages among livestock, cropping, and off-farm income generation within the household and village economy
- the role of (changing) property rights and related determinants and institutional processes of change
- the determinants of formation and maintenance of social capital and of local-level institutions that enhance the sustainable use of forest and arable land

Notes

1   The natural population growth rate of 3.5 per cent measured in the community level survey through recall questions on the number of people residing in the village at the time of the survey and ten years previously, correcting for the number of people emigrating and immigrating, is considerably higher than the national estimate of 2.9 per cent for the period of 1980 to 1989. We note that our growth rate is based on quite simple, and therefore, imprecise questions on population. Growth rates, obtained from census data at two points in time, are admittedly much more exact. Second, the rate reported here is not weighted by the initial size of the village (in comparison with other villages) so that high population growth rates observed in small villages biases our estimate upwards. When we weigh the population growth rate by the size of each village in the sample, the weighted population growth rate for all survey regions as an aggregate is 3.0 per cent. In other words, when correcting for the faster population growth in smaller villages, our estimates coincide very closely with the national ones.

2   On land law in Madagascar, see Keck et al; 1994; Rakotomanga, 1976; Rakotonirainy, 1984.

3   This result coincides with an estimate by the Economist Intelligence Unit in 1990, cited in Keck et al., 1994.

4   Higher rural incomes could possibly be achieved by growth in the rural nonfarm sector. While this chapter focuses on agricultural income growth, the promotion of nonfarm enterprises (for example, for food processing and marketing and for provision of rural services) can be an important strategy for overall rural growth. However, the success of this strategy depends to a large extent on the relative magnitude of forward and backward linkages of the (dominant) farm sector with the nonfarm sector. Islam (1997) finds that the growth multiplier was estimated between 1.35 to 1.90, i.e. $1 US of additional farm income increases nonfarm rural income by $0.35 US to $0.90 US. On farm-nonfarm growth linkages, see, for example, Hazell (1983) and Hazell and Haggblade (1993).

5   To test whether these instruments are good ones, an F-test was performed to test the joint significance of the instrumental variables in the first-stage regression. The F-statistic is the ratio of the explained variation in the dependent variable and the unexplained variation, adjusted for the number of independent variables. The probability of error resulting from the F-test for the estimated coefficients of the instrumental variables is 0.74 for equation (1) (outreach); 0.07 for equation (2) (rice yield); 0.00 for equation (3)

(net immigration); 0.08 for equation (4) (wage rate); 0.02 for equation (5) (change in upland); and 0.49 for equation (6) (soil fertility).

6   All descriptive statistics in this and the following tables are weighted averages, using the sampling weights computed for the stratified random sampling frame.

7   On interlinked credit cum marketing transactions in rural Madagascar, see Barrett, 1997a.

8   As Pender and Kerr (1996) point out, improved access to credit (or higher initial liquid assets of the household or village) is not expected to have an effect on conservation investment and soil fertility, if capital markets are perfect, that is, if every household can borrow and save as much as it wants at the prevailing market rate. However, empirical evidence leads to the rejection of the assumption of a perfect credit market in rural Madagascar.

12 Summary

MANFRED ZELLER, BART MINTEN, CLAUDE RANDRIANARISOA,
CÉCILE LAPENU, and ELIANE RALISON

In Madagascar, the policy objectives related to poverty alleviation, food security and good nutrition, the protection of the environment, and agricultural and economic growth are linked. The pursuit of only one policy objective may have a negative impact on others, and a neglect of the tradeoffs may lead to pathways of development which prove costly and detrimental to the welfare of current and future generations. This book on 'Beyond Market Liberalization: Welfare, Income Generation, and Environmental Sustainability in Rural Madagascar' analyzed the impact of policy variables on farm and off-farm income generation, food and nonfood consumption, and nutritional status of rural households. Apart from the household-level analysis presented in the book, this summary also draws on the community-level analysis of chapter 11 which focused on the critical triangle of development.

This summary seeks to present an overview of the results of the book. We begin with the five major policy issues which emanate from our analysis. We then briefly provide some data on the magnitude of each of the problems and related major causes. In the discussion of causes we limit ourselves mainly to those which can, in principal, be altered by policy. Based on the results of the household and community level analysis presented in this book, we identify five interlinked major policy issues: (1) low agricultural productivity and farm incomes, (2) environmental degradation, (3) low level of "healthy" diversification of rural incomes, (4) high food insecurity and malnutrition, and (5) large inequalities in income and welfare. In the following, we discuss the magnitude of these problems and their main underlying causes.

Environmental Degradation, Low Agricultural Productivity, and Farm Income

We discuss the first two policy issues together as they are closely linked. The direct and immediate cause for low agricultural productivity, low yields, and resultant low farm income is the low level of use of modern inputs, such as high-yield seed, fertilizer, and pesticides. Low yields increase the necessity for households to cultivate more land. Since the terracing of new irrigated riceland requires large up-front investments which become economical only with a long planning horizon (which food-insecure households cannot afford to adopt), households choose to take more upland into cultivation, thus encroaching on grassland, bush, and forest. As land becomes more scarce, the fallow period is reduced, leading to increased degradation of soils as little or no fertilizer is applied to replenish soil nutrients.

The IFPRI/FOFIFA data show an average rice yield of 1.4 tons per hectare for early rice and 2 tons per hectare for main harvest rice in the lowlands. Upland rice ('riz tanety') shows yields of 1.4 ton per hectare compared to 1.0 ton per hectare for slash and burn cultivated rice (riz tavy). Yields of upland crops are similarly low. While some progress has been made, through for example, improved planting material for potatoes, yields remain very low by international standards. Only 19 per cent of the rural households use mineral fertilizer – but only on 8 per cent of the area – and 9 per cent use improved varieties of rice seed. Even if mineral fertilizer is applied, the quantities are significantly below recommended doses, reaching only 55 kg per hectare.

Crop production is plagued by a number of covariant risk factors, that is risks which affect not only a single person, but many households in the community at the same time. The survey households reported that 80 per cent of their planted rice area faced production problems, such as those related to water (rains too late, inundation, drought), crop diseases, or losses due to insects and animals. The area in upland crops was similarly affected by covariant risks (maize, 82 per cent; beans, 85 per cent; cassava, 69 per cent).

Moreover, the community level data reveals that rice yields and soil fertility have declined. Over the last ten years, it is estimated that yields have declined between 10 and 30 per cent, depending on the type of rice. The highest decline has been noticed for upland rice and for 'slash and burn' cultivated rice. Almost 90 per cent of the communities reported soils as less fertile than ten years previously. This percentage is lower in the Vakinankaratra where land prices and fertilizer use are higher compared to the other regions. Since income from crop and livestock production constitutes the major share of total average monthly household income (47,466 ariary out of 65,103 ariary, i.e. 73 per cent), the low level of household income is largely driven by low agricultural productivity. Furthermore, while income from rice production constitutes almost

60 per cent of total income, about 60 per cent of farmers are still net buyers of rice.[1]

The econometric analysis investigated the determinants of adoption of seed and fertilizer, of the level of input expenditures in rice and upland production, as well as the causal factors of total value of lowland and upland production, and of marketed surplus. Moreover, our community level analysis, partly contained in this book and partly contained in several working papers of the IFPRI/FOFIFA series (Lapenu et al., 1998; Minten et al., 1998; Zeller et al., 1998b), investigated the causal factors based on the community level data. Using this causal analysis, we identify several major causes which are discussed in the following.

Access to Credit

Liquidity constraints in rural households appear to have a significant negative impact on input intensity, rice and upland yields, total farm production, crop income, and level and length of on-farm storage, and therefore on the magnitude of seasonal price spreads. The participation in group-based savings and credit institutions was found to significantly increase rice yields, improve soil fertility of uplands, and reduce the pressure for households to cultivate new upland in their villages, thus preserving forest, grassland, and bush.

In the regression analysis, the access to credit was estimated to be a significant and robust determinant of higher agricultural productivity, higher farm incomes, and reduction of pressure on natural resources. In the survey, access to credit was measured by asking each individual adult female and male in the household to estimate the maximum amount that he or she expects to be able to borrow from either formal sources (i.e. banks, cooperatives, etc.) or from informal sources (i.e. friends, relatives, shopkeepers, landlords, moneylenders). Only 52 out of almost 600 survey households reported to have access to formal credit. Most formal rural credit in Madagascar is at present only available to members of community-based group or village bank schemes. In the IFPRI/FOFIFA sample, which includes major intervention areas of microfinance programs, 13 per cent of adult males were members of programs providing credit. The participation rate of women was below 5 per cent. The data from the community level survey indicates that about 11 per cent of households participate in member based financial programs in 1997. However, on a national scale, an upper-limit estimate of the percentage of rural households having access to formal credit is likely to hover around 5 per cent.

On average, for all households, 16 per cent of the gross value of agricultural production is spent on the acquisition of agricultural inputs. The significant and sizable effects of access to credit – of which the elasticity controlling for endogeneity for total income is estimated at 12 per cent – are explained by the severe liquidity constraints that force rural households to choose second-best strategies for production, consumption, and asset portfolios. Liquidity constraints are especially severe during the planting season when agricultural inputs need to be purchased, but the price of the average calorie consumed is about 50 per cent higher than after harvest. Female-headed households have the additional financial burden of paying male farm workers for soil preparation. Vulnerable households also include those with many children or little land. Clear indicators of the severe liquidity constraints in rural Madagascar include households selling rice at harvest time, and buying it back four to seven months later at up to double the price; the low use of agricultural inputs despite its high pay-off, i.e. a $10 US investment results in an estimated average pay-off of $19 US to $25 US half a year later; and the large seasonal fluctuations in calorie intake and nutritional status which are already at critically low levels. The aggregate effect of credit access on total household income (net of all payments for inputs, labor, and interest) not only includes income effects from improved crop production, but also from other income-generating activities (livestock, off-farm microenterprises) and from more cost-effective asset and debt portfolio and consumption stabilization strategies (e.g. storing own rice for home consumption instead of selling at harvest at low price).

The estimated income effects of credit access are for the average household. These effects are presumably larger for households and individuals with more severe liquidity constraints and higher marginal returns to capital, i.e. women and poor households. Female-headed households, households with more dependents, and poorer households use significantly fewer modern agricultural inputs. Much of this pattern, we believe, is explained by the low risk-bearing capacity and liquidity constraints of these socioeconomic groups. It is to be noted that our estimate of the income impact of credit access also includes the effects of improved savings options and access to consumption credit as well as extension services which come along with participation in member based financial institutions in Madagascar. A disentangling of these individual effects is impossible without a larger panel data set including households participating in microfinance programs that offer different financial and nonfinancial services.

Low Level of Rural Infrastructure

The low level of rural infrastructure leads to higher input prices and lower output prices at the farmgate level, as well as higher transportation and transaction costs for farmers acquiring seeds and fertilizer. Our analysis indicates that paved roads are available in only 8 per cent of the rural communities and the average distance and time that it takes to reach a market are 10 kms and more than 2 hours. Higher travel time to a paved road leads to more extensive land use, lower input expenditures, and less orientation towards cash crops. While no effort was made to estimate economic effects of road construction on regions as a whole, it seems that the presence of road infrastructure leads to a significant variation in factor use as well as migration.

Weak Production Response to Changes in Input and Output Prices

While larger farmers were found to have a significant and sizable response of agricultural area and marketed surplus to changes in agricultural input and output prices in general, the response to price change for the majority of subsistence farmers was found to be weak and highly insignificant. Net buyers of rice that are producers of rice have a highly insignificant response to higher rice prices. Net buyers of rice are frequently female-headed households, possess less land, are often wage laborers, and have more dependents in the household. The analysis of consumption shows that these socioeconomic groups are disproportionately hurt by a rice price increase through its negative effect on the level of food expenditure and calorie intake. This causal pathway explains for example, why we find in the Fianarantsoa HT, a rice-deficient region, that a higher rice price lowers the demand for fertilizer by the average farm household. This result is likely a result of the need to buy rice in the planting season when liquidity constraints are high; thus a choice is made between food or planting fields. The aggregate weak and insignificant supply response with respect to agricultural input and output prices is explained by a host of underlying structural factors, such as low risk-bearing capacity of poor households and existence of severe crop production risks, credit constraints (as discussed above), high transaction costs in accessing input and output markets, an inadequate agricultural extension system, and apparently small and insignificant productivity effects of available seed technology under prevalent farm conditions.

Covariant Risks Affecting Crop Production

The frequency and severity of covariant risks leading to crop failures or severe yield losses reduce the incentive for risk-averse farmers to invest in inputs as the downside risk of low or negative gross margins may increase with higher input use. Three types of production risks can be distinguished: climatic risk, risk of plant diseases, and risks related to rural insecurity. Our analysis shows that climatic risk induces farmers to use less inputs and to switch from lowland to upland production while more rural insecurity leads to less upland cultivation.

Insufficient Irrigation Systems

In the survey regions, the percentage of the area under irrigation was reported to have declined by an average 6 per cent over the previous ten years. The positive effect of irrigation on agricultural yields and income seems mostly to be caused by a reduction of the yield-reducing impact of covariant risks.

Declining Soil Fertility and Increased Use of Marginal Lands

Seventy per cent of the villages reported problems with silt in the lowlands. The average fallow period for upland has declined significantly over the prior ten years; from 40 per cent to one-third of the cycle. The analysis further indicates that more marginal upland is taken into production with a negative effect on yields. Migration, mostly motivated by a desire to improve living standards and generally directed towards regions and villages with fertile but not yet cultivated land is a major determinant for taking new forest- and grassland under cultivation. Food insecurity, poverty, and interregional inequalities, are the major causes of migration into rural areas and the resultant reduction in natural resources. Improved rice yields on irrigated lowlands via agricultural intensification, was found to have a positive and significant effect on upland soil fertility and reduced the pressure to cultivate more upland.

Inadequate Extension and Research System

About 23 per cent of farmers surveyed did not know about improved rice varieties. Only 50 per cent of the farmers interacted directly with an agricultural extension agent over the previous year. Moreover, these consultations seem to have had little effect on agricultural yields and income. Our estimates indicate that extension services only slightly increase rice yields and have little effect on most other variables.

Quite disturbing is the finding that improved rice varieties seem not to play a significant role in increasing yields. This appears to be consistent with the fact that only 8 per cent of farmers use improved seed for irrigated rice, and then not on all their fields. In some areas, the low adoption rate seems to be caused by the unavailability or high transaction costs of acquiring improved seed. In other areas, such as the Vakinankaratra, where access to input and output markets is relatively good, the low adoption rate of improved rice varieties suggests that they do not offer much economic benefit over the locally produced, recycled seed.

We conclude that increased rice productivity will contribute to the conservation of natural resources in Madagascar while at the same time tending to reduce the level of rice prices with beneficial effects on food security and poverty. We further conclude that policies focused on an agricultural intensification strategy will also contribute to achieving environmental objectives, such as preservation of soil fertility. Rice remains the key crop in Madagascar. However, productivity increases in rice need to be complemented by increased diversification into other crops and off-farm enterprises so as to reduce the extent of seasonal food insecurity and malnutrition and to benefit poorer socioeconomic groups that do not rely on rice as a cash crop but depend on wage labor and upland crops (i.e. potatoes, maize, cassava) for food and income.

Low Level of 'Healthy' Diversification of Rural Incomes

Income from crop and animal production constitutes 73 per cent of total income of households on average in rural areas. Incomes from wage labor, off-farm enterprises, and other sources account for the remainder. Our results suggest that the diversification into other income sources is largely driven by large labor-to-land ratios in land-poor households and by the overall need to reduce risk exposure. Little of the income diversification or outside agriculture suggests a 'healthy' diversification driven by new-income generating activities.

A clear exception to this otherwise quite general finding is the region of the Vakinankaratra where there has been a 'healthy' diversification out of rice and into dairy production, fruits and vegetables, animal production, and off-farm microenterprises. In this region, rice represents only 50 per cent of total household income (compared to 60 per cent for the average of all other regions) and 28 per cent of the commercial surplus (compared to 45 per cent in other regions). This lower dependence on rice as a food and cash crop, and the higher degree of income diversification, results in a much shorter and less severe lean preharvest period compared to other regions, with beneficial effects on stabilizing food consumption and nutritional status. Our analysis of the panel households of all the regions shows that households could further increase the degree of income diversification. As we conclude below, the long term and sizable investments in the Vakinankaratra in agricultural research and extension, agro-industry, and infrastructure during the past twenty or thirty years seem to have enabled this positive trend to emerge.

Covariate risks, such as drought, cyclones, and crop diseases are responsible for the high variability of crop income. About 73 per cent of crop income is from rice production in all regions. An increase in the occurrence of weather calamities was found to significantly reduce input expenditures and the adoption of modern agricultural technology. Covariant risks seem to hurt wealthier farmers relatively more than poorer farmers. Our analysis appears to further suggest that irrigation can reduce the impact of these risks, and improve the stability of income.

The share of crop income in total household income is lowest for the poorest income quartile. The poorest derive 35 per cent of their income from rural wage labor. However, the demand for rural wage labor, and the level of wages, is highly dependent on agricultural production and productivity. Based on the community level analysis, we estimated an elasticity of the wage rate with respect to yields of 0.33. Thus, while wage laborers benefit from agricultural intensification, increases in profits from rice production are, as expected, only partially shared with them. The remainder of the gains from productivity increases due to increasing rice yields must therefore accrue to the owners of the capital and land used in rice production. This pattern is relevant for the issue of high and increasing inequality in welfare among rural households, and which cautions against a strategy that simply focuses on rice. While increases in rice yields would also benefit the poor, landowners and therefore wealthier farmers would relatively gain more, thus leading to increased income inequality in rural areas.

Because rural wages are dependent on agriculture and agricultural productivity, rural wage income is highly correlated with crop income. For this reason, wage income is not a good measure to diversify agricultural income risk. It is 'unhealthy' diversification, mainly driven by the lack of land and other opportunities. The low level of diversification within agriculture and the dominance of rice as a crop and food, and the small role of truly non-agricultural income opportunities, raises concerns as it renders the majority of rural households highly vulnerable to weather and other covariant risks. Our regression analysis identifies several forces driving the degree of income diversification.

Level of Education

More educated households were found to have a significantly higher share of income from microenterprises in their total household incomes. This result suggests that literacy is an important factor for obtaining significant income from off-farm enterprises.

Gender

Women are more likely to engage in an off-farm microenterprise than men. In the total sample, there were 167 female entrepreneurs compared to 124 males. While men specialize in commerce, mostly food trade, women are disproportionately engaged in handicrafts.

Poverty

Poverty and lack of access to land, is the major factor in causing households to diversify out of self-employed farm income into wage income. Earning a significant share of total income from wages is a reliable indicator of poverty in rural Madagascar.

Access to Credit and Business Management Training

A weakly significant and positive effect of access to credit on the share of crop income in total income is found. This result, we suppose, is mainly caused by the fact that most programs focus on crop or livestock credit. Few cater to the demand for savings and credit services by microentrepreneurs. The existing off-farm enterprises are small-scale activities which do not require much working capital and do not generate much employment for nonfamily members. With our data and analysis, we cannot determine whether it is the lack of credit for off-farm enterprises or the lack of demand for services and goods generated by more capital-intensive microenterprises that explains the low capitalization of existing enterprises.

Covariant Risks

A higher incidence of covariant climatic risks significantly induces households to cultivate more upland, presumably because the impact of such events on rice production seems to be higher than on rainfed upland. This causal pattern implies that farmers in high risk areas forgo intensification of rice fields and instead extensify agricultural production on the uplands. Improving irrigation systems, as noted above, or crop breeding research could reduce the effect of covariant risks and relieve pressure on natural resources.

Insufficient Access to Infrastructure and the Negligible Role of Agro-Industry

Apart from the Vakinankaratra and selected other pockets in the country, the insufficient access to infrastructure (markets, roads, communications) leads to a low degree of agricultural commercialization, resulting in weak forward and backward linkages of agricultural growth for the demand for goods and services produced by off-farm enterprises. As the demand for nonfood goods and services in general is highly elastic with respect to increases in income, and considering that agricultural income is the major share of household income, sizable demand effects for off-farm services and goods will only be generated by increasing farm income.

Food Insecurity, Malnutrition, and Large Income and Welfare Inequalities

Improving food security has been and must remain at the center of food, agriculture, and environmental policy in Madagascar. The results of the analysis in this book on caloric consumption and nutritional status of preschoolers largely coincide with previous surveys and studies such as SECALINE and EPM.

Food Security and Nutritional Status

On average for all households, we found a daily consumption of 2,695 calories per adult-equivalent, 2,094 calories per capita, and 54 grams of protein per capita in 1997. These values are very close to the daily minimum food intake levels of 2,837 calories per adult-equivalent, 2,133 calories per capita, and 56 grams of protein. However, the average picture hides a large share of households which suffer from transitory or chronic food insecurity and malnutrition. Between 14 and 18 per cent of households were found to consume less than 60 per cent of the required minimum calorie intake. The incidences of moderate and severe food insecurity are highest in Fianarantsoa C/F and Ranomafana, followed by Fianarantsoa HT, and are lowest in the Vakinankaratra and the Majunga regions. In all regions, rice is the major food staple, providing on average, 60 per cent of total calories consumed. On average, 47 per cent of preschool children are found to be 'stunted' in all regions; 5 per cent were acutely malnourished; and 28 per cent were 'wasted'.

While food insecurity and poor diets are largely caused by the overall level of poverty, and while marginal increases in income significantly raise the quantity and quality of food consumption, its effect on calorie intake is estimated as very low with an elasticity of 0.1. The elasticity of intake of calories from animal products, an indicator of food quality, is much higher at 0.48. This means that raising incomes by 1 per cent increases calorie intake only by 0.1 per cent. This is consistent with results found in other poor developing countries. Hence, raising incomes of Malagasy households alone will not solve the food insecurity and malnutrition problem. While we did not undertake an econometric analysis of the causes of malnutrition (as this would have required the collection of data beyond the scope of this research program precisely describing food consumption, health, water, sanitary environment, and care of children), the descriptive analysis suggests, again consistent with studies conducted in other countries, that levels of malnutrition in cross sections of households do not quickly decrease as income or food expenditures increase. Malnutrition is caused by a complex set of factors (i.e. water quality, food preparation, care, frequency and type of meals, vaccination and exposure to diseases) so that the partial effect of income on malnutrition is likely to be low. The incidence of sickness was found to be very high; 11.3 per cent of children aged 7 to 11 years were reported to have been sick in the two days prior to the survey (Ralison and Lapenu, 1998). We expect that nonfood inputs into good nutrition (i.e. care, improved water and housing conditions) are very important in determining nutritional status.

Changes in Food Security and Welfare

In order to obtain a sense of how rural households perceive the recent changes in their livelihood and welfare due to changes in the socioeconomic and agroecological environment, the survey questionnaire included a few qualitative questions. Each head of household was asked how, compared to five years earlier, various welfare indicators had changed. We used five simple indicators of welfare: (1) quantity of food consumed by the household; (2) quality of food consumed by the household; (3) quality and availability of drinking water; (4) health status of household members; and (5) housing conditions of the family.

Table 12.1   Overall welfare and quantity of food consumed, 1997 compared to 1992

Reported change	Quantity of food consumed (% of households)	Overall welfare (% of households)
Worsened	41	38
Remained	29	30
Improved	30	31

Source: Data from the 1997 IFPRI/FOFIFA household survey

These results, reported in Table 12.1, suggest that there were winners and losers over the past five years, with the aggregate for all regions on average showing a slight, but not overwhelming worsening of how households felt about their welfare. The heads of households were further asked what the major causes of any positive or negative change were. At an aggregate level for all households and for each of the wealth quartiles in the sample, including the poorest quartile, the number of households gaining in terms of food security due to recent changes in market prices and market conditions was found to always outweigh the number of losers. However, the ratio of winners to losers is more favorable for the wealthier household quartiles than for the two poorer quartiles. In other words, the wealthier households seem to have benefited more frequently from recent changes in agricultural input and output markets than the poor.

At an aggregate level, 50 per cent of those households who improved their food situation reported that favorable changes in market prices and related conditions were the major cause. In comparison, adverse changes in market prices or in other market conditions were reported by household heads to constitute the major cause of greater food insecurity in only 30 per cent of cases. Thus, the adjustments in markets were reported by the household heads as a major causal factor in improving their food security.

It is disturbing that risks appear to be the major driving forces for sliding into greater poverty. We note that idiosyncratic risk factors, such as disease, old age, accident, and death, along with covariant risks, mainly natural calamities such as drought and cyclone, are the overriding reasons that households reported as causing the deterioration in living standards. Covariant risks seem to more frequently affect the wealthy than the poor while the poor report to be slightly more hurt by idiosyncratic risks which negatively impact on their labor which is their major production factor.

The occurrence of these risks seems to have been the major cause in making households more food insecure over the five year period. The lack of a formal social safety net, the inadequacy of health and other social services, and the lack of access to financial services which assist in efficient consumption smoothing (i.e. savings products to hold precautionary savings, access to insurance substitutes) may all contribute to the vulnerability of particularly poor households to these shocks. The results indicate that the contribution of the informal safety net in insuring against idiosyncratic and covariant risks is quite limited as the share of income from gifts and remittances received in total household income is only 536 ariary per month on average for all households. This is less than 1 per cent of total monthly income.

Future research appears to be warranted to better understand the dynamics of moving in and out of poverty, and to explore the costs, benefits, and limits of private and informal markets for providing safety net services, and identify sustainable policy interventions which efficiently can complement existing private safety net mechanisms. Moreover, in view of the positive and significant effects of improved credit access on household income, future research on the cost structure and sustainability of rural financial institutions in Madagascar appears warranted.

Concluding Remarks

The results of the analysis in this book suggest that market reform and the corresponding adjustments in rural markets had, on average, a positive effect on food security for the rural households as an aggregate. However the changes benefited the wealthier households relatively more than poorer households thus leading to more inequality. This conclusion is consistent with the regression results yielding an elastic supply response by wealthier farmers with respect to the rice price and a price-elastic demand for rice as food. The data further suggest that major reasons for sliding into food insecurity and poverty are the occurrence of idiosyncratic risks, and for wealthier households, idiosyncratic and covariant risks. In a nutshell, the overall worsening trend in welfare of households is caused by the occurrence of such risks, and the lack of ability at the household and community levels to effectively insure against them. Due to the lack of income diversification, incomes of rural households are 'lumpy' and at high risk, reinforcing the impact of negative events on food consumption.

Madagascar is a country where the green revolution has yet to take place. The analysis suggests that the hoped-for effects of market liberalization – economic growth and reduced food prices – were not seen because of the price-inelastic aggregate production response of the farm sector. While wealthy farmers were found to have significant price response, the majority of semisubsistence farmers did not produce significantly more for the market as changes in prices not only affected their profits, but at the same time their food budget. Nonprice determinants of agricultural technology adoption and intensification, such as access to education, financial institutions, road infrastructure, agricultural extension, irrigation, and low risk-bearing capacity caused by food poverty and destitution, all play a role in determining the aggregate supply response by the farm sector.

Note

1   To make subsistence and commercial farmers comparable, all agricultural incomes
     include the value of home-consumed production.

Bibliography

Alderman, H. (1986), 'The Effect of Food Price and Income Changes on the Acquisition of Food by Low-income Households', International Food Policy Research Institute, Washington, DC, mimeograph.

Asche, F. and Wessels, C.R. (1997), 'On Price Indices in the Almost Ideal Demand System', *American Journal of Agricultural Economics*, vol. 79, November, pp. 1182-1185.

Badiane, O., Goletti, F., Kherallah, M., Berry, P., Govindan, K., Gruhn, P. and Mendoza, M. (1997), 'Agricultural Input and Output: Marketing Reforms in African Countries', International Food Policy Research Institute, report submitted to BMZ.

Badiane, O., Goletti, F., Lapenu, C., Mendoza, M., Minten, B., Ralison, E., Randrianarisoa, C., Rich, K. and Zeller, M. (1998), 'Executive Summary' in Structure and Conduct of Major Agricultural Input and Output Markets and Response to Reforms by Rural Households in Madagascar, Part I, Introduction and Executive Summary, International Food Policy Research Institute, report submitted to USAID-Madagascar, pp. 17-70.

Baland, J.-M. and Platteau, J.-P. (1998), 'Dividing the Commons - An Assessment of the New Institutional Economics of Property Rights', Photocopy, University of Namur, Belgium.

Barrett, C.B. (1994), 'Understanding Uneven Agricultural Liberalization in Madagascar', *Journal of Modern African Studies*, vol. 32, pp. 449-476.

Barrett, C.B. (1995), 'Madagascar: An Empirical Test of the Market Relaxation - State Compression Hypothesis', *Development Policy Review*, vol. 13(4), pp. 391-406.

Barrett, C.B. (1996a), 'On Price Risk and the Inverse Farm Size - Productivity Relationship', *Journal of Development Economics*, vol. 51, pp. 193-215.

Barrett, C.B. (1996b), 'Urban Bias in Price Risk: The Geography of Food Price Distribution in Low-income Economies', *Journal of Development Studies*, vol. 32(6), pp. 830-849.

Barrett, C.B. (1997a), 'Food Marketing Liberalization and Trader Entry: Evidence from Madagascar', *World Development*, vol. 25, No. 5, pp. 763-777.

Barrett, C.B. (1997b), 'Heteroskedastic Price Forecasting for Food Security Management in Developing Countries', *Oxford Development Studies*, vol. 25, No. 2, pp. 225-236.

Barrett, C.B. (1997c), 'Liberalization and Food Price Distributions: ARCH-M Evidence from Madagascar', *Food Policy*, vol. 22, No. 2, pp. 155-173.

Barrett, C.B. and Dorosh, P.A. (1996), 'Farmers' Welfare and Changing Food Prices: Nonparametric Evidence from Madagascar', *American Journal of Agricultural Economics*, vol. 78, August, pp. 656-669.

Benirschka, M. and Binkley, J.K. (1994), 'Land Price Volatility in a Geographically Dispersed Market', *American Journal of Agricultural Economics*, vol. 76, No. 2, pp. 185-195.

Benjamin, D. (1992), 'Household Composition, Labor Markets, and Labor Demand: Testing for Separation in Agricultural Household Models', *Econometrica*, vol. 60(2), pp. 287-322.

Benjamin, D. (1994), 'Can Unobserved Land Quality Explain the Inverse Productivity Relationship?', *Journal of Development Economics*, vol. 46, pp. 51-84.

Berg, E. (1989), 'The Liberalization of Rice Marketing in Madagascar', *World Development*, vol. 17, No. 5, pp. 719-728.

Bertrand, A. (1994), 'Revue Documentaire, Préalable à l'Elaboration d'une Politique et d'une Stratégie de Gestion de Feux de Végétation à Madagascar', ONE/FOFIFA-DRD, 36 p., mimeograph.

Binkley, J.K. and Harrer, B. (1981), 'Major Determinants of Ocean Freight Rates for Grains: An Econometric Analysis', *American Journal of Agricultural Economics*, vol. 63(1), pp. 47-57.

Binswanger, H.P., Khandker, S.R. and Rosenzweig, M.R. (1993), 'How Infrastructure and Financial Institutions Affect Agricultural Output and Investment in India', *Journal of Development Economics*, vol. 41, pp. 337-366.

Boserup, E. (1965), *The Conditions of Agricultural Growth: The Economics of Agrarian Change under Population Pressure*, Aldine Publishing Co, Chicago, Ill., USA.

Bouis, H.E. and Haddad, L.J. (1992), 'Are Estimates of Calorie Income Elasticities Too High?: A Recalibration of the Plausible Range', *Journal of Development Economics*, vol. 39(2), pp. 333-364.

Braun, J. von (1997), 'The Links between Agricultural Growth, Environmental Degradation, and Nutrition and Health: Implications for Policy and Research', in S.A. Vosti and T. Reardon (eds), *Sustainability, Growth, and Poverty Alleviation: A Policy and Agroecological Perspective*, Johns Hopkins University Press, Baltimore, Md., USA, pp. 66-78.

Braun, J. von, and Pandya-Lorch, R. (eds) (1991), 'Income Sources of Malnourished People in Rural Areas: Microlevel Information and Policy Implications', Working Paper on Commercialization of Agriculture and Nutrition, No. 5, International Food Policy Research Institute, Washington, DC.

Braun, J. von, Puetz, D. and Webb, P. (1989), 'Irrigation Technology and Commercialization of Rice in The Gambia: Effects on Income and Nutrition', Research Report No. 75, International Food Policy Research Institute, Washington, DC.

Cameron, L.A. (1999), 'The Importance of Learning in the Adoption of High-Yielding Variety Seeds', *American Journal of Agricultural Economics*, vol. 81, pp. 83-94.

Cropper, M. and Griffiths, C. (1994), 'The Interaction of Population Growth and Environmental Quality', *American Economic Review*, vol. 84(2), pp. 250-254.

Cuevas, C., Hanson, R., Fafchamps, M., Moll, P. and Srivastava, P.(1993), 'Case Studies of Enterprise Finance in Ghana', RPED, March, The World Bank, Washington, DC.

Deaton, A. (1997), *The Analysis of Household Surveys: A Microeconometric Approach to Development Policy*, Johns Hopkins University Press for the World Bank, Baltimore, Md., USA.

Deaton, A.S. and Muellbauer, J. (1980), 'An Almost Ideal Demand System', *American Economic Review*, vol. 70(3), pp. 312-326.

Diagne, A., Zeller, M. and Sharma, M. (1998), 'Determinants of Households Access to and Participation in Formal and Informal Credit Markets in Malawi and Bangladesh', Paper presented at the annual meeting of the American Economic Association, January 3-5, Chicago, USA.

Dodwell, C. (1995), *Madagascar Travels*, Hodder and Stoughton, London.

Dorosh, P. and Bernier, R. (1994), 'Staggered Reforms and Limited Success: Structural Adjustment in Madagascar', in D. Sahn (ed), *Adjusting to Policy Failure in African Economies*, Cornell University Press, Ithaca, N.Y, pp. 332-366.

Dorosh, P., Haggblade, S., Rajemison, H., Ralantoarilolona, B. and Simler, K. (1998), 'Structure et Facteurs Déterminants de la Pauvreté à Madagascar', Cornell Food and Nutrition Policy Program, Cornell University, Ithaca, NY, USA/Institut National de la Statistique, Antananarivo.

Droy, I. (1997), 'Que Sont les Greniers à Riz Devenus? Le Désengagement de l'Etat sur les Grands Périmètres Irrigés de Maravoay et du Lac Alaotra', *Economie de Madagascar,* vol. 2, pp. 63-88.

Fafchamps, M. and Minten, B. (1998), 'Returns to Social Capital Among Agricultural Traders: Evidence from Madagascar', Discussion Paper No. 23, Markets and Structural Studies Division, International Food Policy Research Institute, Washington, DC.

Fafchamps, M. and Minten, B. (1999a), 'Property Rights in a Flea-market Economy', Discussion Paper No. 27, Markets and Structural Studies Division, International Food Policy Research Institute, Washington, DC.

Fafchamps, M. and Minten, B. (1999b), 'Relationships and Traders in Madagascar', *Journal of Development Studies*, vol. 35(6), forthcoming.

Fafchamps, M. and Quisumbing, A.R. (1999), 'Human Capital, Productivity, and Labor Allocation in Rural Pakistan', *Journal of Human Resources*, vol. 34(2), pp. 369-406.

Fauroux, E. (1989), 'Le Boeuf et le Riz dans la Vie Economique et Sociale Sakalava de la Vallée de la Maharivo', ERA, MRSTD/ORSTOM, Antananarivo.

Foster, A., Rosenzweig, M. and Behrman, J. (1997), 'Population Growth, Income Growth and Deforestation: Management of Village Common Land in India', University of Pennsylvania, Brown University, typescript.

Fraslin, J.-H. (1997), 'Quel Crédit pour les Agriculteurs?' *Economie de Madagascar*, vol. 2, pp. 153-174.

Gavian, S. and Fafchamps, M. (1996), 'Land Tenure and Allocative Efficiency in Niger', *American Journal of Agricultural Economics*, vol. 78, pp. 460-471.

Gezon, L. (1997), 'Institutional Structure and the Effectiveness of Integrated Conservation and Development Projects: Case study from Madagascar', *Human Organization*, vol. 56(4), pp. 462-470.

Goetz, S.J. (1992), 'A Selectivity Model of Household Food Marketing Behavior in Sub-Saharan Africa', *American Journal of Agricultural Economics*, vol. 74(2), pp. 444-452.

Goletti, F., Minot, N., Ahmed, R. and Gruhn, P. (1996), 'Vietnam: Rice Market Monitoring and Policy Options Study', International Food Policy Research Institute, Report to the Asian Development Bank, Washington DC.

Goletti, F., Randrianarisoa, C. and Rich, K. (1998), 'How Good are Rice Seeds in Madagascar? The Structure and Performance of the Seed Sector', in Structure and Conduct of Major Agricultural Input and Output Markets and Response to Reforms by Rural Households in Madagascar, Part II, Analysis of Input Distribution and Seed Markets, International Food Policy Research Institute, report submitted to USAID-Madagascar, pp. 15-71.

Greene, W. (1995), LIMDEP, Version 7.0, Chapter 17.4, pp. 309-314.

Greene, W.H. (1993), *Econometric Analysis*, Second Edition, Prentice Hall, Inc., Englewood, New Jersey, USA, pp. 444-485.

Hazell, P. (1983), 'Rural Growth Linkages: Household Expenditure Patterns in Malaysia and Nigeria', Research Report No. 41, International Food Policy Research Institute, Washington, DC.

Hazell, P. and Haggblade, S. (1993), 'Farm-nonfarm Growth Linkages and the Welfare of the Poor', in M. Lipton and J. van der Gaag, *Including the Poor*, World Bank, Washington, DC, pp. 190-204.

INSTAT (1995), 'Enquête Permanente auprès des Ménages: Rapport Principal', UNDP/World Bank/Malagasy Government, Antananarivo.

INSTAT (1998), 'Recensement Général de la Population et de l'Habitat', Tome VI, Migration, Antananarivo.

Islam, N. (1997), 'The Nonfarm Sector and Rural Development - Review of Issues and Evidence', Food, Agriculture and the Environment, Discussion Paper No. 22, August, International Food Policy Research Institute, Washington, DC.

Jacoby, H.G. (1998), 'Access to Markets and Benefits of Rural Roads: A Nonparametric Approach', World Bank, DRG, mimeograph.

Jarosz, L. (1993), 'Defining and Explaining Tropical Deforestation: Shifting Cultivation and Population Growth in Colonial Madagascar (1896-1940)', *Economic Geography*, vol. 69(4), pp. 366-379.

Jodha, N. (1985), 'Population Growth and the Decline of Common Property Resource in India', *Population and Development Review*, vol. 11(2), pp. 247-264.

Keck, A., Sharma, N.P. and Feder, G. (1994), 'Population Growth, Shifting Cultivation, and Unsustainable Agricultural Development: A Case Study from Madagascar', World Bank Discussion Paper No. 234, Africa Technical Department Series, The World Bank, Washington, DC.

Kikuchi, M. and Hayami, Y. (1980), 'Inducements to Institutional Innovations in an Agrarian Community', *Economic Development and Cultural Change*, vol. 29(1), pp. 21-36.

Kristjanson, P. and Martin, J. (1991), 'More than Free Markets are Needed: the Case of a Peasant Millionaire in Madagascar', *Choices*, Fourth Quarter, vol. 6(4), pp. 19-21.

Kumar, S. (1994), 'Adoption of Hybrid Maize in Zambia: Effects on Gender Roles, Food Consumption, and Nutrition', Research Report No. 100, International Food Policy Research Institute, Washington, DC.

Lapenu, C., Zeller, M., Minten, B., Ralison, E., Randrianaivo, D. and Randrianarisoa, C. (1998), 'Extensification Agricole et Son Effet sur les Pratiques Agricoles, la Fertilite du Sol et les Resources Naturelles', *Cahier de la Recherche sur les Politiques Alimentaires*, No. 11, Mars, IFPRI-FOFIFA, Antananarivo.

Larson, B.A. (1994), 'Changing the Economics of Environmental Degradation in Madagascar: Lessons from the National Environmental Action Plan Process', *World Development*, vol. 22(5), pp. 671-689.

Mendoza, M. and Randrianarisoa, C. (1998), 'The Structure and Behavior of Agricultural Traders in Madagascar', in Structure and Conduct of Major Agricultural Input and Output Markets and Response to Reforms by Rural Households in Madagascar, Part III, Agricultural Output Markets and Price Behavior, International Food Policy Research Institute, report submitted to USAID-Madagascar, pp. 16-77.

Ministère de l'Agriculture (1997), 'Document de Politique Agricole et Alimentaire', Août, document provisoire.

Minten, B. (1999), 'Infrastructure, Market Access, and Agricultural Prices: Evidence for Madagascar', Discussion Paper No. 26, Markets and Structural Studies Division, International Food Policy Research Institute, Washington, DC.

Minten, B. and Mendoza, M. (1999), 'Agricultural Price Policies, Price Behavior, and Market Integration in Madagascar', Working Paper, Markets and Structural Studies Division, International Food Policy Research Institute, Washington, DC, forthcoming.

Minten, B., Randrianarisoa, C. and Zeller, M. (1998), 'Niveau, Evolution, et Facteurs Déterminants des Rendements du Riz à Madagascar', *Cahier de la Recherche sur les Politiques Alimentaires*, No. 8, IFPRI-FOFIFA, Antananarivo.

Oldeman, L.R. (1990), 'An Agro-climatic Characterization of Madagascar', Technical Paper No. 21, ISRIC, Wageningen, The Netherlands.

Pender, J. and Kerr, J. (1996), 'Determinants of Farmers' Indigenous Soil and Water Conservation Investments in India's Semi-arid Tropics', Discussion Paper No. 17, Environment and Production Technology Division, International Food Policy Research Institute, Washington, DC.

Pingali, P., Bigot, Y. and Binswanger, H.P. (1987), *Agricultural Mechanization and the Evolution of Farming Systems in Sub-Saharan Africa*, Johns Hopkins University Press, Baltimore, Maryland, USA.

Pitt, M., Rosenzweig, M. and Gibbons, D. (1995), 'The Determinants and Consequences of the Placement of Government Programs in Indonesia', in D. Van der Walle and K. Nead (eds), *Public Spending and the Poor*, World Bank, Washington, DC, pp. 114-150.

Pitt, M., Rosenzweig, M. and Hassan, M. (1990), 'Productivity, Health, and Inequality in the Intrahousehold Distribution of Food in Low-Income Countries', *American Economic Review*, vol. 80(5), pp. 1139-1156.

Pryor, F.L. (1990), *The Political Economy of Poverty, Equity, and Growth: Malawi and Madagascar*, Oxford University Press.

Raison, J.P. (1984), 'Les Hautes Terres de Madagascar', Karthala, Paris.

Rakotomanga, G. (1976), 'Le Fokonolisme et le Droit Foncier', University of Madagascar, unpublished dissertation.

Rakotonirainy, G. (1984), 'La Dynamique des Structures Fonciers sur les Hautes Terres Malgaches', Antananarivo, unpublished mimeograph.

Ralison, E. and Lapenu, C. (1998), 'Time Allocation in Rural Malagasy Households', in Structure and Conduct of Major Agricultural Input and Output Markets and Response to Reforms by Rural Households in Madagascar, Part IV, Determinants of Income Generation and Welfare of Rural Households in Madagascar and Implications for Policy, International Food Policy Research Institute, report submitted to USAID-Madagascar, pp. 235-252.

Ralison, E., Minten, B., Randrianarisoa, C., Goletti, F., Zeller, M. and Badiane, O. (1997), 'Le Projet FOFIFA/IFPRI: Présentation, Méthodologie, Echantillon', *Cahier de la Recherche sur les Politiques Alimentaires*, No. 1, IFPRI/FOFIFA, Antananarivo.

Ramarokoto, D. (1997), 'Agriculture: Enjeux et Contraintes de la Libéralisation', *Economie de Madagascar*, vol. 2, pp. 7-12.

Ramiarantsoa, H.R. (1995), *Chair de la Terre, Oeil de l'Eau: Paysanneries et Recomposition de Campagnes en Imerina (Madagascar)*, Orstom Editions, Paris.

Randrianarisoa, C. and Minten, B. (1997), 'Analyse Descriptive du Marché des Intrants Agricoles à Madagascar', *Cahier de la Recherche sur les Politiques Alimentaires*, No. 6, IFPRI/FOFIFA, Antananarivo.

Ravelosoa, J.R. (1996), 'Les Disparités Economiques à l'Heure de la Décentralisation: une Image Régionale de la Consommation des Ménages en 1993/94: Une Analyse Menée à Partir des Données de l'EPM', Madio, No. 9637/E, Instat, Antananarivo.

Ravelosoa, R.J. and Roubaud, F. (1996), 'Dynamique de la Consommation dans l'Agglomération d'Antananarivo sur Longue Période et les Stratégies d'Adaptation des Ménages face à la Crise', *Economie de Madagascar*, vol. 1, pp. 9-40.

Razafimandimby, L. (1997), 'Ajustement dans le Secteur Agricole: Insuffisance des Réformes de Prix et Faiblesse de la Compétivité', October, *Economie de Madagascar*, No. 2, pp. 13-36.

Renkow, M. (1990), 'Household Inventories and Marketed Surplus in Semisubsistence Agriculture', *American Journal of Agricultural Economics,* vol. 72(3), pp. 664-675.

Robilliard, A. (1998), 'L'offre de Riz des Ménages Agricoles Malgaches: Etude Econométrique à Partir d'Enquetes Transversales', Antananarivo, mimeo.

Rosenzweig, M.R. and Wolpin, K.I. (1985), 'Specific Experience, Household Structure, and Intergenerational Transfers: Farm Family Land and Labor Arrangements in Developing Countries', *Quarterly Journal of Economics*, No. 100, Supplement, pp. 961-987.

Roubaud, F. (1997), 'La Question Rizicole à Madagascar: Les Résultats d'une Décennie de Libéralisation', *Economie de Madagascar*, vol. 2, pp. 37-62.

Ruthenberg, H. (1980), *Farming Systems in the Tropics*, 3rd edition, Clarendon Press, Oxford.

Ruttan, V. and Hayami, Y. (1984), 'Toward a Theory of Induced Institutional Innovation', *Journal of Development Studies*, vol. 20(4), pp. 203-223.

Sadoulet, E. and Janvry A. de (1995), *Quantitative Development Policy Analysis*, Johns Hopkins University Press, Baltimore, Md., USA.

SARSA, (1996), 'Rural-urban Dynamics in the Fianarantsoa and Mahajanga High Potential Zones', Madagascar Regional Analysis Project, Clark University, Worcester, Mass., USA.

Scherr, S. and Hazell, P. (1994), 'Sustainable Agricultural Development Strategies in Fragile Lands', Discussion Paper No. 1, Environment and Production Technology Division, International Food Policy Research Institute, Washington, DC.

SECALINE, Projet Sécurité Alimentaire et Nutrition Elargie (1997), 'La Situation Alimentaire et Nutritionnelle à Madagascar; Stratégie Nationale de Sécurité Alimentaire et de Nutrition', Gouvernement Malgache IDA, MAG, No. 2474, 134 p + annexes.

Sharma, M. and Zeller, M. (1999), 'Location Criteria of Non-Government Organizations Providing Credit to the Poor: The Experience in Bangladesh', in D. Bigman and H. Fofack (eds), *Geographical Targeting for Poverty Alleviation: Methodology and Applications,* Forthcoming in the World Bank Regional and Sectoral Studies Series.

Shuttleworth, G. (1989), 'Policies in Transition: Lessons from Madagascar', *World Development*, vol. 17, No. 3, pp. 397-408.

Staatz, J., Dione, J. and Dembele, N. (1989), 'Cereals Market Liberalization in Mali', *World Development*, vol. 17, No. 5, pp. 703-718.

Strauss, J. (1984), 'Marketed Surpluses of Agricultural Households in Sierra Leone', *American Journal of Agricultural Economics*, vol. 66, pp. 321-331.

Udry, C. (1996), 'Efficiency and Market Structure: Testing for Profit Maximization in African Agriculture', Dept. of Econ., Northwestern University, June, mimeograph.

Vosti, S. and Reardon, T. (eds) (1997), *Sustainability, Growth, and Poverty Alleviation: A Policy and Agroecological Perspective*, Johns Hopkins University Press, Baltimore and London, pp. 1-15.

World Bank (1997), 'Le Partenariat Madagascar', Banque Mondiale, Antananarivo.

Zeller, M. (1993), 'Credit for the Rural Poor: Country Case Madagascar', Final report to German Agency for Technical Cooperation., International Food Policy Research Institute, Washington, DC.

Zeller, M. (1994), 'Determinants of Credit Rationing: A Study of Informal Lenders and Formal Credit Groups in Madagascar', *World Development*, vol. 22(12), pp. 1895-1909.

Zeller, M. (1998), 'Determinants of Repayment Performance in Credit Groups: The Role of Program Design, Intragroup Risk Pooling, and Social Cohesion', *Economic Development and Cultural Change*, vol. 46(3), pp. 599-620.

Zeller, M., Schrieder, G., Braun, J. von and Heidhues, F. (1997), 'Rural Finance for Food Security of the Poor: Implications for Research and Policy', *Food Policy Review 4*, International Food Policy Research Institute, Washington, DC.

Zeller, M. and Sharma, M. (1998), 'Rural Finance and Poverty Alleviation', Food Policy Report, International Food Policy Research Institute, Washington, DC.

Zeller, M., Diagne, A. and Mataya, C. (1998a), 'Market Access by Smallholder Farmers in Malawi: Implications for Technology Adoption, Agricultural Productivity and Crop Income, *Agricultural Economics*, special issue, vol. 19, pp. 219-229.

Zeller, M., Minten, B. and Randrianarisoa, C. (1998b), 'La Pauvreté dans les Villages Malgaches', *Cahier de la Recherche sur les Politiques Alimentaires*, No. 9, FOFIFA-IFPRI, Antananarivo.

Zeller, M., Lapenu, C., Minten, B., Randrianaivo, D., Ralison, E. and Randrianarisoa, C. (1999), 'Pathways of Rural Development in Madagascar: An Empirical Investigation of the Critical Triangle Between Environmental Sustainability,

Economic Growth and Poverty Alleviation', *Quarterly Journal of International Agriculture*, vol. 38, No. 2, pp. 105-127.

Zong, P. and Davis, J. (1998), 'Off-farm Employment and Grain Marketable Surplus in China', *Journal of Agricultural Economics*, vol. 49(3), pp. 346-358.